At the Lost and Found

EDWARD CURTIN

Clarity Press, Inc.

ISBN: 978-1-963892-16-1
EBOOK ISBN: 978-1-963892-17-8

In-house editor: Diana G. Collier
Interior design: Becky Luening Book Arts

Library of Congress Control Number: 2025931110

Clarity Press, Inc.
2625 Piedmont Rd. NE, Ste. 56
Atlanta, GA 30324, USA
https://www.claritypress.com

PRAISE FOR
At the Lost and Found

"A sumptuous writer and one of the finest thinkers and essayists I've read. Curtin sees our confusing world with compassionate clarity and profound wisdom."

OLIVER STONE | Writer, multiple Oscar-winning director and screenwriter

"Ed Curtin is our warrior with words. I read Ed to see what his soul is pushing, with doubtful faith and ironic whimsy, into our public conscience. Ed writes like Albert Camus's rebel and Leo Tolstoy's Andrei in *War and Peace.* The unspeakable end we have created by our nuclear politics Ed resists by the resurrection strokes of his pen. Can we find the invincible green stick of happiness in the darkness of our winter? Can we see with Albert and Ed and Leo the invincible summer in us all? Will we walk with joy and courage through the cold of our unconscionably chosen nightmare into the sun? Thank you, Ed, for your beautifully transforming essays."

JAMES W. DOUGLASS | Author, *JFK and the Unspeakable*

"Edward Curtin is a 'contrarian.' Throughout his book, he reveals the unspoken truth and smashes the dominant rhetoric. He explains the art of expression, describing real life and feelings, the beauty of language and civilization, the plurality of thought, the development of numerous friendships with a view to grasping our common reality and the future of humanity. He plunges vividly into political history, describing the era of globalization and "endless propaganda" which has hypnotized an entire generation. A Fabulous Book!"

MICHEL CHOSSUDOVSKY | Professor Emeritus, University of Ottawa

"With these lucid and uncompromising essays, Edward Curtin continues to be one of the few voices of a genuine American radicalism, so urgently needed at this moment. His courageous work unsparingly cuts through the morass of lies, evasions, and official narratives surrounding the unending violence perpetrated by malign powers and states and which corrode our shared world. Curtin's prose is infused with moral clarity and is nourished by the utopian spirit drawn from art and literature."

JONATHAN CRARY | Meyer Schapiro Professor of Modern Art and Theory, Columbia University

PRAISE CONTINUED

"Edward Curtin's *At the Lost and Found* is an extraordinary potpourri of political, philosophical, spiritual, and even musical essays and poetic lyrics, exactly a composition of 'things' that you would find in a 'Lost and Found' shop. The book is a colorful image of Life's realities, dreams and desires, ups and downs—but always with hope and following the Light that must prevail. Reading it will motivate and inspire you; it will give you new vitality and an awakened outlook on the world."

PETER KOENIG | Economist, geopolitical analyst, and author, Geneva, Switzerland

"Edward Curtin is a writer who, through every storm, every gale, and every deluge, does his utmost to keep the fragile candle of truth alight. *At the Lost and Found* is an invaluable collection of essays that shows Edward Curtin's sharp analysis of the connections between art and politics in the struggle for social change, while at the same time exposing the hidden agendas of elite mainstream culture."

CAOIMHGHIN Ó CROIDHEÁIN | Dublin artist, writer, and lecturer

"Amid the machinations of the war machine and the incessant 24/7 propaganda that bombards us at all hours, reading the essays of Edward Curtin is like diving into a deep, clear blue ocean of truth. While confronting dark political deceptions such as 9/11 and the JFK assassination with brutal, take-no-prisoners honesty, this gifted writer and uncompromising truth warrior weaves in personal stories—written like poetic parables—where we find life lessons and meaning in truth and the grandeur of nature, friendship, and love."

ELIZABETH MURRAY | Former Deputy National Intelligence Officer for the Near East, National Intelligence Council Member, Veteran Intelligence Professionals for Sanity (VIPS) and Sam Adams Associates for Integrity in Intelligence

For my children Susanne and Daniel,
that they may find in their father's words
the sound of music and truth.

Table of Contents

Acknowledgments

First and foremost, thanks to my wife Jeanne Lemlin for her love and constant support in every way, without whom you would not be reading this book. To my dear friend Dave Ratcliffe for his friendship and amazing computer help without which I would have been lost. To Jim Douglass for his love, friendship, and uplifting messages of hope no matter how dark the days. And to a wonderful editor, Diana Collier, thank you. Lastly, to the unnamed ones, friends and foes, who have inspired me in ways neither they nor I will ever know.

Introduction

My dear mother, who had an artistic temperament that tended at times toward the sentimental, liked to call me a contrarian. She was right. I think she liked but feared this inclination of mine that started in childhood. It no doubt has many roots, some of which an artful reader may sense in the essays in this book, for while I have written about the lies and coverups of the ruling elites, I have tried to do so in a self-revelatory way, even in the writing where it is couched in pure artifice.

I have always felt that conventional life was a provocation because it hid more than it revealed; that it harbored secrets that could not be exposed or else the make-believe nature of normal life would collapse like a cardboard set. That people were performing for some invisible director that they couldn't or wouldn't recognize. I always wondered why.

There is nothing profound in this tendency of mine, except the powerful force of it throughout my life. Like everyone, I was ushered onto this Shakespearean stage and have acted out many roles assigned to me but always with the inner consciousness that something was amiss. Everyone seemed to be playing someone, but who was the player? Who was I?

Because I grew up in a large literate family where our sizable bookcase was filled with great literary classics, I have always loved to read. I noticed early on that the great writers focused on this performative nature of social life, and this strengthened my burgeoning artist's eye. I particularly remember the family set of Mark Twain's books that drew me in this direction, his humorous ways of puncturing social hypocrisy.

My writing was born within all my reading, including my grandparents' large and colorfully illustrated volume of *Arabian Nights* that I would sneak a peek at from time to time. Then there was my father's witty storytelling where he would regale me with his improvised tales drawn from the metaphoric well of Pinocchio's theatrically duplicitous adventures.

By the time I was a young man, my mind was a vast storehouse of words, phrases, metaphors, tunes, memorized lines of poetry, etc. that sometime I could consciously recall but that often would just pop up like jack-in-the boxes to startle and amuse me. This has continued throughout my life – even as I never tried to remember it all and even tried to forget much of it. My forgettery has always been my faithful servant.

I am telling you this for a few reasons. One is that I have noticed that many writers seem afraid to reveal who they are or what motivates them to write. They hide the personal side behind a false objectivity. This is especially true for writers whose focus is political and involves public and cultural affairs, as does much of mine.

I think of Thoreau's words: "We commonly do not remember that it is, after all, always the first person that is speaking."

And that person, with all their hopes, dreams, desires, politics, ambitions, personal relationships, predilections, habits, faith, despair, etc., informs their work, no matter how seemingly authoritative and objective it may sound. What that person wants from writing or any art is a fair question, just as it is the core existential question for everyone: What do you want and why? What are you seeking by doing what you are doing? What is your goal?

Readers want and need to know something (not everything) about the person whose hand pens the words they are reading. It is a normal human response to ask, "Well, where is this person coming from; what's in it for him?"

It is banal to say that one has learned so much from so many others, but it's very true in my case. Not just the living but all those who have preceded me and whose words and creativity have become part of who I am, my memories, all that I have read, heard, seen, and forgotten but emerges when I write, in ways I realize or not. It is mysterious; it happens through osmosis, but in the end one hopes the result is creative and new and that the writing is a place of epiphanies.

I admit that I am possessed by language and that it proceeds the content of what I write. Maybe words possess me. I don't know, nor do I care. I just know it's so. So the mélange of the wide-ranging and free-wheeling essays that result, their multifarious styles and content, fits with my contrarian personality that seeks to do both astute political analyses and art in luminescent words and sentences that pulsate. I think of them as beyond a cage of categories and intertwined lovers.

I wrote the essays in this book between late summer 2019 and 2024. The topicality of many will be apparent, but I hope you will find in them more than contemporary relevance. I hope you will find me, Ed Curtin, one man who lived through these strange and disturbing years and responded in his own way. One man whose core concerns are essentially no different from the serious contrarian poets, writers, journalists, philosophers, musicians, painters, and artists throughout world history.

There are those who are trying to mechanize us all, to eliminate passion and will, to transmute love into a chemical and hate into a biological aberration. They seem to be succeeding, but they will fail. One reason I have written these essays is to oppose these scoundrels and their ilk who kill and wage endless wars against innocents around the world. Another is to try to create something that will delight and last a little while. I believe that writing is my vocation and that I am answering a call, and if there is any credit due, it is beyond me.

It is a very cruel world, as events over these last few years have confirmed. It is hard to wake up in the morning and hear the news. It leaves one with a sense of lostness that must be fought. The spirit of resistance can be found in many places, including poetry and song. I often remember the words of a poet that my mother had memorized and liked to recite, William Wordsworth, whose romanticism flows in my veins as well. He ended his great poem "Intimations of Immortality" thus: "Thanks to the human heart by which we live,/Thanks to its tenderness, its joys, and fears,/To me the meanest flower that blows can give/Thoughts that do often lie too deep for tears."

Nietzsche was right about writers when he said their work is a personal confession, "a kind of involuntary and unconscious memoir." No doubt this is true for me.

Finally, I hope that in reading this book you will find the words of Yuri Zhivago in the novel of death and resurrection, *Doctor Zhivago,* by the great Russian poet and novelist, Boris Pasternak, echoing in your mind. As he contemplates being possessed by the mystery of inspiration while writing poems, Yuri writes this: "Language, the home and dwelling of beauty and meaning, itself begins to think audible sounds but by virtue of the power and momentum of its inward flow." Since Zhivago means "living" in Russian, it is my wish that these essays live in your memory like the sound of music deeply felt, the same inward flow I felt when writing them.

The End of the Speed Limit on the Highway to Nowhere

There was a time when time was time and space and speed had some human meaning, for people lived within the limits of the natural world of which they were a part.

As Albert Camus said, "In our madness, we push back the eternal limits, and at once dark Furies swoop down upon us to destroy."

The destruction is now upon us.

In former days you could cross over to other people's lives and come back with a different perspective, knowing what was obvious was true and that to exist meant to be composed of flesh and blood like all the others in different places and to be bound by the natural cycles of life and death, spring and fall, summer and winter. There were limits then, on the land, water, and even in the sky, where space too had dimensions and the stars and planets weren't imaginary landing strips for mad scientists and their partners in celluloid fantasies.

In that rapidly disappearing world where people felt situated in space and time, life was not yet a holographic spectacle of repetitive images and words, a pseudo-world of shadowy figures engaging in pseudo-debates on electronic screens with people traveling from one place to another only to find that they never left home. When the mind is homeless and the grey magic of digital propaganda is its element, life becomes a vast circinate wandering to nowhere. The experience of traveling thousands of miles only to see the same chain of stores lining the same road in the same town across a country where the same people live with their same machines and same thoughts in their same lives in their same clothes. A mass society of mass minds in the hive created by cell phones and measured in nanoseconds where the choices are the freedom to choose what is always the same within a cage of categories meant to render all reality a "mediated reality."

Without roots we are like Sisyphus pushing his rock not up the hill but in circles, only to reach what we think is the end is the beginning again. Runners in the circle game.

People's roots were what once gave them distinction, a place to stand against the liquid flow of modernity and its disillusionments. These roots were cultural and geographic, material and spiritual. They went deep. Such rootedness was not a panacea, simply a place to take a stand. It gave a bit of stability, the sense of real existing individuals with identities, histories, ground beneath their feet. It was possible to meet others as different but equally human despite their different roots, and to grasp our common reality. It was the antithesis of globalization, of sameness. It was diversity before there was fake diversity.

The idea of roots has become even more complicated since Simone Weil wrote her well-known book, *The Need for Roots*, in 1943. Even then she admitted this:

> To be rooted is perhaps the most important and least recognized need of the human soul. It is one of the hardest to define.

So I will not try to do so. Like so much in life, its reality involves both a yes and a no, like our relationship to time.

For we have always been time-bound creatures, caught in its mystery, and we always will be. This was true before the invention of clocks, although the clock ushered in a technological revolution from which we've never looked back. Most people are now on speed going nowhere.

I recently looked back at a series of photographs that my parents had taken of me when I was about two years old. They were shot at our home by a professional photographer and got me thinking about three themes that have always fascinated me and which lie at the center of our world today: cameras, clocks, and mirrors. Each plays a significant part in what Guy Debord called *The Society of the Spectacle*:

> In societies dominated by modern conditions of production, life is presented as an immense accumulation of spectacles. . . . The spectacle's estrangement from the acting subject is expressed by the fact that the individual's gestures are no longer his own; they are the gestures of someone else who represents them to him.

I, the only boy with seven sisters, was dressed for the occasion in shorts and a polo shirt with suspenders. Like a little model. An actor on a stage, a player in the spectacle before the spectacle became all-consuming. Some of the photos were of me standing on a couch in front of a large mirror, double images, some with me looking away and others looking into the mirror. Two boys in a mirror world. Images. A few captured me winding up a metal mechanical toy soldier so he could march across the floor to war. Others were of me looking up at a grandfather clock, focused on the time I couldn't have understood; seeing the hands of time I couldn't tell. Those photographs froze me in time as they were meant to do. They lie before me now as afterimages of my earliest memories and my later concerns. Time will decompose the paper they are printed on, just as my memories will disappear with my final journey.

I write these words from the third floor of the old Rogues Harbor Inn to anchor my sojourner's passage through the mists of time. The old clocks throughout this ancient hotel are all stopped. It is and is not comforting. Yet these words move as I write them but stop when I'm done. They too are a double-edged sword. We want to stop time's passage but to live as well, and you can't have both simultaneously. Maybe words are edible, and once they are written they must be eaten. Then they are gone.

After fifty years I have returned to Ithaca, New York for three days and nights. Everything has changed, changed utterly. When

I first arrived here half a century ago, I came to spend a few days with Fr. Daniel Berrigan, S.J., the radical anti-war priest and poet, on my exit from the Marines Corps and my jettisoning of the mechanical soldier's life. I had to move out of the photographs.

The boats are still anchored in the sea-like Cayuga Lake along whose west side lie the towns of Ovid and Ulysses through which my wife and I passed to taste the wine pressed from the vines whose roots sink deep into this earth. To imbibe the fruit of these vines on a beautiful day is to feel happy. The names evoke the traditions of classical Greece and Rome, but when you study history, you realize that the soil then and now is soaked deep with the blood of innocents.

Walking through the ancient deep gorge that leads to the beautiful Taughannock Falls, the tallest free-falling waterfall east of the Mississippi River at 66 meters, beauty dominates your mind. But when you grasp the history of how the native Iroquois tribes were massacred right here by the European settlers who drove them from their roots in this land, the natural beauty turns a darker shade of red.

Is there is any place on this blood-soaked earth where a semi-conscious person can rest easy? For beauty is the beginning of terror, is it not, the terrible realization that, as Rilke said, "every angel is terrible"? And we are the terrible angels, exulting in beauty and often loving life so much that it brings us to tears, for we know it will end, and so we kill others to extend our lives, thinking it will bring us peace, even as we falsely cry peace, peace, when there is no peace.

If we think radically and go to the roots (Latin, *radix*) of human existence, we uncover our double-consciousness, the tragicomic state of laughter and despair, suffering and happiness that has no end. There is no escape for mortals, even though history is replete with so many failed efforts to transcend the limits of the possible. The modern project to achieve perfection and total control is a technological Faustian effort to transcend our humanity, now with artificial intelligence, digital dementia, and the marriage of the human to the machine. This mad quest goes by many names (Lewis Mumford presciently called it *The Myth of the Machine*), but it is always directed by ruling elites to gather more power to themselves. Today it is called the Great Reset, using medical technology and "vaccines" as the leading edge of its spear to disembowel our humanity. It may succeed because so many people have lost a rootedness in the lived spiritual experience of a sacred vision that allows an escape from our enigma. With this loss, they have lost the utopian vision that inspires hope when there is no hope.

The much-maligned English writer, D. H. Lawrence, grasped this in the years after the mass insanity of World War I when he wrote:

> We are all spectres . . . spectres to one another . . . abstracted reality. . . . Shadow you are even to yourself . . . abstracted reality. . . . We are not solid. We don't live in the flesh. Our instincts and intuitions are dead, we live wound round with the winding-sheet of abstraction. And the touch of anything solid hurts us. For our instincts and intuitions which are our feelers of touch and knowing through touch, they are dead, amputated. We walk and talk and eat and copulate and evacuate wrapped in our winding-sheets, all the time wrapped in our winding-sheets.

There's a man I know very well, who, when his brother-in-law died, was given one of his watches. The brother-in-law had been an accountant who saved everything that passed through his hands, from ticket stubs to scraps of notes and old pens and jewelry that his mother had worn eighty years before, including many of her watches. Everything. His passion to save was countered by his speed at getting to the finish line. He was a champion runner, who had grown up in the Depression and his parents were immigrants who worked hard to survive. The watch had never been used. It was a beautiful wind-up watch the man had won as part of a collegiate four-man two-mile relay track team that had set a world record at a major track meet. The man had, through grit and perseverance, won a track scholarship to this prestigious university where he had excelled at running very fast. The back of the watch was inscribed from the Meet Committee with the date, place, and record time.

My friend used the watch regularly, winding it every morning. It ran a few minutes slow every day, insulting the fleet feet of his brother-in-law, who of course was Greek. One day, while winding the watch, the man dropped it, and it stopped. The jeweler said it would be very expensive to repair, so the man decided to set it at 12:00 and leave it at that stop-time. He kept wearing it and when anyone asked him for the time, he'd show it to them, saying it was high noon or midnight at the oasis, or, if they preferred, NOW. Naturally this was received with quizzical looks.

The Contronymal Cage

"Vexilla regis prodeunt Inferni."
[The banners of the king of Hell advance.]
—DANTE ALIGHIERI, *The Divine Comedy: The Inferno*

Try to look ahead and see if you can see what's been coming for decades. Try to climb higher and see the beautiful things that Heaven bears, where we came forth, and once more see the stars and raise a banner of resistance to the King of Hell and all his henchmen. For they are here, and working hard as usual, and indifference will only strengthen their resolve. Don't be deceived by these digital demons. They want to make you think they don't exist. They wish to get you to suspend your disbelief and get lost in the endless looping movie they have created to conceal their real machinations.

For we are living in a world of endless propaganda and simulacra where vast numbers of people are hypnotized and can't determine the difference between the real world of nature, the body, etc. and digital imagery. Reality has disappeared into screens. Simulation has swallowed the distinction between the real world and its representations. Meaning has migrated to the margins of consciousness. This process is not yet complete but getting there.

This may at first seem hyperbolic, but it is not. I wish to explain this as simply as I can, which is not easy, but I will try. I will attempt to be rational, while knowing rationality and the logic of facts can barely penetrate the logic of digital simulacra within which we presently exist to such a large extent. Welcome to the New World Order and artificial intelligence which, if we do not soon wake up to their encroaching calamitous consequences, will result in a world where "we will never know" because our brains will have been reduced to mush and nothing will make sense. The British documentary filmmaker, Adam Curtis, has said in his recent film, *Can't Get You Out of My Head: An Emotional History of the Modern World*, that it's already "pointless to try to understand the meaning of why things happen" and we will never know, but this is a nihilistic claim that leads to resigned hopelessness. We must get such sentiments "out of our heads."

We do not, of course, live in the middle ages like Dante. Hell, purgatory, and heaven seem beyond our ken. Our imaginations have withered together with our grasp on reality. Up/down, good/evil, war/peace—opposites have melded into symbiotic marriages. Most people are ashamed, as the poet Czeslaw Milosz has said, to ask themselves certain questions that the seething infinity of modern relativity has bequeathed us. Space and time have lost all dimensions; the experience of the collapse of hierarchical space and time is widespread. For those who still call themselves religious believers like Dante, "when they fold their hands and lift up their eyes, 'up' no longer exists," Milosz rightly says. The map and the territory are one as all metaphysics are almost lost. And with its loss go our ability to see the advancing banner of the King of Hell, to grasp the nature of the battle for the soul of the world that is now underway. Or if you prefer, the struggle for political control.

One thing is certain: This war for control must be fought on both the spiritual and political levels. The centuries' long rise of technology and capitalism has resulted in the degradation of the human spirit and its lived sense of the sacred. This must be reversed, as it has fundamentally led to the mechanistic embrace of determinism and the disbelief in freedom. Logical thought is necessary, but not mechanistic thought with the deification of reason. Scientific insight is essential, but within its limitation. The spiritual and artistic imagination that transcends materialist, machine thinking is needed now more than ever. We emphatically need to realize that the subject precedes the object and consciousness the scientific method. Only by realizing this will we be able to break free from the trap that is propaganda and digital replications, whose modi operandi are to dissolve the differences between truth and falsity, the imaginary and the real, facts and fiction, good and evil. To play satanic circle games, create double-binds, whose intent and result is to imprison and confuse.

It is akin to asking what is the antonym to the word contronym, which is a word having two meanings that contradict each other, such as "cleave," which means both to cut in half and to stick together. There are many such words.

"What is the opposite of a contronym?" I asked my thirteen-year-old granddaughter, a great reader and writer raised far away from the madding crowd of flickering and looping electronic images. To which, after thinking a few minutes, she correctly replied, "The antonym to a contronym is itself, because it has two opposite meanings. It contradicts itself."

Or as Tweedledee told Alice: "Contrariwise, if it were so, it might be; and if it were so, it would be; but as it isn't, it ain't. That's logic."

And that's the logic used to trap a sleeping public in a collective hallucination of media and machines. A grand movie in which all "opposites" are integrated to tranquilize all anxieties and amuse all boredom so that the audience doesn't realize there is a world outside the Wonderland theater.

A Place to Start

Let me begin with a little history, some fortieth anniversaries that are occurring this year. In themselves, and even in their temporal juxtapositions, they mean little, but they give us a place to anchor our reflections: a sense of time and the progression of developments that have led to widespread digital cognitive warfare and twisted simulations. Widespread unreality rooted in materialist brain research financed by intelligence agencies. Spectacles of spectacles. Turning again to Guy Debord, who puts it thus in *The Society of the Spectacle*:

> Where the real world changes into simple images, the simple images become real beings and effective motivations of hypnotic behavior.

In 1981, Ronald Reagan was sworn in as the U.S. President. He was a bad actor, of course, which meant he would be a good actor (or the reverse of the reverse of the reverse . . .) in a society that was becoming increasingly theatrical, image based, and dominated by what Daniel Boorstin in his classic book, *The Image: A Guide to Pseudo-Events in America*, had earlier termed "pseudo-events." Reagan was the personification of a pseudo-event, a walking illusion, a "benign" Orwellian persona presented to the public to conceal an evil agenda. He was a masked man, one created by Deep-State forces to convince the public it was "morning in America again," even as the banner of an avuncular good guy concealed, right from the start, the treacherous "October Surprise" involving the Iranian hostage crisis. It was an evil opening act to start the charade, for which Reagan received overwhelming popular support and went on to serve two terms as the acting president. The audience was enthralled. In crucial ways, his election marked the beginning of our descent into hell.

Halfway through his two terms, Gary Wills, *In Reagan's America: Innocents at Home,* introduced Reagan as follows:

> The geriatric "juvenile lead" even as President, Ronald Reagan is old and young—an actor, but with only one role. Because he acts himself, we know he is authentic. A professional, he is always the amateur. He is the great American synecdoche, not only a part of our past but a large part of our multiple pasts. This is what makes many of the questions asked about him so pointless. Is he bright, shallow, complex, simple, instinctively shrewd, plain dumb? He is all these things and more. Synecdoche, just the Greek word for "sampling," and we all take a rich store of associations that have accumulated around the Reagan career and persona. He is

just as simple, and just as mysterious, as our collective dreams and memories.

A few weeks after Reagan was sworn in, his newly named CIA Director William Casey (see Robert Parry's book, *Trick or Treason: The 1980 October Surprise Mystery*) made a revealing comment at a meeting of the new cabinet appointees. Casey said, as overheard and recorded by Barbara Honegger who was present, "We'll know our disinformation program is complete when everything the American public believes is false."

Thirdly, in August of 1981, the French sociologist Jean Baudrillard published his seminal book, *Simulacra and Simulation*, in which he set out his theory of simulation where he claimed that a "hyperreal" simulated world was replacing the real world that once could be represented but not replaced. He argued that this simulated world was generated by models of a real world that never existed and so people were living in "hyperreality," or a totally fabricated reality. This was a radical notion, and his claim at the time that this was already total was no doubt an exaggeration. But that was then, not now. Forty years have allowed his nightmarish theory to take on reality. I will return to this subject later.

Technology and the Trap of the Machine Mass Mind

In his classic work, *Propaganda*, Jacques Ellul writes that "An analysis of propaganda therefore shows that it succeeds primarily because it corresponds exactly to a need of the masses ... just two aspects of this: the need for explanation and the need for values, which both spring largely, but not entirely, from the promulgation of news." He wrote that in 1962 when news and world events were rapidly speeding up but were nowhere near as technologically frenzied as they are today. Then, there were radio programs, many newspapers, and a handful of television stations. And yet, even in those days, as the sociologist C. Wright Mills said, the general public was confused and disoriented, liable to panic, and even that degree of information overwhelmed their capacity to assimilate it. In *The Sociological Imagination* he wrote:

> The very shaping of history now outpaces the ability of people to orient themselves in accordance with cherished values. And which values? Even when they do not panic, people often sense that older ways of feeling and thinking have collapsed and that newer beginnings are ambiguous to the point of moral stasis. Is it any wonder that ordinary people feel they cannot cope with the larger worlds with which they are so suddenly confronted? That they cannot understand the meaning of their epoch for their own lives? That—in defense of selfhood—they become morally insensible, trying to remain altogether private individuals? Is it any wonder that they come to be possessed by a sense of the trap?

This trap has been progressively closing ever since. To say this is false nostalgia for the good old days is intellectual claptrap. The evidence is overwhelming, and honest minds can see it clearly and a bit of self-reflection would reveal the inner wounds this development has caused. There are various reasons for this, many intentional, others not: political machinations by the power elites, technological, cultural, religious developments, etc., all rooted in a similar way of thinking. Whereas the wealthy elites have always controlled society, over the recent decades the growth in technological propaganda has increased exponentially. But the machines have been built upon a technical way of thinking that Ellul describes as "the totality of methods rationally arrived at and having absolute efficiency in every field of human activity." This way of thinking is the opposite of the organic, the human. It is all about means without ends, self-generating means whose sole goal is efficiency. Everything is now subordinated to technique, especially people. He says:

> From another point of view, however, the machine is deeply symptomatic: it represents the ideal toward which techniques strives. The machine is solely, exclusively, technique; it is pure technique, one might say. For, wherever a technical factor exists, it results, almost

> inevitably, in mechanization: technique transforms everything it touches into a machine.

If only cell phones shocked the hands that touched them!

I think it is beyond dispute that this sense of entrapment and confusion with its concomitant widespread depression has increased dramatically over the decades and we have come to a dark, dark place. Lost in a dark wood would be an understatement. In the inferno would perhaps be more appropriate.

Who will be our Virgil to guide us through this hell we are creating and show us where it is leading?

The massive use of psychotropic drugs for living through problems is well known. The sense of meaninglessness is widespread. The shredding of social bonds with the journey into a vast digital dementia has resulted in panic and anxiety on an enormous scale. The fear of death and disease permeates the air as religious faith wanes. People have been turned against each other as an hallucinatory cloak of propaganda has replaced reality with the black magic of digital incantations.

I remember how, in 1975, when I was teaching at a Massachusetts university and, sensing a vast unmet need in my students, I proposed a course called "The Sociology of Life, Death, and Meaning." My colleagues balked at the idea and I had to convince them it was worthwhile. I sensed that the fear of death and a growing loss of meaning was increasing among young people (and the population at large) and it was my responsibility to try to address it. My colleagues considered the subject not scientific enough, having been seduced by the positivist movement in sociology. When the enrollment for the course reached 220 plus, my point was made. The need was great. But it was a small window of opportunity for such deep reflections, for by 1980 the cowboy in the white hat had ridden into Washington, a rock star was enthroned in the Vatican and all was once again well with the world. Delusory orthodoxy reigned again. Until....

For the last forty-plus years there has been a progressive dissolution of reality into a theatrical electronic spectacle, beginning with the push for computer generated globalization and continuing up to the latest cell phones. Science, neuroscience, and technology have been deified. Cognitive warfare has been waged against the public mind. The intelligence agencies, war departments, and their accomplices throughout the corporations, media, Hollywood, medicine, and the universities have united to effect this end. Neuroscience and medicine have been weaponized—the objective being to convince the public that they are machines, their brains are computers, and that their only hope is embrace that "reality."

After the actor Reagan rode off into the sunset, his Vice-President and former Director of the CIA (therefore a supreme actor), George H. W. Bush, took the reins and declared the decade of the 1990s the decade of brain research, to be heavily financed by the federal government. In 1992, boy wonder William Clinton, straight out of the fetid fields of Arkansas politics, was elected to carry on this work, not just the brain research but the continuous bombing of Iraq and the slaughters around the world, including of Serbia, but also the work of dismantling welfare and repealing the Glass-Steagall Act, reuniting commercial and investment banking and opening the door for the rich to get super rich and normal people to get screwed. So Clinton fulfilled the duties of the good Republican President that he actually was, and the right-wing played the game of ripping him for being a leftist. It would be funny except that so many believed this game in which all the players operated within the same frame (and of course still do), the play within the play whose real directors are always invisible to the fixated audience.

What is the antonym of a contronym?

When George W. Bush took over, he continued the brain research project with massive federal monies by declaring 2001–2010 the Decade of the Behavior Project.

Then under Obama, whose role model, as he said, was the actor Reagan, and under Trump, whose role model was the guy he played on reality television and whose official role was playing the bad guy to Obama's good guy, the money for the mapping of the brain and artificial intelligence continued flowing from the

Defense Advanced Research Projects Agency (DARPA) and the Office of Science and Technology Project (OSTP).

Three decades and more of joint military, intelligence, and neuroscience work on how to understand brains so as to control them through mind control and computer technology might suggest something untoward was afoot, wouldn't you say?

Create the Problem and Then the "Solution"

If you are still on this twisted path with me, you may feel an increased level of anxiety. Not that it is new, for you have probably felt it for a long time. We both know that free-floating anxiety, like depression and fear, has been a staple of life in the good old USA for decades. We didn't create it and, as C. Wright Mills has said, "Neither the life of an individual nor the history of a society can be understood without understanding both." For our biographies, including anxiety and meaninglessness, take place within social history and social structures, and so we must ask: what are the connections? And are there solutions?

There are drugs, of course, and the caring folks at the pharmaceutical companies who want to see us with Smiley Faces, perky in mind and body, are always glad to provide them for an exorbitant price, one often well hidden in the ledgers of their insurance company partners-in-crime. But still, there is so much else to fear: terrorists, viruses, bad weather, bad breath, my bad, your bad, bad death, etc.

Is there a place upon which to pin this anxiety that floats?

Professor Mattias Desmet, a clinical psychology professor at the University of Ghent in Belgium, has some interesting thoughts about it, but they don't necessarily lead to happy conclusions. I think he is correct in saying that for decades there has been a situation brewing that is the perfect soil for mass formation with a hypnotized public embracing a new totalitarianism, one that has now been made real through COVID-19 with the lockdowns and loss of liberties as we descend with Dante to the lowest depths of the Inferno.

These background developments are the breakdown of social bonds, the loss of meaning making, with its accompanying free-floating anxiety, and the absence of ways to relieve that anxiety short of aggression.

These conditions didn't just "happen," however, but were created by multiple power elite actors with long range plans. If that sounds conspiratorial, that's because it is. That's what the powerful do. They conspire to achieve their goals. The average person, without the awareness, will, inclination, or ability to do investigative sociological research, often falls prey to their designs, and through today's electronic digital media is mesmerized into feeling that the media offer solutions to their anxieties. It provides answers, even when they are propaganda.

As Ellul says, "Propaganda is the true remedy for loneliness." It draws all lost souls to its benevolent siren song. CNN's smiling Sanjay Gupta sedates many a mind and *The New York Times* and *CBS* soothe untold numbers of Mr. and Mrs. Lonely-hearts with sweet nothings straight from the messaging centers of the World Economic Forum and Langley, Virginia. They draw on the need to obey and believe and provide fables that give people a sense of value and belonging to the group, even though the group is unreal. These media can quite easily, but usually subtly, turn their audiences' frenetic, agitated passivity into active aggression towards dissidents, especially when those dissidents have been blamed for endangering the lives of the "good" people.

As has occurred, censorship of dissent is necessary, and this must be done for the common good, even when it is carried out in allegedly democratic societies. In the name of freedom, freedom must be denied. Thus, Biden's declaration of war against domestic dissent.

Mattias Desmet had it right; we are far down the road to totalitarianism.

Simulation and Simulacra

When I was a boy, I did certain boy things that were popular in my generation. For a short period, I constructed model ships and planes from kits. It was something to do when I was constrained to the house because of bad weather. These kits were replicas of famous battle ships or planes and came with decals you could paste on them when you were done. The decals identified these historical vehicles, which were very real or had been. I knew I was making a miniature double of real objects, just as I knew a map of New York City streets corresponded to the real Bronx streets I roamed. The map and my models were simulacra, but not the real thing. The real things were outside somewhere. And I knew not to walk on the map for my wanderings. I knew the difference between reality and models.

Today we are caught in a contronymal cage. As I said, a contronym is a word having two definitions that contradict each other. Two examples are the word bolt, which can mean to lock with a bolt and to flee, and clip, which means to attach and to detach.

There are many such words and there is also a system of thought based on them. It has no name except for the one I give it here, admittedly an awkward one: The Contronymal Circus. Like words that are their own antonyms, this system of thought confuses and traps, as it is meant to do.

Language is of course slippery and equivocal, with words often connoting multiple meanings. But language is also conditioned by history; even my phrasing it that way is an example of using words in a loose and sloppy way, for "history" doesn't exist and can't do anything, people make history, use and shape words for their own designs, even as language then uses them as well.

To say I am making a moot point is an example of my point: Is it arguable or irrelevant to consider? Is that clear?

The political system that is endlessly debated and fixates people's attention is a contronymal system that contains positive and negative poles that cancel each other out while keeping the believer frustrated. Once you are in it, you are trapped because there are no outside references, the simulated system of thought is your cage. Biden vs. Trump is an example of this cage.

The great Irish writer James Joyce was born in 1882 in Ireland, a country that was historically subjected to colonial domination by Great Britain. He realized early on that the English language bequeathed to him was not neutrally aesthetic but through usage was politically charged and that words meant one thing to the colonizers and another to the colonized. In *The Portrait of the Artist As A Young Man*, his autobiographical novel, he has Stephen Dedalus say about his conversation with his condescending Jesuit English-born dean of studies:

> The language in which we are speaking is his before it is mine. How different are the words home, Christ, ale, master on his lips and on mine! I cannot speak or write these words without unrest of spirit. His language, so familiar and so foreign, will always be for me an acquired speech. I have not made or accepted his words. My voice holds them at bay. My soul frets in the shadow of his language.

For language constitutes "reality" as much as describes it. It is political. Therefore, all cultures of resistance need to reclaim the language, which includes not just individual words and their meaning, but phrases, sentences, paragraphs, and narrative structures. When ruling elites can impose language usage on the ruled, they can control their thinking, their sense of "reality," and their belief in what is possible.

This is why poets are so central to the resistance of oppressed people, and by oppressed people I include residents of the United States, who may not yet describe themselves with that term. For when language is corrupted and thought twisted in sinister ways, all efforts to resist the colonizers of the mind are self-defeating. Double binds are not reserved for personal relationships but pertain equally to politics and culture. There is a reason why public discourse about politics (and most everything) in the U.S.A. is so circular in nature, so self-defeating, always ending in a dead-end as the system of oligarchic rule rolls along and even strengthens. Think Bush vs. Gore, Obama vs. McCain, Hillary Clinton vs. Trump, Biden vs. Trump, Trump vs. Harris. Think of what has happened to reading, writing, and speaking skills throughout the society at every level. Functional illiteracy is widespread. Ignorance may not be bliss even when it's folly to be wise, for the inability to grasp the contradictory nature of the story you are thinking in has no happy ending.

In the words of the Palestinian writer Edward Said: "As one critic has suggested, nations themselves *are* narrations. The power to narrate, or to block other narratives from forming and emerging, is very important to culture and imperialism, and constitutes one of the main connections between them."

The French thinker, Jean Baudrillard, cast this language conundrum in terms of simulacra and simulation, simulacra between copies of copies that have no originals. He said:

> Today abstraction is no longer that of the map, the double, the mirror, or the concept. Simulation is no longer that of the territory, a referential being, or a substance. It is the generation by models of a real without origin or reality: a hyperreal. The territory no longer precedes the map, nor does it survive it. It is nevertheless the map that precedes the territory—precession of simulacra—that engenders the territory. . . ."

What I am trying to say is difficult to grasp because it is so twisted. To use language to untwist this example of what the poet William Blake called the "mind-forged manacles" that is the essence of explicit or implicit propaganda is hard, because it involves unveiling the words used and the narratives we imbibe to understand our worlds. It involves grasping the presuppositions of a counterfeit system. It grows much harder by the day because language has been radically reduced to slogans and words to images of images. Artificial Intelligence is further reducing all reality to illusions. We are caged in a system of contradictions, a narrative of contronyms through which we must see.

Here's Baudrillard again:

> It is a question of substituting the signs of the real for the real, that is to say of an operation of deterring every real process via its **operational double,** a programmatic, metastable, perfectly descriptive machine that offers all the signs of the real and short-circuits all its vicissitudes. Never again will the real have a chance to produce itself—such is the vital function of the model in a **system of death,** or rather of anticipated resurrection, that no longer gives the event of death a chance. [my emphasis]

At the end of *Portrait of the Artist as a Young Man*, Joyce, the great wordsmith and experimenter with form who would go on to write *Ulysses* and *Finnegan's Wake*, has Stephen Dedalus declare that he will leave Ireland to go and "forge in the smithy of my soul the uncreated conscience of my race."

It is time for us to also leave, to abandon a way of thinking that offers us the false choice of the evil of two lessers in a corrupt system. We have been sold a counterfeit bill of goods, one forged in the devious minds of deans of deception who make Stephen's interlocuter look like an obnoxious amateur.

When Baudrillard wrote *Simulacra and Simulation in 1981*, he was telling us that something fundamental had changed and would change far more in the future.

Translated into plain English (French intellectuals can be difficult to understand), he was saying that in much of modern life, reality has disappeared into its signs or models. And within these signs, these self-enclosed systems, distinctions can't be made because these simulacra contain, like contronyms, both their positive and negative poles, so they cancel each other out while holding the believer imprisoned in amber. Once you are in them, you are trapped because there are no outside references, the simulated system of thought or machine is your universe, the only reality. There is no dialectical tension because the system has swallowed it. There is no critical negativity, no place for the rebel to stand outside it because the simulacrum encompasses the positive and negative in a circulatory process that makes everything equivalent but the "positivity" of the simulacrum itself. A simple example would be the double-bind, the circular process that short circuits choice by offering alternatives that trap the chooser either way. You are inside the whale: "The virtual space of the global is the space of the screen and the network, of immanence and the digital, of a dimensionless space-time."

In the case of my model airplanes, there were real planes that my replicas were based on. I knew that. Baudrillard was announcing that the world was changing and children in the future would have a difficult time distinguishing between the real and its simulacra. Not just children but all of us have arrived at that point, thanks to digital technology, where to distinguish between the real and the imaginary is very hard. Thus, the purpose of video games: To mechanize brains. Thus, the purpose of all the brain research funded by the Pentagon: To control brains via the interface of people with machines. This is a fundamental reason why the ruling elites, under the cover of COVID-19, have been pushing for an online digitized world through which they can amass even greater control via control over people's sense of reality. Are we watching a video of the real world or a video of a model of the real world? How to tell the difference? Was that a false flag—or what?

The weather report says that there is a 31% chance of rain tomorrow at 2 P.M., and people take that seriously, even though only a genuine blockhead would not realize that this is not based on reality but on a computer model of reality and a reality that is unreal a second degree over, since it has yet to occur. Yet that everyday example is normal today. It's a form of hypnosis. The map precedes the territory.

But it gets even weirder as a regular perusal of the news confirms. A very strange warped sense of reality unconnected to digital technology is widespread. There recently was a news report about a Mohammed Ali drawing that sold for $425,000. The drawing could have been done by a child with a marker. It depicts a stick figure Ali in a boxing ring standing with arms raised in victory over a fallen opponent. From the fallen boxer's head a speech bubble rises with these words: "Ref, he did float like a butterfly and sting like a bee." It is factually true that Ali knocked many opponents on their asses and raised his arms in victory. So when he drew his stick drawing he was probably remembering that. Therefore his drawing, a representation of his memory of reality and imagination, is two degrees removed from the real. For no opponent uttered those words from his back on a canvas. They are Ali's signature words, how he liked to present himself on the world's stage, part of his act, for he was a quintessential performer, albeit an unusual one with courage and a social conscience. Obviously, his drawing is not art but a crude little sketch. Whoever spent nearly half a million dollars for it, did so either for an investment (there are questions concerning reality and illusion in that field of endeavor) or as a form of magical appropriation, similar to getting a famous person's signature to "capture" a bit of their immortality. Either way it's more than weird, even though not uncommon. It is its commonness that makes it emblematic of this present era of copies and simulacra, the mumbo jumbo magic that disappears the real into simulated images.

Take the recent case of the TV actor William Shatner, who played a spaceship captain named Captain Kirk on a very popular television series, *Star Trek,* a show filled with kitsch wisdom loved by hordes of desperadoes. All unreal but taken close to the fanatics' hearts. He's been in the news recently for taking a ride into earth's sub orbit on a spacecraft owned and operated by Amazon billionaire Jeff Bezos. Bezos gave the ninety-year-old actor a comp ride up and away supposedly because he was a big *Star Trek* fan. In keeping with the pseudo-spiritual theme of this business venture and PR stunt, the spacecraft was called the New Shepard, presumably to distinguish it from the Old Shepard, whom we must assume is dead as Nietzsche said a few years ago. Sometimes these billionaires are so busy making money that they forget to tune in to the latest news. Bezos was announcing his new religion, a blending of P. T. Barnum and technology. Anyway, pearls of "spiritual" wisdom, like those uttered on the old TV series, greeted the public following Shatner's trip. Ten minutes up and down isn't three days and nights, but he was up to the task. A guy playing an actor playing a spaceship pilot playing a TV personage on a public relations business stunt flight. "Unbelievable," as he said. Who is copying whom?

Baudrillard offers the example of The Iconoclasts from centuries past:

> . . . whose millennial quarrel is still with us today. This is precisely because they predicted the omnipotence of simulacra, the faculty the simulacra have of effacing God from the conscience of man, and the destructive annihilating truth that they allow to appear—that deep down God never existed, even that God himself was never anything but his own simulacrum—from this came their urge to destroy the images.

We are now awash in epiphanies of representation, as Daniel Boorstin noted in *The Image* in the 1960s and which everyone can notice as those little rectangular boxes are constantly raised everywhere to capture what their operators might unconsciously think of as a world they no longer think is real, so they better capture it before it fully evaporates. Such acquisitive image taking bespeaks an unspoken nihilism, secret simulations that signify the death sentence of their referents.

So let's just say simulacra are traps wherein the real is no longer real but a hyperreal that seems realer than real, while concealing its unreality.

This goes much further than the use of digital technology. It involves the entire spectrum of techniques of mind control and propaganda. It includes politics, medicine, economics, COVID-19, the lockdowns and vaccines, etc. Everything.

Let me end with one small example. A trifle, you'll agree. I began by noting the election of the actor Ronald Reagan in 1980. Then the quote from the CIA Director Casey: "We'll know our disinformation program is complete when everything the American public believes is false."

Then came the CIA actor George H. W. Bush, the two-faced Bill Clinton, George W. Bush the son of the CIA man, Obama,

Trump, and Biden. Rather shady characters all, depending usually on your political affiliations. Suppose, however, that these seven men are an acting troupe in the same play, which is a highly sophisticated simulacrum that plays in loops, and that the object of its architects is to keep the audience engaged in the show and rooting for their favorite character. Suppose this self-generating spectacle has a name: *The Contronym Circus*. And suppose that at the very heart of its ongoing run, one of the lead characters, who had been reared from birth to play a revolutionary role, one that demanded many masks and contradictory faces that could be used to reconcile the personae of the other six actors and perhaps reconcile the Rashomon-like story, suppose that character was Barack Obama, and suppose he was reared in a CIA family and later just "happened" to become President, where he became known as "the intelligence president" because of his intimate relationship with the CIA. And suppose he gave the CIA everything it wanted.

Would you think you were living in a simulacrum?

Or would you say Jeremy Kuzmarov's report at *CovertAction Magazine,* "A Company Family: The Untold History of Obama and the CIA" was a simulation of the most scurrilous kind?

Or would you feel lost in the wood in the middle of your life, heading with Dante down to hell?

"'I was thinking,' said Alice very politely, 'which is the best way out of this wood. It's getting so dark. Would you tell me, please?'

"But the fat little men [Tweedledum and Tweedledee] only looked at each other and grinned."

Yet it is no laughing matter. If we want to get through this hell we are traversing, we had better clearly recognize those who are carrying the Banner of the King of Hell. Identify them and stop their advance. It is a real spiritual war we are engaged in, and we either fight for God or the devil, but first we have to distinguish one from the other.

Chance Encounters as the Walls Close In

"A treasure stumbled upon, suddenly; not gradually accumulated, by adding one to one. The accumulation of learning, 'adding to the sum-total of human knowledge'; lay that burden down, that baggage, that impediment. Take nothing for your journey; travel light."

—NORMAN O. BROWN, *Love's Body*

These are "heavy" times, colloquially speaking. Forebodings everywhere. Everything broken. People on edge, nervous, filled with anxiety about they know not what since it seems to be everything. The economy, politics, elections, endless propaganda, the wars in Ukraine and against Gaza, censorship, the environment, nuclear war, COVID/vaccines, a massive worldwide collapse, the death of democratic possibilities, the loss of all innocence as a very weird and dangerous future creeps upon us, etc. Only the most anesthetized don't feel it.

The anxiety has increased even as access to staggering amounts of knowledge—and falsehoods—has become available with the click of a button into the digital encyclopedia. The CIA's MK-Ultra mind control program has gone digital. The more information, the more insubstantial the world seems, but it is not an insubstantiality that connects to hope or faith but to despair. Across the world people are holding their breath. What's next?

Roberto Calasso, the late Italian writer, wrote that we live in "the unnamable present," which seems accurate. Information technology, with its easily available marriage of accurate and fraudulent information, affects people at the fathomless depths of the mind and spirit. Yet it is taken-for-granted that the more such technological information there is available, as well as the ease with which one can add one's two-cents to it, is a good thing, even as those powerful deep-state forces that control the Internet pump out an endless stream of purposely dissembling and contradictory messages. Delusions of omnipotence and chaos everywhere, but not in the service of humanity. Such chaos plays in chords D and C—Depressing and Controlling.

In the midst of this unnamable present, all of us need to dream of beauty and liberation even as we temporarily rely on digital technology for news of the wider world. For the local news we can step outside and walk and talk to people, but we can't endlessly travel everywhere, so we rely on the Internet for reports from elsewhere. Even as we exercise great effort to discern facts from fictions through digital's magic emanations, we hunger for some deeper experiences than the ephemerality of this unnamable world. Without it we are lost in a forest of abstractions.

While recently dawdling on a walk, I stopped to browse through tables of free books on the lawn of my local library. I was looking for nothing but found something that startled me: a few descriptive words of a child's experience. I chanced to pick up an old (1942), small autobiography by the English historian, A. L. Rowse—*A Cornish Childhood.* The flyleaf informed me that it was the story of his pre-World War I childhood in a little Cornish village in southwestern England. The son of a china-clay worker and mother of very modest means, Rowse later went on to study at Oxford and became a well-known scholar and author of about a hundred books. In other words, a man whose capacious mind was encyclopedic long before the Internet offered its wares of information about everything from A to Z.

Since my grandfather, the son of an Irish immigrant father and English mother, had spent his early years working in a bobbin factory in Bradford, England, a polluted mill town in the north, before sailing at age 11 from Liverpool to New York City aboard the *Celtic* with his four younger siblings sans parents, I had an interest in what life was like for poor children in England during that era. How circumstances influenced them: two working-class boys, one who became an Oxford graduate and well-known author; the other who became a NYC policeman known only to family and friends. The words Rowse wrote and I read echoed experiences that I had had when young; I wondered if my grandfather had experienced something similar. Rowse writes this on pages 16–17 where I randomly opened the book:

> A little group of thatched cottages in the middle of the village had a small orchard attached; and I remember well the peculiar purity of the blue sky seen through the white clusters of apple-blossom in spring. I remember being moon-struck looking at it one morning early on my way to school. It meant something for me; what I couldn't say. It gave me an unease at heart, some reaching outwards toward perfection such as impels men into religion, some sense of the transcendence of things, of the fragility of our hold upon life . . . . I could not know then that it was an early taste of aesthetic sensation, a kind of revelation which has since become a secret touchstone of experience for me, an inner resource and consolation. . . . In time it became my creed—if that word can be used of a religion which has no dogma, no need of dogma; for which this ultimate aesthetic experience, this apprehension of the world and life as having value essentially in the moment of being apprehended *qua* beauty, I had no need of religion. . . . in that very moment it seemed that time stood still, that for a moment time was held up and one saw experience as through a rift across the flow of it, a shaft into the universe. But what gave such poignancy to the experience was that, in the very same moment that one felt time standing still, one knew at the back of the mind, or with another part of it, that it was moving inexorably on, carrying oneself

> and life with it. So that the acuity of the experience, the reason why it moved one so profoundly, was that at bottom it was a protest of the personality against the realization of its final extinction. Perhaps, therefore, it was bound up with, a reflex action from, the struggle for survival. I could get no further than that; and in fact have remained content with that.

I quote so many of Rowse's words because they seem to contain two revelations that pertain to our current predicament. One a revelation that opens onto hope; the other a revelation of hopelessness. On the one hand, Rowse writes beautifully about how a patch of blue sky through apple blossoms (and his reading Wordsworth's *Intimations of Immortality*) could open his heart and soul to deep aesthetic consolation. Calasso, in discussing "absolute literature" and the *Bhagavad Gita in Literature and the Gods*, refers to this experience with the word *ramaharsa* or horripilation, the happiness of the hairs. It is that feeling one has when one experiences a thrill so profound that a shiver goes down one's spine and one experiences an epiphany. Your hairs and other body parts stand up, whether it's from a patch of blue, a certain spiritual or erotic/love encounter, or a line of poetry that takes your breath away. Such a thrill often happens through a serendipitous stumbling.

For Rowse, the epiphany was bounded, like a beautiful bird with its wings clipped; it was an "aesthetic experience" that seemed to exclude something genuinely transcendent in the experiential and theological sense. Maybe it was more than that when he was young, but when this scholar described it in his 39th year, this intellectual could only say it was aesthetic.

C. S. Lewis, in the opening pages of *The Abolition of Man*, echoing Coleridge's comment about two tourists at a waterfall, one who calls the waterfall pretty and the other who calls it sublime (Coleridge endorsing the latter and dismissing the former with disgust), writes, "The feelings which make a man call an object sublime are not sublime feelings but feelings of veneration." In other words, the sublime nature of a patch of blue sky through apple blossoms in the early morn cannot be reduced to a person's subjective feelings but is objectively true and a crack into the mystery of transcendence. To see it as a protest against one's personal extinction and to be content to "get no further than that" is to foreclose the possibility that what the boy felt was not what the man thought; or to quote Wordsworth about what seems to have happened to Rowse: "Shades of the prison house begin to close/Upon the growing boy," and that is that.

But we are even a longer way gone from when Rowse wrote his remembrances. In our secular Internet age, first society and now its technology, not aesthetics or the religion of art, have replaced God for many people, who, like Rowse, have lost the ability to experience the divine. It embarrasses them. Something—an addiction to pseudo-knowledge?—blocks their willingness to be open to surpassing the reasoning mind. We think we are too sophisticated to bend that low even when looking up. "The pseudomorphism between religion and society" has passed unobserved, as Calasso puts it:

> It all came together not so much in Durheim's [French sociologist 1858–1917] claim that "the religious is the social," but in the fact that suddenly such a claim *sounded natural*. What was left in the end was naked society, but invested now with all the powers inherited, or rather burgled, from religion. The twentieth century would see its triumph. The theology of society severed every tie, renounced all dependence, and flaunted the distinguishing feature: the tautological, the self-advertising. The power and impact of totalitarian regimes cannot be explained unless we accept that the very notion of society has appropriated an unprecedented power, one previously the preserve of religion. . . . **Being anti-social would become the equivalent of sinning against the Holy Ghost**. . . . Society became the subject above all subjects, for whose sake everything is justified.

For someone like Rowse, the Oxford scholar and bibliophile, writing in the midst of WW II about his childhood before WW I, an exquisite aesthetic explanation suffices to explain his experience, one that he concludes was perhaps part of an evolutionary reflex action connected to the struggle for survival. Thus, this epiphany of beauty is immured in sadness rather than opening out into affirmation. Lovely as his description is, it is caged in inevitability, as if to say: Here is your bit of beauty on your way to dusty death. It is a denial of freedom, of spiritual reality, of what Lewis refers to for brevity's sake as "the Tao," what the Chinese have long meant as the great thing, the correspondence between the outer and the inner, a reality beyond causality and the controlling mind.

Now even beauty has been banned behind machine experiences. But the question of beauty is secondary to the nature of reality and our connection to it. The fate of the world depends upon it. When the world is too much with us and doom and gloom are everywhere, where can we turn to find a way forward to find a place to stand to fight the evils of nuclear weapons, poverty, endless propaganda, and all the other assorted demons marauding through our world?

It will not be to machines or more information, for they are the essence of too-muchness. It will not come from concepts or knowledge, which Nietzsche said made it possible to avoid pain. I believe it will only come from what he suggested: "To make an experiment of one's very life—this alone is freedom of the spirit, this then became for me my philosophy." And before you might think, "Look where it got him, stark raving mad," let me briefly explain. Nietzsche may seem like an odd choice to suggest as insightful when it comes to openness to a spiritual dimension to experience since he is usually but erroneously seen as someone who "killed God." Someone like Gandhi might seem more appropriate with his "experiments with truth." And of course, Gandhi is very appropriate. But so too are Emerson, Thoreau, Jung, and many others, at least in my limited sense of what I mean by experiment. I mean experimenting-experiencing (both derived from the same Latin word, *expereri*, to try or test, like the word essay) by assuming through an act of faith or suspension of disbelief that if we stop trying to control everything and open ourselves to serendipitous stumbling, what may seem like simply beautiful aesthetic experiences may be apertures into a spiritual energy of which we were unaware. James W. Douglass explores this possibility in his tantalizing book, *Lightning East to West: Jesus, Gandhi, and the Nuclear Age,* when he asks and then explores this question: "Is there a spiritual reality, inconceivable to us today, which corresponds in history to the physical reality which Einstein discovered and which led to the atomic bomb?"

I like to think that my grandfather, although a man not very keen on things spiritual, might have, in his young years amidst the grime and fetid air of Bradford, chanced to look up and saw a patch of blue sky through the rising smoke and felt the "happiness of the hairs" that opened a crack in his reality to let the light in.

Roberto Calasso quotes this from Nietzsche:

> That huge scaffolding and structure of concepts to which the man who must clings in order to save himself in the course of life, for the liberated intellect is merely a support and a toy for his daring devices. And should he break it, he shuffles it around and ironically reassembles it once more, connecting what is least related and separating what is closest. By doing so he shows that those needful ploys are of no use to him and that he is no longer guided by concepts but by intuitions.

I have an intuition that there are hierophanies everywhere, treasures to be stumbled upon—by chance. If we let them be.

The Subtleties of Anti-Russia Leftist Rhetoric

While the so-called liberal and conservative media—all stenographers for the intelligence agencies—pour forth the most blatant propaganda about Russia and Ukraine that is so conspicuous as such that it is comedic if it weren't so dangerous, the self-depicted cognoscenti also ingest subtler messages, often from the alternative media.

A woman I know and who knows my sociological analyses of propaganda contacted me to tell me there was an excellent article about the war in Ukraine at *The Intercept*, an on-line publication funded by billionaire Pierre Omidyar that I have long considered a leading example of much deceptive reporting wherein truth is mixed with falsehoods to convey a "liberal" narrative that fundamentally supports the ruling elites while seeming to oppose them. This, of course, is nothing new since it's been the modus operandi of all corporate media in their own ideological and disingenuous ways, such as *The New York Times, CBS,* the *New York Post,* the *Washington Post*, the *New York Daily News, Fox News, CNN, NBC*, etc. for a very long time.

Nevertheless, out of respect for her judgment and knowing how deeply she feels for all suffering people, I read the article. Written by Alice Speri, its title sounded ambiguous—"The Left in Europe Confronts NATO's Resurgence After Russia's Invasion of Ukraine"—until I saw the subtitle that begins with these words: "Russia's brutal invasion complicates . . ." But I read on. By the fourth paragraph, it became clear where this article was going. Speri writes that "In Ukraine, by contrast [with Iraq], it was Russia that had staged an illegal, *unprovoked invasion*, and U.S.-led support to Ukraine was understood by many *as crucial to stave off even worse atrocities* than those the Russian military had already committed." [my emphasis]

While ostensibly about European anti-war and anti-NATO activists caught on the horns of a dilemma, the piece goes on to assert that although U.S./NATO was guilty of wrongful expansion over many years, Russia has been an aggressor in Ukraine and Georgia and is guilty of terrible war crimes, etc.

There is not a word about the U.S. engineered coup in 2014, the CIA and Pentagon backed mercenaries in Ukraine, or its support for the neo-Nazi Azov Battalion and Ukraine's years of attacks on the Donbass where many thousands have been killed. It is assumed these actions are not criminal or provocations. And there is this:

> The uncertain response of Europe's peace activists is both a reflection of a brutal, *unprovoked invasion that stunned the world* and of an anti-war movement that has grown smaller and more marginalized over the years. The left in both Europe and the U.S. have struggled to respond to a wave of support for Ukraine that is at cross purposes with a decades long effort to untangle Europe from a U.S.-led military alliance. [my emphasis]

In other words, the article, couched in anti-war rhetoric, was anti-Russia propaganda. When I told my friend my analysis, she refused to discuss it and got angry with me, as if I therefore were a proponent of war. I have found this is a common response.

This got me thinking again about why people so often miss the untruths lying within articles that are in many parts truthful and accurate. I notice this constantly. They are like little seeds slipped in as if no one will notice; they work their magic nearly unconsciously. Few do notice them, for they are often imperceptible. But they have their effects and are cumulative and are far more powerful over time than blatant statements that will turn people off, especially those who think propaganda doesn't work on them. This is the power of successful propaganda, whether purposeful or not. It particularly works well on "intellectual" and highly schooled people.

For example, in a recent printed interview, Noam Chomsky, after being introduced as a modern day Galileo, Newton, and Descartes rolled into one, talks about propaganda, its history, Edward Bernays, Walter Lippman, etc. What he says is historically accurate and informative for anyone not knowing this history. He speaks wisely of U.S. media propaganda concerning its unprovoked war against Iraq and he accurately calls the war in Ukraine "provoked." And then, concerning the war in Ukraine, he drops this startling statement:

> I don't think there are "significant lies" in war reporting. The U.S. media are generally doing a highly creditable job in reporting Russian crimes in Ukraine. That's valuable, just as it's valuable that international investigations are underway in preparation for possible war crimes trials.

In the blink of an eye, Chomsky says something so incredibly untrue that unless one thinks of him as a modern day Galileo, which many do, it may pass as true and you will smoothly move on to the next paragraph. Yet it is a statement so false as to be laughable. The media propaganda concerning events in Ukraine has been so blatantly false and ridiculous that a careful reader will stop suddenly and think: Did he just say that?

So now Chomsky views the media, such as *The New York Times* and its ilk, that he has correctly castigated for propagandizing for the U.S. in Iraq and East Timor, to use two examples, as doing "a highly creditable job in reporting Russian crimes in Ukraine," as if suddenly they were no longer spokespeople for the CIA and U.S. disinformation. And he says this when we are in the midst of the greatest propaganda blitz since WW I, with its censorship, Disinformation Governance Board, de-platforming of dissidents, etc., that border on a parody of Orwell's *Nineteen Eighty-Four.*

Even slicker is his casual assertion that the media are doing a good job reporting Russia's war crimes after he earlier has said this about propaganda:

> So it continues. Particularly in the more free societies, where means of state violence have been constrained by popular activism, it is of great importance to devise methods of manufacturing consent, and to ensure that they are internalized, becoming as invisible as the air we breathe, particularly in articulate educated circles. Imposing war-myths is a regular feature of these enterprises.

This is simply masterful. Explain what propaganda is at its best and how you oppose it and then drop a soupçon of it into your analysis. And while he is at it, Chomsky makes sure to praise Chris Hedges, one of his followers, who himself recently wrote an article—"The Age of Self-Delusion"—that also contains valid points appealing to those sick of wars, but which also contains the following words:

> *Putin's revanchism* is matched by our own.
>
> The disorganization, ineptitude, and low morale of the Russian army conscripts, along with the repeated intelligence failures by the Russian high command, apparently convinced Russia would roll over Ukraine in a few days, exposes the lie that Russia is a global menace.
>
> 'The Russian bear has effectively defanged itself,' historian Andrew Bacevich writes.
>
> But this is not a truth the war makers impart to the public. Russia must be inflated to become a global menace, *despite nine weeks of humiliating military failures.* [my emphasis]

Russia's revanchism? Where? Revanchism? What lost territory has the U.S. ever waged war to recover? Iraq, Syria, Cuba, Vietnam, Yugoslavia, etc.? The U.S.'s history is a history not of revanchism but of imperial conquest, of seizing or controlling territory, while Russia's war in Ukraine is clearly an act of self-defense after years of U.S./NATO/Ukraine provocations and threats, which Hedges recognizes. "Nine weeks of humiliating military failures"?—when they control a large section of eastern and southern Ukraine, including the Donbass. But his false message is subtly woven, like Chomsky's, into sentences that are true.

"But this is not a truth the war makers impart to the public." No, it is *exactly what* the media spokespeople for the war makers—i.e. *The New York Times* (Hedges former employer, which he never fails to mention and for whom he covered the Clinton administration's savage destruction of Yugoslavia), *CNN*, *Fox News*, *The Washington Post*, the *New York Post*, etc.—impart to the public every day for their masters. Headlines that read how Russia, while allegedly committing daily war crimes, is failing in its war aims and that the mythic hero Zelensky is leading Ukrainians to victory. Words to the effect that "The Russian bear has effectively defanged itself" presented as fact.

Yes, they do inflate the Russian monster myth, only to then puncture it with the myth of David defeating Goliath.

But being in the business of mind games (too much consistency leads to clarity and gives the game away), one can expect them to scramble their messages on an ongoing basis to serve the U.S. agenda in Ukraine and further NATO expansion in the undeclared war with Russia, for which the Ukrainian people will be sacrificed. Orwell called it "doublethink":

> Doublethink lies at the very heart of Ingsoc, since the essential act of the Party is to use conscious deception while retaining the firmness of purpose that goes with complete honesty. To tell deliberate lies while genuinely believing in them, to forget any fact that has become inconvenient, and then, when it becomes necessary again, to draw it back from oblivion for just so long as it is

> needed, to deny the existence of objective reality and all the while to take account of the reality one denies—all this is indispensably necessary. . . . with the lie always one step ahead of the truth.

Revealing while concealing and interjecting inoculating shots of untruths that will only get cursory attention from their readers, the writers mentioned here and others have great appeal for the left intelligentsia. For people who basically worship those they have imbued with infallibility and genius, it is very hard to read their sentences carefully and smell a skunk. The subterfuge is often very adroit and appeals to readers' sense of outrage at what happened in the past—e.g. the George W. Bush administration's lies about weapons of mass destruction in Iraq.

Chomsky, of course, is the leader of the pack, and his followers are legion, including Hedges. For decades they have been either avoiding or supporting the official versions of the assassinations of JFK and RFK, the attacks of September 11, 2001 that led directly to the war on terror and so many wars of aggression, and the recent COVID-19 propaganda with its devastating lockdowns and crackdowns on civil liberties. They are far from historical amnesiacs, of course, but obviously convey the message that these foundational events are of no importance, for otherwise they would have addressed them. If you expect them to explain, you will be waiting a long time.

In a recent article—"How the organized Left got COVID wrong, learned to love lockdowns and lost its mind: an autopsy"—Christian Parenti writes this about Chomsky:

> Almost the entire left intelligentsia has remained psychically stuck in March 2020. Its members have applauded the new biosecurity repression and calumniated as liars, grifters, and fascists any and all who dissented. Typically, they did so without even engaging evidence and while shirking public debate. Among the most visible in this has been Noam Chomsky, the self-described anarcho-syndicalist who called for the unvaccinated to

> "remove themselves from society," and suggested that they should be allowed to go hungry if they refuse to submit.

Parenti's critique of the left's response (not just Chomsky's and Hedges') to COVID also applies to those foundational events mentioned above, which raises deeper questions about the CIA and NSA's penetration of the media in general, a subject beyond the scope of this analysis.

For those, like the liberal woman who referred me to *The Intercept* article, who would no doubt say of what I have written here: Why are you picking on leftists? my reply is quite simple.

The right-wing and the neocons are obvious in their pernicious agendas; nothing is really hidden; therefore they can and should be opposed. But many leftists serve two masters and are far subtler. Ostensibly on the side of regular people and opposed to imperialism and the predations of the elites at home and abroad, they are often tricksters of beguiling rhetoric that their followers miss. Rhetoric that indirectly fuels the wars they say they oppose.

Smelling skunks is not as obvious as it might seem. Being nocturnal, they come forth when most people are sleeping.

The Life and Public Assassination of President John F. Kennedy

What is the truth, and where did it go?
Ask Oswald and Ruby, they oughta know
"Shut your mouth," said the wise old owl
Business is business, and it's a murder most foul
Don't worry, Mr. President
Help's on the way
Your brothers are coming, there'll be hell to pay
Brothers? What brothers? What's this about hell?
Tell them, "We're waiting, keep coming"
We'll get them as well
—BOB DYLAN, "Murder Most Foul"

Why President Kennedy was publicly assassinated by the CIA sixty-one years ago has never been a more important question. All pseudo-debates to the contrary—including the numerous and growing claims that it was not the U.S. national security state but the Israelis that assassinated the president—which exonerates the CIA while suggesting the Israeli government controlled the CIA, a false claim—the truth about the assassination has long been evident. There is nothing to debate unless one is some sort of intelligence operative, has an obsession, or is out to make a name or a buck. I suggest that all those annual JFK conferences in Dallas should finally end, but my guess is that they will be rolling along for many more decades. To make an industry out of a tragedy is wrong. And these conferences are so often devoted to examining and debating minutiae that are a distraction from the essential truth.

As for the corporate mainstream media, they will never admit the truth but will continue as long as necessary to titillate the public with lies, limited hangouts, and sensational non-sequiturs. To do otherwise would require admitting that they have long been complicit in falsely reporting the crime and the endless coverup. That they are arms of the CIA and NSA.

The Cold War, endless other wars, and the nuclear threat John Kennedy worked so hard to end have today been inflamed to a fever pitch by U.S. leaders in thrall to the forces that killed the president. President Joseph Biden, like all the presidents that followed Kennedy, is JFK's opposite, an unrepentant warmonger, not only in Ukraine with the U.S. war against Russia and the U.S. nuclear first-strike policy, but throughout the world—the Middle East, Africa, Syria, Iran, and on and on, including the push for war with China.

Nowhere is this truer than with the U.S. support for the current Israeli genocide of the Palestinians in Gaza, a slaughter supported by Biden and Trump and also by Robert Kennedy, Jr., who, ironically, was campaigning for the presidency on the coattails of JFK and his father Senator Robert F. Kennedy, who would be appalled by his unequivocal support for the Israeli government. Kennedy, Jr. has said that he would rather lose the election than turn against Israel. By such support and his silence as the slaughter in Gaza continues, RFK, Jr. is, contrary his other expressed opinions, supporting a wide range of war-related matters that involve the U.S.- Israel alliance, which is central to the military-industrial forces running U.S. foreign policy. To say this is dispiriting is a great understatement, for RFK, Jr., a very intelligent man, knows that the CIA killed his uncle and father, and he is campaigning as a spiritually awakened man intent on ending the U.S. warfare state, something impossible to accomplish when one gives full-fledged support to Israel.

The Biden administration is doing all in its power to undo the legacy of JFK's last year in office when on every front he fought for peace, not war. It is not hard to realize that all presidents since John Kennedy have been fully aware that a bullet to the head in broad daylight could be their fate if they bucked their bosses. They knew this when they sought the office because they were run by the same bosses before their election. Small-souled men, cowards on the make, willing to sacrifice millions to their ambition.

I believe that the following article is important reading. It is not based on speculation but on well-sourced facts, and it will make clear the importance of President Kennedy and why his assassination lay the foundation for today's dire events. In this dark time, when the world is spinning out of control, the story of his great courage in the face of an assassination he expected, can inspire us to oppose the systemic forces of evil that control the United States and are leading the world into the abyss.

LIST OF SECTIONS

Despite a treasure-trove of new research and information having emerged over the last sixty-one years, there are many people who still think who killed President John Fitzgerald Kennedy and why are unanswerable questions. They have drunk what Dr. Martin Schotz has called "the waters of uncertainty" that result "in a state of confusion in which anything can be believed but nothing can be known, nothing of significance, that is."[1]

Then there are others who cling to the Lee Harvey Oswald "lone-nut" explanation proffered by the Warren Commission.

Both these groups agree, however, that whatever the truth, unknowable or allegedly known, it has no contemporary relevance but is old-hat, ancient history, stuff for conspiracy-obsessed people with nothing better to do. The general thinking is that the assassination occurred more than a half-century ago, so let's move on.

Nothing could be further from the truth, for the assassination of JFK is the foundational event of modern American history, the Pandora's box from which many decades of tragedy have sprung.

Pressured to Wage War

From the day he was sworn in as President on January 20, 1961, John F. Kennedy was relentlessly pressured by the Pentagon, the Central Intelligence Agency, and by some of his own advisers to wage war—clandestine, conventional, and nuclear.

To understand why and by whom he was assassinated on November 22, 1963, one needs to apprehend this pressure and why President Kennedy consistently resisted it, and the consequences of that resistance.

It is a key to understanding the current state of our world today and why the United States has been waging endless foreign wars and creating a national security surveillance state at home since JFK's death.

---

1 E. Martin Schotz, *History Will Not Absolve Us: Orwellian Control, Public Denial, and the Murder of President Kennedy* (Kurtz, Ulmer, & DeLucia Book Publishers, 1996).

A War Hero Who Was Appalled By War

It is very important to remember that Lieutenant John Kennedy was a genuine Naval war hero in WW II, having risked his life and been badly injured while saving his men in the treacherous waters of the south Pacific after their PT boat was sunk by a Japanese destroyer. His older brother Joe and his brother-in-law Billy Hartington had died in the war, as had some of his boat's crew members.

As a result, Kennedy was extremely sensitive to the horrors of war, and when he first ran for Congress in Massachusetts in 1946, he made it explicitly clear that avoiding another war was his number one priority. This commitment remained with him and was intensely strengthened throughout his brief presidency until the day he died, fighting for peace.

Despite much rhetoric to the contrary, this anti-war stance was and is unusual for a politician, especially during the 1950s and 1960s. Kennedy was a remarkable man, for even though he assumed the presidency as somewhat of a cold warrior vis à vis the Soviet Union in particular, his experiences in office rapidly chastened that stance. He very quickly came to see that there were many people surrounding him who relished the thought of war, even nuclear war, and he came to consider them as insane and very dangerous.

A Prescient Perspective

Yet even before he became president, then Senator Kennedy gave a speech in the U.S. Senate that sent shock waves throughout Washington, D.C.[2] In 1957 he came out in support of Algerian independence from France, in support of African liberation generally, and against colonial imperialism. As chair of the Senate's African Subcommittee in 1959, he urged sympathy for African

2 James W. Douglass, *JFK and the Unspeakable: Why He Died & Why It Matters* (Orbis Books, 2008), pp. 8 & 212.

James DiEugenio, *Destiny Betrayed*, 2nd Edition (Skyhorse Publishing, 2012), pp. 17–33.

independence movements as part of American foreign policy. He knew that continued colonial policies would only end in more bloodshed because the voices of independence would not be denied, nor should they.

The speech caused an international uproar, and Kennedy was harshly criticized by Eisenhower, Nixon, John Foster Dulles, and even members of the Democratic party, such as Adlai Stevenson and Dean Acheson. But it was applauded throughout Africa and what was then called the third world.

Yet he continued throughout his 1960 campaign for president to raise his voice against colonialism worldwide and for a free Africa. Such views were anathema to the foreign policy establishment, including the CIA and the burgeoning military industrial complex that Dwight Eisenhower belatedly warned against in his Farewell Address, delivered nine months after approving the Bay of Pigs invasion of Cuba in March 1960, a juxtaposition that revealed the hold the Pentagon and CIA had and has on sitting presidents.[3]

Patrice Lumumba

One of Africa's anti-colonial and nationalist leaders was the charismatic Congolese leader Patrice Lumumba, who in June 1960 had been become the first democratically elected leader of Congo, a country savagely raped and plundered for more than half a century by Belgium's King Leopold II for himself and multinational mining companies. Kennedy's support for African independence was well-known and especially feared by the CIA, which together with Brussels, considered Lumumba, and Kennedy for supporting him, as threats to their interests in the region.

So, three days before JFK's inauguration, together with the Belgium government, the CIA had Lumumba brutally assassinated after torturing and beating him. This murder had been approved

3 *Eisenhower Farewell Address (Best Quality) - 'Military Industrial Complex' WARNING,* Ewafa YouTube video [16:14] (speech given January 17, 1961). https://www.youtube.com/watch?v=OyBNmecVtdU

by President Eisenhower in August 1960 at an NSC meeting where he gave Allen Dulles, the Director of the CIA, the approval to "eliminate" Lumumba.

Then on January 26, 1961, when Dulles briefed the new president on the Congo, he did not tell JFK that they had already assassinated Lumumba nine days before. This was meant to keep Kennedy on tenterhooks, to teach him a lesson. On February 13, 1961, Kennedy received a phone call from his UN ambassador Adlai Stevenson informing him of Lumumba's death. There is a photograph by Jacques Lowe of the horror-stricken president answering that call that is harrowing to view. It was an unmistakable message of things to come, a warning.[4]

Dag Hammarskjöld, Indonesia, and Sukarno

One of Kennedy's central allies in his efforts to support third world independence was U.N Secretary-General Dag Hammarskjöld. He had been deeply involved in peacekeeping in the Congo and efforts to resolve disputes in Indonesia, the latter being an extremely important country that was central to JFK's concerns. Hammarskjöld was killed in a plane crash on September 18, 1961, while on a peacekeeping mission to the Congo. Substantial evidence exists that he was assassinated and that the CIA and Allen Dulles were involved. Kennedy was devastated to lose such an important ally.

Kennedy's Indonesia strategy involved befriending Indonesia as a Cold War ally as a prerequisite for his Southeast Asian policy of dealing with Laos and Vietnam and finding peaceful resolutions to smoldering Cold War conflicts. Hammarskjöld was central to these efforts. The CIA, led by Dulles, strongly opposed Kennedy's strategy in Indonesia. In fact, Dulles had been involved in treacherous maneuverings in Indonesia for decades. President Kennedy

---

4 See David Talbot, *The Devil's Chessboard: Allen Dulles, the CIA, and the Rise of America's Secret Government* (Harper Collins, 2015), pp. 375–89 and the photographs at the book's center.

supported the Indonesian President Sukarno, whom Dulles opposed.

Two days before Kennedy was killed on November 22, 1963, he had accepted an invitation from Indonesian President Sukarno to visit that country the following spring. The aim of the visit was to end the conflict (*Konfrontasi*) between Indonesia and Malaysia and to continue Kennedy's efforts to support post-colonial Indonesia with economic and developmental aid, not military. It was part of his larger strategy of ending conflict throughout Southeast Asia and assisting the growth of democracy in newly liberated post-colonial countries worldwide.

Of course, JFK never went to Indonesia in 1964, and his peaceful strategy to bring Indonesia to America's side and to ease tensions in the Cold War was never realized, thanks to Allen Dulles. And Kennedy's proposed withdrawal from Vietnam, which was premised on success in Indonesia, was quickly reversed by Lyndon Johnson after JFK's murder. Soon both countries would experience mass slaughter engineered by Kennedy's opponents in the CIA and Pentagon. In Indonesia, Sukarno would be forced out and replaced by General Suharto, who would rule with an iron fist for the next thirty years, massacring at will with American support.[5]

The Bay of Pigs

In mid-April 1961, less than three months into his presidency, a trap was set for President Kennedy by the CIA and its Director, Allen Dulles, who knew of Kennedy's reluctance to

---

5 Greg Poulgrain, *The Incubus of Intervention: Conflicting Indonesian Strategies of John F. Kennedy and Allen Dulles*, (Strategic Information and Research Development Centre, 2015).

Edward Curtin and Greg Poulgrain, "The CIA's Involvement in Indonesia and the Assassinations of JFK and Dag Hammarskjold," *Global Research*, November 22, 2020. https://www.globalresearch.ca/the-cias-involvement-in-indonesia-and-the-assassinations-of-jfk-and-dag-hammarskjold/5537193

Greg Poulgrain, *JFK vs. Allen Dulles: Battleground Indonesia* (Simon & Schuster, 2020).

invade Cuba. They assumed the new president would be forced by circumstances at the last minute to send in ground forces to back the invasion that they had planned. The CIA and generals wanted to oust Fidel Castro, and in pursuit of that goal, trained a force of Cuban exiles to invade Cuba. This had started under President Eisenhower. Kennedy refused to go along, and the invasion was roundly defeated. The CIA, military, and Cuban exiles bitterly blamed Kennedy.

But it was all a sham. Classified documents uncovered in 2000 revealed that the CIA had discovered that the Soviets had learned the date of the invasion more than a week in advance and had then informed Cuban Prime Minister Fidel Castro, but—and here is a startling fact that should make people's hair stand on end—the CIA never told the President. The CIA knew the invasion was probably doomed before the fact but went ahead with it anyway.

Why? So they could and did afterwards blame JFK for the failure.

This treachery set the stage for events to come. For his part, sensing but not knowing the full extent of the set-up, Kennedy fired CIA Director Allen Dulles—(who, in an absurdity, was later named to the Warren Commission investigating his death) and his assistant, General Charles Cabell (whose brother Earle Cabell, to further the absurdity, was the mayor of Dallas on the day Kennedy was killed)—and said he wanted "to splinter the CIA in a thousand pieces and scatter it to the winds."

Not the sentiments to endear him to a secretive government within a government whose power was growing exponentially.[6]

Afterwards Kennedy said to his friends Dave Powell and Ken O'Donnell, "They were sure I'd give in to them and send the go-ahead order to the [Navy's aircraft carrier] *Essex*. They couldn't believe that a new president like me wouldn't panic and save his own face. Well, they had me figured all wrong."[7]

---

6 Vernon Loeb, "Soviets Knew Date of Cuba Attack," *Washington Post*, April 29, 2000. https://www.archives.gov/research/alic/reference/military/cuban-missile-crisis.html

7 Robert F. Kennedy, Jr., *American Values* (Harper Collins, 2018), p. 117.

Kennedy Responds After the Bay of Pigs Treachery

The stage was now set for events to follow as JFK, now even more suspicious of the military-intelligence people around him, and in opposition to nearly all his advisers, consistently opposed the use of force in U.S. foreign policy.

In 1961, despite the Joint Chief's demand to put combat troops into Laos—advising 140,000 by the end of April—Kennedy bluntly insisted otherwise as he ordered Averell Harriman, his representative at the Geneva Conference, "Did you understand? I want a negotiated settlement in Laos. I don't want to put troops in." The president knew that Laos and Vietnam were linked issues, and since Laos came first on his agenda, he was determined to push for a neutral Laos.

Also in 1961, he refused to accede to the insistence of his top generals to give them permission to use nuclear weapons in Berlin and Southeast Asia. Walking out of a meeting with his top military advisors, Kennedy threw his hands in the air and said, "These people are crazy."

In March 1962, the CIA, in the person of legendary operative Edward Lansdale, and with the approval of the Chairman and every member of the Joint Chiefs of Staff, presented to the president a pretext for a U.S. invasion of Cuba. Code-named *Operation Northwoods,* the false-flag plan called for innocent people to be shot in the U.S., boats carrying Cuban refugees to be sunk, a terrorism campaign to be launched in Miami, Washington D.C., and other places, all to be blamed on the Castro government so that the public would be outraged and call for an invasion of Cuba.[8]

Kennedy was appalled and rejected this pressure to manipulate him into agreeing to terrorist attacks that could later be used against him. He already knew that his life was in danger and that the CIA and military were tightening a noose around his neck. But he refused to yield.

---

8 "Pentagon Proposed Pretexts for Cuba Invasion in 1962," The National Security Archive, April 30, 2001. https://nsarchive2.gwu.edu/news/20010430/

As early as June 26, 1961, in a White House meeting with Soviet Premier Nikita Khrushchev's spokesperson, Mikhail Kharlamov, and Alexei Adzhubei, Khrushchev's son-in-law, when asked by Kharlamov why he wasn't moving faster to advance relations between the two countries, Kennedy said, "You don't understand this country. If I move too fast on U.S.-Soviet relations, I'll either be thrown into an insane asylum, or be killed."[9]

He refused to bomb and invade Cuba as the military wished during the Cuban missile crisis in October 1962. The Soviets had placed offensive nuclear missiles and 60,000 support troops in Cuba to prevent another U.S. invasion. American aerial photography had detected the missiles. This was understandably unacceptable to the U.S. government. While being urged by the Joint Chiefs and his trusted advisors to order a preemptive nuclear strike on Cuba, JFK knew that a diplomatic solution was the only way out, short the death of hundreds of millions of people that he wouldn't accept. Only his brother, Robert, and Secretary of Defense Robert McNamara stood with him in opposing the use of nuclear weapons. In the end, after thirteen incredibly tense days, Kennedy and Soviet Premier Nikita Khrushchev miraculously found a way to solve the crisis and prevent the use of those weapons. Premier Khrushchev had promised to take the Soviet missiles out of Cuba in return for Kennedy's pledge not to invade, which Kennedy gave. Furthermore, JFK sent RFK to meet with Soviet ambassador Anatoly Dobrynin to secretly promise to Khrushchev's demand that the U.S. then withdraw their missiles from Turkey.

Afterwards, JFK told his friend John Kenneth Galbraith that "I never had the slightest intention of doing so."[10]

The Fateful Year 1963

Then on June, 10 1963 he gave an historic speech at American University in which he called for the total abolishment of nuclear

9 Pierre Salinger, *P.S.: A Memoir* (St. Martin's Press, 1995), p. 253

10 See Douglass, *JFK and the Unspeakable*, chapters 1–3.

weapons, the end of the Cold War and the "Pax Americana enforced on the world by American weapons of war," advocating instead a movement toward "general and complete disarmament."[11]

A few months later he signed a Limited Test Ban Treaty with Nikita Khrushchev.

In October 1963 he signed National Security Action Memorandum 263 calling for the withdrawal of 1,000 U. S. Military troops from Vietnam by the end of the year and a total withdrawal by the end of 1965.[12]

All this he did while secretly engaging in negotiations with Soviet Premier Nikita Khrushchev via the KGB's Georgi Bolshakov,[13] Norman Cousins, the journalist and editor of *The Saturday Review*, and Pope John XXIII, and with Cuba's Prime Minister Fidel Castro through various intermediaries, one of whom was French Journalist Jean Daniel. Of course, secret was not secret when the CIA was involved.

In an interview with Daniel on October 24, 1963, Kennedy said:

> I approved the proclamation Fidel Castro made in the Sierra Maestra, when he justifiably called for justice and especially yearned to rid Cuba of corruption. I will go even further: to some extent it is as though Batista was the incarnation of a number of sins on the part of the United States. Now we will have to pay for those sins. In the matter of the Batista regime, I am in agreement with the first Cuban revolutionaries. That is perfectly clear.

Such sentiments were anathema, shall we say treasonous, to the CIA and top Pentagon generals. These clear refusals to go to war with Cuba, to emphasize peace and negotiated solutions

11 *President John F. Kennedy's "Peace Speech,"* video of 1963 speech, C-SPAN video [27:06]. https://www.youtube.com/watch?v=0fkKnfk4k40

12 See James K. Galbraith, "Exit Strategy," *Boston Review,* October/November 2003.

13 Pierre Salinger, *With Kennedy* (Doubleday & Co., 1966), p. 198.

to conflicts, not war, to order the withdrawal of all military personnel from Vietnam, to call for an end to the Cold War, and his decision to engage in private, back-channel communications with Cold War enemies marked Kennedy as an enemy of the national security state. They were on a collision course.

The Assassination on November 22, 1963

Once in the presidency, Kennedy underwent a deep metanoia, a spiritual transformation, from Cold Warrior to peacemaker. He came to see the generals who advised him as devoid of the tragic sense of life and as hell-bent on war. And he was well aware that his growing resistance to war had put him on a dangerous collision course with those generals and the CIA. On numerous occasions he spoke of the possibility of a military coup d'état against him.

On the night before his trip to Dallas, he told his wife, "But, Jackie, if somebody wants to shoot me from a window with a rifle, nobody can stop it, so why worry about it."

And we know that nobody did try to stop it because they had planned it. But not from a sixth-floor window.

Who Killed Him?

If the only things you read, watched, or listened to since 1963 were the mainstream corporate media (MSM), you would be convinced that the official explanation for JFK's assassination, *The Warren Commission*, was correct in essentials. You would be wrong because those media have for all these years served as mouthpieces for the government, most notably for the CIA that infiltrated and controlled them long ago. Total control of information requires media complicity, and in the JFK assassination and in all matters of importance, the CIA and MSM are synonyms. The corporate media are the propaganda arm of the CIA.

So they report that *The Warren Commission* claim that the president was shot by an ex-Marine named Lee Harvey Oswald, firing three bullets from the 6th floor of the Texas School Book Depository as Kennedy's car was driving away from him. But this is patently false for many reasons, including the claim that one of these bullets, later to be termed "the magic bullet," would have had to pass through Kennedy's body and zigzag up and down, left and right, to strike Texas Governor John Connolly who was sitting in the front seat, causing seven wounds in all, with the bullet only to be found later in pristine condition on a stretcher in Parkland Hospital.

The absurdity of that claim, the key to the government's assertion that Oswald killed Kennedy, is only visually reinforced and made ridiculous by the famous Zapruder film that clearly shows the president being shot from the front right, and as the right front of his head explodes, he is violently thrown back and to his left as Jacqueline Kennedy climbs on to the car's trunk to retrieve a piece of her husband's skull and brain.

This video evidence is clear and simple proof of a conspiracy.[14]

Who Was Lee Harvey Oswald?

But there is another way to examine it.

If Lee Harvey Oswald, the man the *Warren Commission* said killed JFK, was connected to the intelligence community, the FBI and the CIA, then we can logically conclude that he was not "a lone-nut" assassin or not the assassin at all. There is a wealth of evidence to show how from the very start Oswald was moved around the globe by the CIA like a pawn in a game, and when the game was done, the pawn was eliminated in the Dallas police headquarters by Jack Ruby two days later.

James W. Douglass, in *JFK and the Unspeakable: Why He Died and Why It Matters,* the most important book to read on the matter, asks this question:

> Why was Lee Harvey Oswald so tolerated and supported by the government he betrayed?

---

14 *Zapruder Film HD* [00:26]. JFK Assassination Truth Youtube channel. https://youtu.be/bgZYMau2rug

This is a key question.

After serving as a U.S. Marine at the CIA's U-2 spy plane operating base in Japan with a Crypto clearance (higher than top secret, a fact suppressed by the Warren Commission) and being trained in the Russian language, Oswald left the Marines and defected to the Soviet Union. After denouncing the U.S., rejecting his American citizenship, working at a Soviet factory in Minsk, and taking a Russian wife—during which time Gary Powers' U-2 spy plane is shot down over the Soviet Union—he returned to the U.S. with a loan from the American Embassy in Moscow, only to be met at the dock in Hoboken, New Jersey by a man, Spas T. Raikin, a prominent anti-communist with extensive intelligence connections recommended by the State Department.

He passed through immigration with no trouble, was not prosecuted, moved to Fort Worth, Texas where, at the suggestion of the Dallas CIA Domestic Contacts Service chief, he was met and befriended by George de Mohrenschildt, an anti-communist Russian, who was a CIA asset. De Mohrenschildt got him a job four days later at a graphic arts company that worked on maps for the U.S. Army Map Service related to U-2 spy missions over Cuba.

Oswald was then shepherded around the Dallas area by de Mohrenschildt who in 1977—on the day he revealed he had contacted Oswald for the CIA and was to meet with the House Select Committee on Assassinations' investigator, Gaeton Fonzi—allegedly committed suicide.

Oswald then moved to New Orleans in April 1963 where he got a job at the Reilly Coffee Company owned by CIA-affiliated William Reilly. The Reilly Coffee Company was located in close vicinity to the FBI, CIA, Secret Service, and Office of Naval Intelligence offices and a stone's throw from the office of Guy Bannister, a former Special Agent in charge of the FBI's Chicago Bureau, who worked as a covert action coordinator for the intelligence services, supplying and training the anti-Castro paramilitaries meant to ensnare Kennedy. Oswald then went to work with Bannister and the CIA paramilitaries.

From this time up until the assassination, Oswald engaged in all sorts of contradictory activities, one day portraying himself as pro-Castro, the next day as anti-Castro, with many of these theatrical performances being directed from Bannister's office. It was as though Oswald, on the orders of his puppet masters, was enacting multiple and antithetical roles in order to confound anyone intent on deciphering the purposes behind his actions and to set him up as a future "assassin."

Douglass persuasively argues that Oswald "seems to have been working with both the CIA and FBI," as a provocateur for the former and an informant for the latter. Jim and Elsie Wilcott, who worked at the CIA Tokyo Station from 1960–64, in a 1978 interview with the *San Francisco Chronicle*, said, "It was common knowledge in the Tokyo CIA station that Oswald worked for the agency."

When Oswald moved to New Orleans in April 1963, de Mohrenschildt left Dallas for Washington, D. C. where he met with CIA officials, having asked the CIA for and been indirectly given a $285,000 contract to do a geological survey for Haitian dictator "Papa Doc" Duvalier, which he never did, but for which he was paid. He never saw Oswald again.

Ruth and Michael Paine then entered the picture on cue. She had been introduced to Oswald by de Mohrenschildt. In September 1963, Ruth Paine drove from her sister's house in Virginia to New Orleans to pick up Marina Oswald and bring her to her house in Dallas to live with her. Back in Dallas, Ruth Paine conveniently got Oswald a job in the Texas Book Depository where he began work on October 16, 1963.

Ruth, along with Marina Oswald, was the Warren Commission's critically important witness against Oswald. Allen Dulles, who JFK had fired but who amazingly served as a key member of the Warren Commission, questioned the Paines during the course of it, studiously avoiding any revealing questions.

The Paines had extensive intelligence connections. Thirty years after the assassination a document was declassified showing Ruth Paine's sister Sylvia worked for the CIA. Her father traveled throughout Latin America on an Agency for International

Development (notorious for CIA front activities) contract and filed reports that went to the CIA. Her husband Michael's stepfather, Arthur Young, was the inventor of the Bell helicopter and Michael's job there gave him a security clearance. Her mother was related to the Forbes family of Boston and her lifelong friend, Mary Bancroft, worked as a WW II spy with Allen Dulles and was his mistress.

From late September until November 22, various "Oswalds" are later reported to have simultaneously been seen from Mexico City to Dallas. Two Oswalds were arrested in the Texas Theatre, the real one taken out the front door and an impostor out the back.

As Douglass says, "There were more Oswalds providing evidence against Lee Harvey Oswald than the Warren Report could use or even explain."

Even J. Edgar Hoover knew that Oswald impostors were used, as he told LBJ concerning Oswald's alleged visit to the Soviet Embassy in Mexico City. He later called this CIA ploy, "the false story re Oswald's trip to Mexico . . . their (CIA's) double-dealing," something that he couldn't forget.

It was apparent that a very intricate and deadly game was being played at high levels in the shadows.

We know Oswald was blamed for the President's murder. But if one fairly follows the trail of the crime, it becomes blatantly obvious that government forces were at work. Douglass and others have amassed layer upon layer of evidence to show how this had to be so.

Who Had the Power to Withdraw the President's Security?

To answer this essential question is to finger the conspirators and to expose, in Vincent Salandria's words, "the false mystery concealing state crimes."[15]

---

15 *The JFK Assassination: A False Mystery Concealing State Crimes,* video of Vincent Salandria's address at the Coalition on Political Assassinations Conference, Dallas, Texas, November 20, 1998 [1:25:44], rat haus reality press YouTube channel. https://www.youtube.com/watch?v=zkP5xtYT92k

Oswald, the mafia, anti-Castro Cubans could not have withdrawn most of the security that day. Dallas Sheriff Bill Decker withdrew all police protection. The Secret Service withdrew the police motorcycle escorts from beside the president's car where they had been the day before in Houston, and took agents off the back of the car where they were normally stationed to obstruct gunfire. The Secret Service admitted there were no Secret Service agents on the ground in Dealey Plaza to protect Kennedy, but we know from evidence that during and after the assassination there were people in Dealey Plaza impersonating Secret Service agents. The Secret Service approved the fateful, dogleg turn (on a dry run on November 18) where the car almost came to a halt, a clear security violation. The House Select Committee on Assassinations concluded this, not some conspiracy nut.

Who could have squelched the testimony of all the doctors and medical personnel who claimed the president had been shot from the front in his neck and head, testimony contradicting the official story?

Who could have prosecuted and imprisoned Abraham Bolden, the first African-American Secret Service agent personally brought on to the White House detail by JFK, who warned that he feared the president was going to be assassinated? (Douglass interviewed Bolden seven times and his evidence on the aborted plot to kill JFK in Chicago on November 2—a story little known but extraordinary in its implications—is riveting.)

The list of all the related people who turned up dead, the evidence and events manipulated, the inquiry squelched, distorted, and twisted in an ex post facto cover-up clearly point to forces within the government, not rogue actors without institutional support.

The evidence for a conspiracy organized at the deepest levels of the intelligence apparatus is overwhelming. James Douglass presents it in such depth and so logically that only one psychologically invested in the mainstream narrative would not be deeply moved and affected by his book, the essential book to read on the matter, where there is still more from him and other researchers who have cut the Gordian Knot of this false mystery with a few brief strokes.

Oswald, the Preordained Patsy

Three examples will suffice to show that Lee Harvey Oswald, working as part of a U.S. Intelligence operation, was set up to take the blame for the assassination of President Kennedy, and that when he said while in police custody that he was "a patsy," he was speaking truthfully. These examples make it clear that Oswald was deceived by his intelligence handlers and had been chosen without his knowledge, long before the murder, to take the blame as a lone, crazed killer.

First, Kennedy was shot at 12:30 PM CT. According to the *Warren Report*, at 12:45 PM a police report was issued for a suspect that perfectly fit Oswald's description. This was based on the testimony of Howard Brennan, who said he was standing across from the Book Depository and saw a white man, about 5'10" and slender, fire a rifle at the president's car from the sixth-floor window. This was blatantly false because easily available photographs taken moments after the shooting show the window open only partially at the bottom about fourteen inches, and it would have been impossible for a standing assassin to be seen "resting against the left windowsill," (the windowsill was a foot from the floor), as Brennan is alleged to have said. He would have therefore had to have been shooting through the glass. The description of the suspect was clearly fabricated in advance to match Oswald's.

Then at 1:15 PM in the Oak Cliff neighborhood of Dallas, Police Officer J.D. Tippit was shot and killed. At 1:50 PM, Lee Harvey Oswald was arrested in the Texas Theater and taken out the front door where a crowd and many police cars awaited him, while a few minutes later a second Oswald is secretly taken out the back door of the movie theater. (To read this story of the second Oswald and his movement by the CIA out of Dallas on a military aircraft on the afternoon of November 22, 1963, documented in great detail by James W. Douglass, will make your hair stand on end.[16])

Despite his denials, Oswald, set up for Kennedy's murder based on a prepackaged description, is arraigned for Tippet's murder at 7:10 PM. It was not until the next day that he was charged for Kennedy's.

The Message to Air Force One

Secondly, while Oswald is being questioned about Tippit's murder in the afternoon hours after his arrest, Air Force One has left Dallas for Washington with the newly sworn-in president, Lyndon Johnson, and the presidential party. Back in D.C., the White House Situation Room is under the personal and direct control of Kennedy's National Security Advisor, McGeorge Bundy, a man with close CIA ties who had consistently opposed JFK on many matters, including the Bay of Pigs and Kennedy's order to withdraw from Vietnam.

As reported by Theodore White in *The Making of the President 1964*, Johnson and the others were informed by the Bundy-controlled Situation Room that "there was no conspiracy, learned of the identity of Oswald and his arrest. . . ."[17]

Vincent Salandria, one of the earliest and most astute critics of the Warren Commission, put it this way in his book, *False Witness*:

> This was the very first announcement of Oswald as the lone assassin. In Dallas, Oswald was not even charged with assassinating the President until 1:30 A.M. the next morning. The plane landed at 5:59 P.M. on the 22nd. At

16 See Douglass, *JFK and the Unspeakable,* pp. 287–304.

Also, "Oswald's Doubles" at https://ratical.org/ratville/JFK/Unspeakable/TwoLHOs.html

17 Theodore White, *The Making of the President, 1964* (Atheneum, 1965), p. 48.

See also, Gerald S. Strober and Debra Strober, *Let Us Begin Anew: An Oral History of the Kennedy Presidency* (Perennial, 1993), pp. 450–51.

that time the District Attorney of Dallas, Henry Wade, was stating that "preliminary reports indicated more than one person was involved in the shooting ... the electric chair is too good for the killers." Can there be any doubt that for any government taken by surprise by the assassination—and legitimately seeking the truth concerning it—less than six hours after the time of the assassination was too soon to *know* there was no conspiracy? This announcement was the first which designated Oswald as the lone assassin....

I propose the thesis that McGeorge Bundy, when that announcement was issued from his Situation Room, had reason to know that the true meaning of such a message when conveyed to the Presidential party on Air Force One [and to a separate plane with the entire cabinet that had turned around and was headed back over the Pacific Ocean] was not the ostensible message which was being communicated. Rather, I submit that Bundy . . . was really conveying to the Presidential party the thought that Oswald was being designated the lone assassin before any evidence against him was ascertainable. As a central coordinator of intelligence services, Bundy in transmitting such a message through the Situation Room was really telling the Presidential party that an unholy marriage had taken place between the U.S. Governmental intelligence services and the lone-assassin doctrine. Was he not telling the Presidential party peremptorily, "Now, hear this! Oswald is the assassin, the sole assassin. Evidence is not available yet. Evidence will be obtained, or in lieu thereof evidence will be created. This is a crucial matter of state that cannot await evidence. The new rulers have spoken. You, there, Mr. New President, and therefore dispatchable stuff, and you the underlings of a deposed President, heed the message well." Was not Bundy's

Situation Room serving an Orwellian double-think function?[18]

Oswald's Prepackaged Life Story

Finally, Air Force Colonel Fletcher Prouty adds a third example of the CIA conspiracy for those who need more evidence that the government has lied from the start about the assassination.

Prouty was Chief of Special Operation in the Pentagon before and during the Kennedy years. He worked for CIA Director Allen Dulles supporting the clandestine operations of the CIA under military cover. He had been sent out of the country to the South Pole by the aforementioned CIA operative Edward Lansdale (Operation Northwoods) before the Kennedy assassination and was returning on November 22, 1963. On a stopover in Christchurch, New Zealand, he had heard a radio report that the president had been killed but knew no details. He was having breakfast with a U.S Congressman at 7:30 AM on November 23, New Zealand time. A short time later, which was approximately 4:30 PM Dallas time, November 22, four hours after the assassination, he bought the Christchurch newspaper and read it together with the Congressman.

The newspaper reports from the scene said that Kennedy had been killed by bursts of automatic weapons fire, not a single shot rifle, firing three separate shots in 6.8 seconds, as was later claimed to have been done by Oswald. But the thing that really startled him was that at a time when Oswald had just been arrested and had not even been charged for the murder of Officer Tippit, there was already elaborate background information on Oswald, his time in Russia, his association with Fair Play for Cuba Committee in New Orleans, etc. "It's almost like a book written five years later," said Prouty. "Furthermore, there's a picture of Oswald, well-dressed in a business suit, whereas, when he was picked up on the streets

18 Vincent J. Salandria, *False Mystery: Essays on the JFK Assassination* (ratical.org, 2017). https://www.ratical.org/ratville/JFK/FalseMystery/index.html

of Dallas after the President's death, he had on some t-shirt or something....[19]

"Who had written that scenario? Who wrote that script ... So much news was already written ahead of time of the murder to say that Oswald killed the President and that he did it with three shots.... Somebody had decided Oswald was going to be the patsy.... Where did they get it, before the police had charged him with the crime? Not so much 'where,' as 'why Oswald?'"

Prouty, an experienced military man working for the CIA in the Pentagon, accused the military-intelligence "High Cabal" of killing President Kennedy in an elaborate and sophisticated plot and blaming it on Oswald, whom they had for years set up in advance as part of a fake defector program run by the CIA. They brought him back to the U.S. on June 13, 1962 and had him escorted to Fort-Worth, Texas where he was introduced to his CIA handler de Mohrenschildt. The evidence for a government plot to plan, assassinate, cover-up, and choose a patsy in the murder of President John Kennedy is overwhelming.

Five years after JFK's assassination, we would learn, to our chagrin and his glory, that the president's younger brother, Senator Robert F. Kennedy, equally brave and unintimidated, would take a bullet to the back of his head in 1968 as he was on his way to the presidency and the pursuit of his brother's killers. The same cowards struck again.

Their successors still run the country and must be stopped.

---

19 David T. Ratcliffe, *Understanding Special Operations and Their Impact on the Vietnam War Era: 1989 Interview with L. Fletcher Prouty* (Rat House Reality Press, 1999), p. 215

Bob Dylan's Midnight Message to JFK's Ghost

"For murder, though it have no tongue,
will speak with most miraculous organ."
—HAMLET

On May 1, 1962, President John Kennedy was meeting in the Oval Office with a group of Quakers who were urging him to do more for peace and disarmament. As he kept explaining the great political opposition he was facing within his own government, they kept urging him to do more. He listened very closely to their words and finally said, "You believe in redemption don't you." By the next spring he had turned decisively toward the peacemaking the Quakers had urged upon him, resulting in his murder in the fall by treacherous government forces, led by the CIA, that had opposed him all along.

Now, March 27, 2020, that Dylan has burst forth from behind his many masks and gifted the world with his incandescent new song about the assassination, with a title taken from *Hamlet*, from the mouth of the ghost of the dead King of Denmark –"Murder Most Foul"– we have entered a new day in an odd way. For those who have wondered over the years if Dylan had "sold out," here is their answer. For those who have wondered if he would go to his grave reciting the words of T.S. Eliot's J. Alfred Prufrock—"I am no Prince Hamlet nor was meant to be"—Dylan rolls out Hamlet's booming response. Not only does this song lay bare the truth of the most foundational event in modern American history, but it does so in such a powerfully poetic way and at such an opportune time that it should redeem Dylan in the eyes of those who ever doubted him.

I say "should," but while the song's release has garnered massive publicity from the mainstream media, it hasn't taken long for that media to bury the truth of his words about the assassination under a spectacle of verbiage meant to damn with faint praise. As the media in the celebrity culture of the spectacle tend to do, the emphasis on the song's pop cultural references is their focus, with platitudes about the assassination and "conspiracy theories," as well as various shameful and gratuitous digs at Dylan for being weird, obsessed, or old. As the song says, "they killed him once and they killed him twice," so now they can kill him a third time, and then a fourth, ad infinitum. And now the messenger of the very bad news must be dispatched along with the dead president.

The media like their Hamlets impotent and enervated, but Dylan has come out roaring like a bull intent on avenging his dead president.

He has the poet's touch, of course, a hyperbolic sense of the fantastic that draws you into his magical web in the pursuit of deeper truth. In many ways he's like the Latin American magical realist writers who move from fact to dream to the fantastic in a puff of wind.

Dylan is our Emerson. His artistic philosophy has always been about movement in space and time through song. Always moving, always restless, always seeking a way back home through song, even when, or perhaps because, there are no directions. "An artist has got to be careful never to arrive at a place where he thinks he's at somewhere," he's said. "You always have to realize that you are constantly in a state of becoming and as long as you can stay in that realm, you'll be alright."

Sounds like living, right?

Sounds like Emerson, also. "Life only avails, not the having lived. Power ceases in the instant of repose; it resides in the moment of transition from a past to a new state, in the shooting of the gulf, in the darting to an aim. Thus one fact the world hates, that the soul becomes."

"Murder Most Foul" is Dylan's soul becoming.

"A song is like a dream, and you try to make it come true. They're like strange countries that you have to enter. You can write a song anywhere.... It helps to be moving. Sometimes people who have the greatest talent for writing songs never write any because they are not moving," he wrote in *Chronicles.*

"Murder Most Foul" is a moving song in every sense of the word—a trip to truth.

Dylan has long been accused of abandoning his youthful idealism and protest music. I think this is a bum rap. He was never a protester, though his songs became anthems of the civil rights and anti-war movements. There is no doubt that those songs were inspirational and gave people hope to carry on the good fight. But in turning in a more oblique and circumspect musical direction, following his need to change as the spirit of inspiration moved him, Dylan's songs came to inspire in a new way. You could always tell his sympathies lay with the oppressed and downtrodden, but for decades he didn't shout it, with perhaps the one exception being the powerful, hard-hitting, and mesmeric *Hurricane* in 1975. With that one he stepped into the ring to brawl.

But for the most part over the years, a listener has had to catch his drift. If you go to the music, and dip into his various stylistic changes over the decades, however, you will find a consistency of themes. He deals with essentials like all great poets. Nothing is excluded. His work is paradoxical. Yes, he's been singing about death since twelve, but it has always been countered by life and rebirth. There is joy and sadness; faith and doubt; happiness and suffering; injustice and justice; romance and its discontents; despair and hope. His music possesses a bit of a Taoist quality mixed with a Biblical sensibility conveyed by a hopelessly romantic American. He has fused his themes into an incantatory delivery that casts a moving spell of hope upon the listener. He is nothing if not a spiritual spellbinder; similar in many ways to that other quintessential American, the Beat poet Allen Ginsberg, whose best work was a poetic quest for an inspired salvific poetry.

While speaking the unspeakable truth about President John Kennedy's murder might seem hopeless, it is actually a sign of great hope. For our only hope is in telling the truth, which Dylan has done.

This is art, not theory, and art of a special kind since Dylan is an artist at war with his art. His songs demand that the listener's mind and spirit be moving as the spirit of creative inspiration moved Dylan. A close listening will force one to jump from line to line, verse to verse—to shoot the gulf—since there are no bridges to cross, no connecting links. The sound carries you over and keeps you moving forward. If you're not moving, you'll miss the meaning.

I have no wish to explicate the poet's brilliant work. It speaks for itself. It says far more than it specifically says about a system rotten to the core, a country where everything went wrong since "The day the killers blew out the brains of the king/Thousands were watching, no one saw a thing."

If you listen to Dylan's piercing voice and follow the lyrics closely, you might be startled to be told, not from someone who can be dismissed as some sort of disgruntled "conspiracy nut," but by the most famous musician in the world, that there was a government conspiracy to kill JFK, that Oswald didn't do it, and that the killers then went for the president's brothers.

> Your brothers are comin', there'll be hell to pay
> Brothers? What brothers? What's this about hell?
> Tell them, "We're waiting, keep coming," we'll get
> them as well

This is an in-your-face tale, set to music with a barely tinkling piano, a violin, and a soupçon of percussion, whose lightest words, as Hamlet's father's ghost said to him:

> Would harrow up thy soul, freeze thy young blood,
> Make thy two eyes like stars start from their spheres,
> Thy knotty and combinèd locks to part,
> And each particular hair to stand on end

Like quills upon the fretful porcupine.

"Murder Most Foul" truly startles. It is a redemptive song. Dylan holds the mirror up for us. He unlocks the door to the painful and sickening truth. He shoves the listener in and, as he writes in *Chronicles,* "your head has to go into a different place. Sometimes it takes a certain somebody to make you realize it."

Dylan is our certain somebody. In these dark times he has offered us his voice.

You believe in redemption, don't you?

Interview Most Foul

The mainstream corporate propagandists never have had any interest in the truth and consequences of JFK's assassination by the national security state led by the CIA. They still make no connection between it and where this society finds itself today. Dylan's words fall on deaf ears:

What's new, pussycat? What did I say?
I said the soul of a nation been torn away
And it's beginning to go into a slow decay

Imagine this: A so-called presidential historian for a major television network publishes an interview in the most famous newspaper in the world with the most famous singer/songwriter in the world, who has recently written an explosive song accusing the U.S. government of a conspiracy in the assassination of the most famous modern American president, and the interviewer never asks the singer about the specific allegations in his song except to ask him if he was surprised that the song reached number one on the Billboard hit list and other musical and cultural references that have nothing to do with the assassination.

Imagine no more. For that is exactly what Douglas Brinkley, CNN's presidential historian, has just done with his June 12, 2020, interview with Bob Dylan in *The New York Times*. The interview makes emphatically clear that Brinkley is not in the least interested in what Dylan has to say about the assassination of the President of the United States, John F. Kennedy, whose murder most foul marks in the most profound way possible the devolution of the U.S. into the cesspool it has become.

Brinkley has another agenda.

He introduces the interview by sketching in his relationship with Dylan and tells us that he therefore felt "comfortable" reaching out to him in April after Dylan had released his song about the JFK assassination, "Murder Most Foul." He conveniently links to a *New York Times* piece by John Pareles wherein Pareles writes about the surprise song release, "The assassination of John F. Kennedy is its core and central trauma—'the soul of a nation been torn away/and it's beginnin' to go into a slow decay'—while Dylan tries to find answers, or at least clues, in music."

That is simply false—for Dylan emphatically does not *try* to find answers or clues to JFK's murder, but boldly *states* his answer. If you listen to his piercing voice and follow the lyrics closely, you might be startled to be told, not from someone who can be dismissed as some sort of disgruntled "conspiracy nut," but by the most famous musician in the world, that there was a government conspiracy to kill JFK, that Oswald didn't do it, and that the killers then went for the president's brothers.

But neither Pareles nor the presidential historian interviewer Brinkley wants to hear Dylan's answer. It was already clear that the corporate mainstream media were in the process of diverting readers from the core of Dylan's message.

Brinkley continues this coverup under the guise of promoting Dylan's upcoming album, *Rough and Rowdy Ways*, while showing his appreciation for Dylan's music and his genius and asking questions that emphasize cultural and musical allusions in the new album and making certain to not allow Dylan's explosive message any breathing room.

Here is Brinkley's opening question, the only semi-direct one the presidential historian deems worthy of asking about "Murder Most Foul" and the assassination of an American president. This question opens the interview and shuts the door on further inquiry. It is a ridiculous question as well:

> Was "Murder Most Foul" written as a nostalgic eulogy for a long-lost time?
>
> To which Dylan responds:
>
> To me it's not nostalgic. I don't think of "Murder Most Foul" as a glorification of the past or some kind of send-off to a lost age. It speaks to me in the moment. It always did, especially when I was writing the lyrics out.

Could Brinkley really think he was asking a serious question? Nostalgia? What, for a brutal assassination, as Dylan describes it:

> Being led to the slaughter like a sacrificial lamb
> . . . .
> Shot down like a dog in broad daylight
> . . . .
> The day that they blew out the brains of the king
> Thousands were watching, no one saw a thing

No, the presidential historian knew the question wasn't serious. Did he think Dylan was *nostalgic* about the bloody murder of a man he calls the king, as he sings the part of Hamlet sending his midnight message of truth and revenge to JFK's ghost? Of course not. Brinkley was doing what all the mainstream corporate media do: Making sure the truth was hidden behind a stream of pop cultural references and questions that would appeal to *The New York Times'* aging readers who are nostalgic for their youth as they contemplate old age and death.

When Dylan answers one of his questions about his recent song, "I Contain Multitudes," by saying "it is trance writing," he uses a word that applies to this *New York Times* interview. It is a trance-inducing interview meant to do what the *Times* has been doing for nearly six decades: obfuscating the truth about the murder of President Kennedy by the national security state led by the CIA. The same CIA that has always found a most receptive mouthpiece in the *Times*.

This interview, that begins with a witless question about nostalgia, ends with the question all the aging baby boomer *Times'* readers were waiting to hear Brinkley ask Dylan:

> How is your health holding up? You seem to be fit as a fiddle. How do you keep mind and body working together in unison?

From nostalgia to health more or less sums up this interview. "What is the truth and where did it go?" Dylan asks.

Brinkley makes sure the truth is gone by asking other questions to take your head to places where you won't see a thing. It's quite a magic trick.

Drinking Coffee in the Early Morning Rain and Thinking of Donald Rumsfeld

It's been raining incessantly for three days. It is a cool early morning in the beginning of July and I have just made a cup of coffee. Now an electrical power outage has occurred and so I am sitting in a rocking chair in the semi-darkness, savoring my coffee and feeling thankful that I made it in time. I have a close relationship with coffee and the end of night and the break of day. As for time, that is as mysterious to me as the fact that I am sitting here in its embrace. The electric clocks have stopped. I think: To exist—how amazing!

More than the coffee, however, I am luxuriating in the sound of the tumbling rain. Its beautiful music creates a cocoon of peace within which I find temporary joy. The joy of doing nothing, of pursuing no purpose. Of knowing that whatever I do it will never be enough, for me or anyone, and the world will continue turning until time stands still, or whatever time does or is according to those who invented it. I will be gone and others will have arrived and the water will flow from the skies and the clocks will still tell people what they don't know—what time is—although they will continue to tell it.

A few weeks ago, when this area was in a mini-drought, the local newspaper, in the typical wisdom of such cant, had a headline that said "there is a threat of rain later this week." They are experts at threats. This is the corporate media's purpose. Rain is a threat, joy is a threat, doing nothing is a threat, the sun is a threat—but the real threats they conceal. To create fear seems to be their purpose, as they do not tell us about the real threats. Their purpose is not to tell the truth, but if you listen closely you can still hear it.

In the middle of the night I woke up to go to the bathroom, and outside the small bathroom window I watched the rain engulfing the lower roof and sluicing down the shingles in two heavy streams. I thought how the desiccated mind of the headline writer must be feeling now, but then I realized that he or she was asleep, as usual. There is a moist world and a dry one, and the corporate media is run by arid souls who would like to make the world a desert like their masters of war in Washington.

Then as I sit here my brief peace is roiled by the memory of reading Tacitus, the Roman historian, and his famous quote of Calgacus, an enemy of Rome:

> These plunderers of the world [the Romans], after exhausting the land by their devastations, are rifling the ocean: stimulated by avarice, if their enemy be rich; by ambition, if poor; unsatiated by the East and by the West: the only people who behold wealth and indigence with equal avidity. To ravage, to slaughter, to usurp under false titles, they call empire; and where they make a desert, they call it peace.

I think of former Secretary of Defense Donald Rumsfeld on his recent deathbed. Here was a man whose entire life was dedicated to the American Empire. He spent all his allotted time making war or making money from the spoils of war. He was a desert maker, a slaughterer for the Empire. No doubt he died very rich in gold.

I can no longer hear the rain because my mind is filled with the louder thought of what Rumsfeld thought as he lay dying. Was he sorry? Did he believe in God or was his god Mars, the Roman god of war? Did he smile a bloody smile or say he was sorry and beg for forgiveness from all his innocent victims? Did he see the faces of the Iraqi children that he slaughtered? Or did he pull an Eichmann and say, "I will leap into my grave laughing"?

Your guess is as good as mine, but mine leans toward the bloody smile of a life well spent in desert making. But that is a "known unknown."

Rolling thunder and a lightning strike in the east jolt me back from my deaf dark thoughts. The sound of the rain returns. The coffee tastes great. Peace returns with the unalloyed gift of the ravishing rain.

Yet the more I sit and listen and watch it soundly stipple the garden and grass, the more thoughts come to me, as my father once told me: Thoughts think us as much as we think thoughts. It's what we do with our thoughts that count, he said, and like lightning, if we don't flash when we are given the gift of life, when we're gone, it will be as if we never were, like the lightning before it flashed.

Thomas Merton's prophetic words from his hermitage in the Kentucky woods in 1966 think me:

> Let me say this before rain becomes a utility that they can plan and distribute for money. By "they" I mean the people who cannot understand that rain is a festival, who do not appreciate its gratuity, who think that what has no price has no value, that what cannot be sold is not real, so that the only way to make something *actual* is to place it on the market. The time will come when they will sell you even your rain. At the moment it is still free, and I am in it. I celebrate its gratuity and its meaninglessness.

There are moments in many lives when, if one is lucky, they are initiated into a ritual that sustains them throughout life. To others these experiences can easily seem paltry and meaningless, but to the receiver they offer a crack into deeper dimensions of being and becoming. For me it was my introduction to coffee during a hurricane.

My father had driven my mother, three of my sisters, and me to Jones Beach on Long Island. This was before people checked the weather every minute. The sky in the southwest grew darker as we drove, but on we went. The beach was deserted except for some gulls and the parking lot was empty. My father parked the car close to the beach and while my sisters and mother sat in the car, and my mother, listening to the weather reports, issued warnings to us, my father and I ran like wild dogs into the heavy surf despite her admonitions that the hurricane from the south was arriving sooner than expected. It started to rain hard. The surf picked up. We swam and got battered and shouted exultantly and came out shaking with the chills. A pure white sea gull landed on my wet head and my father laughed. Awe-struck, I stood stock still and my shaking stopped. In its mouth the sea gull held a purple ribbon, which it dropped at my feet as it flew off. I grabbed the ribbon and we jogged up to the concession building where there was one man working. My father ordered coffee and a hot chocolate for me. But they had run out of hot chocolate. So my father ordered two coffees and filled mine with three or four sugars. I had never sampled coffee and didn't like the smell, but my father said to drink it, with the sugar it will taste good and it will warm you up. It strangely tasted like hot chocolate. We toasted our adventure as I drank my Proustian madeleine at eleven-years-old.

I had put the ribbon on the counter as we drank. When we were going back to the car, I noticed there were words on the ribbon. They said: Rest in peace. I have long lost the ribbon but retain its message.

So now every morning between the end of night and the break of day, I sit with my coffee and listen. And even when it isn't raining, I watch the birds emerge from their nightly rests to greet the day with their songs. They tell me many things, and they are all free.

This morning I am wondering if Donald Rumsfeld ever heard them.

I suspect their message was an "unknown unknown" for him, just like the gift of rain. He preferred the rain of death from the skies in the form of bombs and missiles. He was only doing his job.

He made a desert and called it peace.

A Gentrified Little Town Goes to Pot

"In my little town/ I grew up believing/
God keeps his eye on us all."
—SIMON AND GARFUNKEL, "My Little Town"

Hello my old friends Paul and Art,

I'm just sitting here chilling out in the silent darkness of a late night spinning some discs and thinking your song is great but even great songs age as do we all and so I want to tell you that as a NYC born and bred boy like you guys who moved out to the country decades ago that in my little town many young people grew up not believing that God keeps his eye on us all because they grew up not believing in God, and even many of their parents, baby-boomer believers in hands-off parenting and meditation and yoga weekends and you can be anything you want rainbow roads, didn't keep an eye on them, not at all, since the parents thought of themselves as super cool and so the kids were allowed to fend for themselves in a most culturally liberal life-style way, and then, when the kids got confused and screwed up and did various drugs, especially a lot of pot following on the Ritalin they were given for their "disabilities" and the anti-depression meds that fell out of the families' medicine cabinets and of course booze, and I guess I should add some heroin and the other shit that's around—man, it's crazy—the parents were dumbfounded and couldn't understand what went wrong and why their kids, even as they aged, were still kids like they the parents were, caught in a stream of lostness, an existential despair unaware of its despair, to quote my old friend Søren K, so they lived in a haze of smoke and mirrors and that darkness you guys sang about where they suffered from socially-induced attention deficit disorder and floated in a culture of self-awareness and eclectic New-Ageism feasting on organic food and nostalgia for penny candy and days at summer camp even as the town they settled in became an up-scaled high-tech movie set for millionaires in which the cool people could mingle with cooler people as the celebrities came and went and the out-of-towners all dressed in black like walking shades brought their money from Wall St. and high tech and financial institutions and the little town acquired a reputation as the hippest coolest gayest Democratic place to visit and move to especially after 9/11 even before the town went to pot and SARS-CoV-2 walked in and the town allowed 10 or so recreational pot stores to open in its small space and the lines of the desperadoes waiting for their legal fixes wound round and round and all the heads were spinning and dizzy with dreams of mashed potatoes and brownies unlike mom used to make but the money kept pouring in and the press went wild with popular stories of weed and more weed and the true believers in this enormous and shattering breakthrough of legal pot and brilliant entrepreneurial instant millionaires that would end their chronic pains and everyone would be dreamily happy and relaxed as they awaited redemption at the hands of the latest politician to ride to the rescue and save the country and ease all the pain caused by Mr. Pumpkin Head and his ilk, like what would be better, man, if you know what I mean, but there's something a little weird with all this crazy excitement about getting high legally and paying for what you can grow, but I guess the town likes the tax revenue but I'm thinking what's happened to old-fashioned DIY Yankee initiative and cool stuff like that in a town where the American Revolution was fought to allow the rich to build their McMansions and buy up the land to raise llamas and place Buddha statues and even their own little churches on and stuff like that but maybe I'm starting to get off topic a bit here so I should probably stop now while I'm ahead and on a high note about revolution and making the world safe for weed which should be the goal even though I'm not so sure aging hippies and their hipster kids will know how to use the stuff responsibly and stay off the road to ruin and avoid accidents while high and just chill out like I'm sure the USA will do once we get rid of the orange man and vote with my little town to return a Democrat to the White House so we can assume our responsibility to protect all those countries threatened by madmen like Gaddafi and Assad and maybe even do something about that demon Putin that will allow us little town folks to feel safe as once again God and the NSA keep their eyes on us all even while we are getting high which is our god given right as god fearing Americans and we return to the old values that we all shared before we went down the New Jersey Turnpike looking for America, guys, Kathy ain't the only one sleeping and your singer not the only one lost if you get my drift.

Here's to chilling,

EJ

The CIA Does "Soulful Work"

Back in the late 1980s and early 1990s, a spate of books and articles extolling the word "soul" became the rage in the U.S. A. Soul became the chic word. It popped up everywhere. Everything seemed to acquire soul—cars, toasters, underwear, cats' pajamas, assorted crap, kitsch, etc. Soul sold styles from boots to bras to bibelots from *The New York Times* to *O Magazine*.

The vogue in soul talk spread to every domain as everyone was commodified and capital was financialized. While political, economic, and ecological reality spun out of regular people's control and they felt unable to feel connected to a religious tradition that cut through the materialistic and war miasma, they were ravaged with a hunger to devour, to consume. It was soul propaganda, highbrow New Ageism at its finest, the religious equivalent of an old-fashioned Ralph Lauren interior. It was the era of consuming souls in a society that had become a spiritual void. At least for those who had become divorced from their bodies and tradition at its best. Fantasy started to rapidly replace reality.

The great popularizer of this new sense of soul and self (though no-self would be more accurate) was Thomas Moore, the author of the best-selling book—*Care of the Soul*, "a pathbreaking lifestyle handbook" and soon to be soul franchise (*The Soul of Sex, Soul Therapy, The Soul of Christmas*, etc.) His works replaced the idea of an existential self with a precious, epicurean conception. "You have a soul, the tree in front of your house has a soul, but so too does the car parked under the tree," he said, adding that things "have as much personality and independence as I do." Ah, soul!

Not soul as I once learned in Catholic school: the essence of human freedom and consciousness in God united with the body.

Definitely not soul as the essence of a person bound by conscience to God and other human beings.

Not soul as in "For what shall it profit a man if he should gain the whole world and lose his soul."

Not even soul as the dictionary defines it: "the immortal essence of an individual life."

Although I have seen this soul-talk used for decades now to sell all sorts of bullshit and thought I couldn't be surprised by any more usage, I just stumbled on one that took my breath away. I read in *Life Undercover*, a memoir by RFK, Jr.'s presidential campaign manager, daughter-in-law, and former CIA spy under nonofficial cover in the Middle East, Southeast Asia, and North Africa, Amaryllis Fox (Kennedy), that CIA work is "soulful work." I didn't know this. I thought its job was to spy, kill, and foment chaos for its Wall St handlers (with certain exceptions being some analysts who gather information). I recall former CIA Director Mike Pompeo saying, "I was the CIA director. We lied, we cheated, we stole. It's—it was like—we had entire training courses. It reminds you of the glory of the American experiment." Or as my friend Doug Valentine, an expert on the CIA, puts it, the CIA is "Organized Crime," not a bunch of soul-force workers out to feed the hungry and clothe the naked. He writes:

> CIA and military intelligence units now operate out of a global network of bases, as well as secret jails and detention sites operated by complicit secret police interrogators. Their strategic intelligence networks in any nation are protected by corrupt warlords and politicians, the "friendly civilians" who supply the death squads that in fact are their private militias, funded largely by drug smuggling and other criminal activities.

Yet Fox effusively thanks her CIA colleagues for their great work and for making her the woman she has become. "Your allegiance is to the flag, to the Constitution, to some higher power, be that God or Love," she writes in gratitude. For some reason, I don't think the assassinated JFK or RFK would buy her love talk; rather, they may quote another eloquent Irish American, the playwright Eugene O'Neill: "God damn you, stop shoving your rotten soul in my lap."

The man Fox is trying to elect president of the U.S., Robert F. Kennedy, Jr., also wrote a memoir—*American Values*—that revolves around an indictment of the CIA for an endless series of crimes: "What are we going to do about the CIA?" he quotes his father saying to his aide Fred Dutton at the beginning of JFK's presidency, before both Kennedys were killed by the soulful CIA. Kennedy Jr. wrote, "Critics warned that the 'tail' of the covert operations branch would inevitably wag the dog of intelligence gathering (espionage). And indeed, the clandestine services quickly subsumed the CIA's espionage function as the Agency's intelligence analysts increasingly provided justification for the CIA's endless interventions." Fifty years later his campaign manager Fox Kennedy—you can't make such weirdness up—married to RFK, III, is touting the soulful work of the Agency. She replaced Dennis Kucinich, who was a strong a supporter of the Palestinians. Is Fox and RFK, Jr.'s relationship a matter of what the Boss says to Luke in the iconic movie *Cool Hand Luke*—"What we got here is failure to communicate"—or the kind of communication that takes place in elite circles behind closed doors? So RFK, Jr. can support the Israeli genocide of the Palestinians.

Sometimes sick people utter truths that lead to sardonic assent. They remind you of history that is so shameful you cringe. Fox and Pompeo also seem to live in separate realities, their psyches twisted by some deep evil force for which they both worked.

And here we are in another presidential election year. When you think about presidential politics, you have to laugh. I like to laugh so I think about them from time to time. It's always a bad joke, but that's why they are funny. It makes no difference whether the president is Ford, Nixon, Carter, Reagan, George H. W. Bush, Clinton, Bush Jr., Obama, Trump, Biden, or anyone who tries to square the oval office for their special sort of big change that never comes. Those who tell you with a straight face that the lesser of two (or more) evils is better than nothing have not studied history. They choose the evil of two lessers and wash their hands. They live on pipe dreams, as Eugene O'Neill put it in *The Iceman Cometh*:

> To hell with the truth! As the history of the world proves, the truth has no bearing on anything. It's irrelevant and immaterial, as the lawyers say. The lie of a pipe dream is what gives life to the whole misbegotten mad lot of us, drunk or sober.

I am reminded of advice I was given during the immoral and illegal Vietnam War when I had decided to apply for a discharge from the Marines as a conscientious objector. But if you don't go to the war, people said to me with straight faces, some poor draftee will. The military needs good people. To which I would often respond: Like the country needs good commanders-in-chief such as Lyndon Johnson and Richard Nixon. It's like what people say about buying a lottery ticket when your odds are 1 in 500,000,000—someone has to win. Ha! Ha! Never reject the system is always the message.

Contemplating U.S. history for the past fifty-five plus years confirms the continuity of government policy for war, economic policies that enrich the wealthy at the expense of the working class, and the massacre of the innocent around the world. But we can pretend otherwise. For an egregious recent example, the leading candidates in the 2024 election—Biden, Harris, Trump, and RFK, Jr.—all stand firmly behind the Israeli genocide in Gaza that any human being with a soul would condemn.

That these men are controlled by the Israel Lobby is obvious, but we can pretend otherwise.

That this is corruption is obvious, but we can pretend otherwise.

We can pretend and pretend and pretend all we want because we are living in a pretend society.

What's that old Rodney Dangerfield joke: the problem with happiness is that it can't buy you money? Well, the problem with presidential politics is it can't buy you the truth, but if you do it right it can fetch you money, a lot of corrupt money to help you rise to the pinnacle of a corrupt government. For the truth is that the CIA/NSA run U.S. foreign war policy, and the presidents are figureheads, actors in a society that lost all connection to reality on November 22, 1963.

Scott Ritter has recently written about the CIA and its spearheading of the U.S. war against Russia through Ukraine:

> Now, amid such a tense environment, it appears the C.I.A. has not only green-lighted an actual invasion of the Russian Federation, but more than likely was involved in its planning, preparation and execution.
>
> Never in the history of the nuclear era has such danger of nuclear war been so manifest.
>
> That the American people have allowed their government to create the conditions where foreign governments can determine their fate and the C.I.A. can carry out a secret war which could trigger a nuclear conflict, eviscerates the notion of democracy.

If this is soulful work, God help us.

Ask the 45,000 + dead Palestinians in Gaza whose voices cry out for justice while the top presidential contenders cheer on the Israeli/U.S. slaughter.

"The terrible truth is," writes Douglas Valentine, "that a Cult of Death rules America and is hell-bent on world domination."

And yes, presidential politics is a funny diversion from that reality. Eugene O'Neill could be humorous also. He played the Iceman theme to perfection, the Grim Reaper of two faces.

There was a tale circulating in the 1930s that a man came home and called upstairs to his wife, "Has the iceman come yet?" "No," she replied, "but he's breathing hard."

Media Pseudo-Debates and the Silence of Leftist Critics

You've heard of them, no doubt, the U.S. rulers who can't rule too well and are always getting surprised by events or fed bad advice by their underlings. Their "mistakes" are always well intentioned. They stumble into wars through faulty intelligence. They drop the ball because of bureaucratic mix-ups. They miscalculate the perfidy of the elites whom allegedly they oppose while ushering them into the national coffers out of necessity since they are too big to fail. They never see the storm coming, even as they create it. Their incompetence is the retort to all those nut cases who conjure up conspiracy theories to explain their actions or lack thereof. They are innocent. Always innocent.

They and their media mouthpieces offer Americans, who are most eager to accept what Lutheran pastor and anti-Nazi dissident Dietrich Bonhoeffer, executed at age thirty-nine by Hitler, called cheap grace: "Cheap grace is the grace we bestow on ourselves. Cheap grace is the preaching of forgiveness without requiring repentance. . ."

These incompetents are, in the immortal words of the New York newspaper columnist Jimmy Breslin, "The Gang Who Couldn't Shoot Straight."

Except they could and can.

They've actually shot a lot of people, here and abroad. It's one of their specialties. But they mean well. They screw up sometimes, but they mean well. They care, even while they kill millions with their guns and bombs. But they have their followers.

As another dissident thirty-nine-year-old pastor, executed by the American state, Martin Luther King, Jr. said: "Nothing in the world is more dangerous than sincere ignorance and conscientious stupidity."

Mainstream Media Pseudo-Debates

The U.S. rulers have their defenders. Most are corporate mainstream journalists whose jobs are to defend the ruling elites of both political parties. They will criticize across the political divides depending on their organizations' political leanings at the moment. But they will never attack the fundamentals of the oligarchic war system since they are part of it. Their jobs depend on it. So *CNN* and *The New York Times* will obsessively attack Trump while *Fox News* will do the same to Obama or Biden. This is a game.

These days such massive media conglomerates are seemingly starkly divided and basically serve as adjuncts of one political party or the other. They are essentially political propagandists for either the Democrats or the Republicans and have abandoned any pretense to be anything else. They speak to their respective audiences in self-enclosed vacuums. They promote the divide that runs down the middle of the USA, a divide they helped to create.

Some have argued that this radical division of the media turf is because of economic and business factors—that the media organizations and their "journalists" have seen this strategy as the path to greater profits. There is probably some truth in this. But it is a small part.

For all sides of the corporate media serve the same overarching political function: to divide and conquer the population; to set the so-called left against right; middle America against the east and west coasts; white against black; working class against middle-class; men against women; husbands against wives, etc. To keep people, who in reality should be allies, fighting with each other. It is a classic strategy of divide-and-conquer that is carried out by the mainstream media pursuant to their unstated mandate.

It is not an accident and has been conducted with a vengeance in recent years.

And crucially, it is anchored in the false premise of left vs. right with a reasonable center somewhere in between. Such a center has never existed. While left and right might once have been useful categories, they have long since outlived their usefulness. They now just serve to engender pseudo-debates.

Pseudo-debates are not new, but they are highly effective. They are debates based on false premises. In this case, the premise is that the massive corporate media conglomerates are not part of the same system of control and containment of the population but are genuine opponents in the battle for truth and democracy. Accept this premise and you have entered into endless debates leading nowhere. It is a classic method of intelligence agencies to sow uncertainty and confusion and to have people following Alice down the rabbit hole, tumbling and tumbling into an endless void as they argue continually about nothing.

Dr. E. Martin Schotz has brilliantly explicated this trick in the case of the assassination of President Kennedy ("Certainly no honest person could ever accept the 'single bullet theory'") where people are still debating a false mystery almost sixty years after the fact. He writes:

> The lie is that there is a mystery to debate. And so we have pseudo-debates. Debates about meaningless disputes, based on assumptions which are obviously false. . . . Perhaps many people think that engaging in pseudo-debate is a benign activity. That it simply means that people are debating something that is irrelevant. This is not the case. I say this because every debate rests on a premise to which the debaters must agree, or there is no debate. In the case of pseudo-debate the premise is a lie. So in the pseudo-debate we have the parties to the debate agreeing to purvey a lie to the public. And it is all the more malignant because it is subtle. The unsuspecting person who is witness to the pseudo-debate does not understand that he is being passed a lie. He is

> not even aware that he is being passed a premise. It is so subtle that the premise just passes into the person as if it were reality. This premise—that there is uncertainty to be resolved—seems so benign. It is as easy as drinking a glass of treated water. But the fact remains that there is no mystery except in the minds of those who are willing to drink this premise. The premise is a lie, and a society which agrees to drink such a lie ceases to perceive reality. This is what we mean by mass denial.

The entire corporate media ideological spectrum operates under the umbrella of oligarchic control, something that is not new, just more egregious with every passing day. More in your face. The corporate media serve as the mouthpieces for those oligarchs, but they try to convince their separate audiences that this isn't so. They give people enemies—false ones. Objects to hate.

Just like symptoms are not the disease, they give people a focus upon which to rivet their attention while the disease goes unattended. As with a drug addict, the taking of drugs is not the fundamental problem, although it becomes one and might kill you. The problem is why one takes drugs; what is it that one feels needs to be tranquilized and silenced. Or, as the writer William Saroyan once flippantly said regarding the claim that smoking causes cancer: "You may tend to get cancer from the thing that makes you want to smoke, not from the smoking itself."

The corporate mainstream media are the drug that serves to hide the core truth of an oligarchic cancerous warfare state drunk on power and using propaganda to play both sides. Everyone has become pawns in their game.

A recent example serves to illustrate a method in their madness. There is a new, ongoing *Spotify* podcast—"Renegades: Born in the USA"—featuring Barack Obama and the singer Bruce Springsteen in conversation. Two rebels—it's of course ridiculous—but there it is. Two super rich celebrities stroking each other's egos in an upper-class setting. One a singer, who rose to prominence out of nowhere as the voice of the small-town beleaguered working class; the other, a mixed-race politician who rose to prominence out of nowhere from a family background redolent of the CIA. Two icons of popular and political culture crossing over with a smooth patina of mixed-arts bullshit telling listeners they/we need to return to the good old days when political centrism served the great American ideal that they both share. People are supposed to take this conversation between "buddies" seriously, as the two sit maskless with their feet seemingly touching at a time when people are told to wear masks and avoid close contact with those outside their households. As Bruce strums his guitar, any half-way sentient people would realize they were being played, even while the meaning of the song was so twisted that they were enjoying it.

Left-wing Gatekeepers

Then, if we switch from the mainstream corporate media to alternative voices, especially prominent ones on the left, we notice something even stranger.

I think most readers would agree that the two seismic events of the last twenty years are the current COVID-19 issue and the September 11, 2001 attacks. The latter, not only because of all the victims that died that day, but for how it led to so much death and destruction around the world, the endless war on terror, the invasions of Afghanistan, Iraq, Libya, Syria, etc., the ensuing loss of basic liberties and privacy via the Patriot Act, etc. The former for obvious current reasons of death and further loss of basic liberties under the lockdowns as governments throughout the world institute unprecedented measures of control, etc. Clearly these two events stand out over the decades. They bookend twenty years of massive U.S. war crimes, the growth of the national security complex, an obscene increase in wealth for the wealthiest, and the loss of privacy and civil liberties for all.

And as everyone knows, September 11th and COVID-19 have resulted in great controversies and much debate because of their serious implications and the obvious questions about the official story lines raised by many respectable writers and researchers of varying political perspectives. At the very least, one would expect that leftist/liberal critics of the so-called Deep State and the machinations of the elite's wars and propaganda would have engaged in these discussions about these two seminal events or written analytic articles about them.

But for a core group of prominent left/liberal critics, these two subjects have been avoided like they are of no importance. No debates, no discussions, no analyses—simply silence, as if they didn't happen and there was nothing to discuss. Cases closed: the government has spoken. Let us move on to more important matters.

But that is wrong. For example, in about a dozen closely reasoned books of his own and with other international researchers, David Ray Griffin has raised innumerable questions that show that the official September 11 story is full of holes. Canadian writer Graeme MacQueen has written a devastating critique of the linked anthrax attacks that followed September 11, showing clearly that they were a U.S. government operation. I myself have raised significant questions about what I call the linguistic mind-control associated with the attacks in "Why I Don't Speak of 9/11 Anymore." The dissident literature is enormous.

A few of Griffin's points are illustrative of the many anomalies in the official account. There are so many, and not just from Griffin but from other researchers, that I will mention just a few about the building collapses—what Griffin calls "miracles of science." The contradictions about the hijackers are also voluminous.

Here are a few such scientific miracles:

The Twin Towers and WTC 7 were the only steel-framed high-rise buildings ever to come down without explosives or incendiaries. The Twin Towers, each of which had 287 steel columns, were brought down solely by a combination of airplane strikes and jet-fuel fires. WTC 7 was not even hit by a plane, so it was the first steel-framed high-rise to be brought down solely by ordinary building fires. These World Trade Center buildings also came down in free fall—the Twin Towers in virtual free fall, WTC 7 in *absolute* free fall—for over two seconds. Although the collapses of the WTC buildings were not overtly aided by explosives, they imitated the kinds of implosions that can only be induced by demolition companies. In the case of WTC 7, the structure came down symmetrically (straight down, with an almost perfectly horizontal roofline), which meant that all 82 of the steel support columns had to fall simultaneously, although the building's few fires had a very *asymmetrical pattern.* The South Tower's upper 30-floor block changed its angular momentum in midair and then disintegrated.

I could go on and on with examples. The simple point is that there are so many absurdities in the official story that to ignore them is an act of intellectual and moral betrayal. Anyone who has closely studied the government's *9/11 Commission Report* knows it is highly fictional.

The same is true for dissenting voices on the COVID-19 issue. There has been an enormous amount of well-reasoned critiques of the official version of the COVID-19 narrative: *Global Research*, *Off-Guardian*, *The Brownstone Institute*, and *Children's Health Defense* are a few of the publications that have investigated the matter, one that has been an anathema for the corporate mainstream media. All present many articles by serious writers who raise innumerable questions and make irrefutable points about the matter. And there are very many doctors and medical researchers who have raised disturbing questions arising out of their research and clinical practice.

And again, the point is not simple agreement with the dissenters' arguments, but the need to engage their critiques. Here too the silence is resounding, for it says, "we buy the official account."

Consider these few:

The man who invented the test used to determine the so-called COVID positive test results, the Nobel Prize winning chemist, Kary Mullis, has said that the test cannot do that, it is not a diagnostic test, and therefore all the test results are meaningless. Additionally, there is serious doubt that the virus called SARS-CoV-2 causes a disease called COVID-19 since there is no evidence that the virus has ever been isolated. Assuming for argument's sake, however, that the PCR test can detect a specific virus, even Anthony Fauci and the World Health Organization (one hour after Biden was sworn into office), have both said that the PCR test, in order to have any accuracy, must be performed at cycles below 35 thresholds while for a year those tests have been done at thresholds much higher, resulting in vast numbers of false positives. Cycle thresholds are the levels at which the PCR test is said to detect a sample of the COVID-19 virus.

Furthermore, eminent voices such as Michel Chossudovsky and Peter Koenig at *Global Research*, Robert Kennedy, Jr. at *Children's Health Defense*, and Catte Black and Kit Knightly at *Off-Guardian* have for a long time been vociferously objecting to the official narrative with a vast amount of additional analyses involving the consequences of the widespread lockdowns. Such dissidents have had to fight against an organized campaign of censorship that should raise the alarm for anyone who cares about truth.

For leftists who remain silent on these fundamental issues, I can assure them that these critiques of the official explanations of September 11, 2001 and COVID-19 are not right-wing conspiracies but are the work of leftists digging deep for truth.

It is therefore more than odd that certain left/liberal writers completely avoid these issues. One must assume, therefore, that they accept the official explanations for these events, just as this coterie of leftist/liberal critics dismiss the voluminous and detailed critiques of the Warren Commission and the assassination of President Kennedy. From their silence one can assume that they view these matters as of no importance because the authorities have given us the truth.

One such deceased left-wing writer, who can stand in for the group of living writers to whom I allude, was the well-known and often brilliant journalist Alexander Cockburn, the founder of *Counterpunch Magazine*. In Cockburn's case, however, and to his credit even though he had no idea what he was talking about regarding September 11, 2001 and the JFK assassination, he did not remain silent but expressed his bile in ways he thought piercing but which made him appear quite ignorant. Cockburn had a sharp tongue and liked to ridicule anyone who disagreed with him. He excoriated all who questioned the JFK assassination or September 11 as "conspiracy nuts," "lunatics" involved with "kookery."

Echoing the CIA's conspiracy meme, his name calling was offensive and his ignorance of these matters extraordinary. But he was a star leftist, an untouchable. Few wished to criticize him. He started with the assumption that government stupidity, incompetence, and screw-ups allow these terrible events to happen, and then without a shred of evidence, concluded that is indeed why they happened. All evidence and logic to the contrary, he derisively dismissed as the work of fools. Only Cockburn and a government that admits mistakes were made were right. His arguments on these matters were pseudo-debates based on premises he conjured out of thin air.

He was a master incompetent of the incompetence theory, one that many prominent leftists follow today, such as a recent passing comment by one of them on the COVID-19 matter as a *mishandling* by the ruling elite. The implicit assumption being that the basic government and mainstream media tale is correct and all would be far better if the Trump administration hadn't screwed up. Nothing further is forthcoming or necessary. Let us proceed on the assumption that the official account is true and that the government's inept response is the problem. Failure of leadership. Government negligence. Incompetence.

And anyone who even harbors a suspicion that there may be more to the story is engaging in conspiratorial thinking. Of course, this is the same response given to those who for twenty years have researched and questioned the government's account of September 11, 2001. The 9/11 omission story. The fictional account that will dominate the news as the twentieth anniversary approaches this September. Will any of those liberal/leftists who have remained silent all these years let it pass as truth? I suspect so but hope not.

The Need for Dialogue

So we have pseudo debates on one hand and silence on the other when what is required is not self-censorship but open critical dialogue on these fundamental matters. "There comes a time when silence is betrayal," said Martin Luther King from the pulpit of Riverside Church on April 4, 1967, when he condemned the Vietnam War and broke his own silence in opposition to many of his advisers. A year later to the day, like JFK, he was murdered by the warfare state he condemned. Like Senator Robert Kennedy two months later. They were killed by very competent people.

Dr. Martin E. Schotz wrote twenty-six years ago in *History Will Not Absolve US* that those he had in mind for their defense of the Warren Commission were "such individuals as Noam Chomsky, Alexander Cockburn, the editors of *The Nation* magazine, and, if everyone remembers, I.F. Stone as well. I think the positions of these individuals are very important because in their surprising (to us) dishonesty and willingness to cooperate with the warfare state in covering up the crime, there is obviously something to be learned."

Yes, there is. It is time for all people of good will to stop finding excuses for the ruling elites, whether through incompetence theories or the silent refusal to publicly engage the government and its critics on the most important issues of our time—September 11, 2001 and COVID-19. Those Schotz names above are heroes for many on the liberal/left today who follow in their stead. It's as though they have found it necessary to mimic their teachers' lessons. Better logic would have them analyzing the premises of September 11 and COVID-19. Start with the basics. Be explicit. Tell us why you are silent.

It's time to graduate from this school of denial.

The Online Double-Bind

The trap was set at least twenty-five years ago and the mice jumped at the smell of cheese. I am referring to the introduction of the computer as a mass necessity and the Internet that followed. I was slow to enter the trap, "forced" finally in 2007 by the college where I was teaching. Up to that point I was just a member of The Lead Pencil Club, whose motto was "a speed bump on the information superhighway" and whose membership list numbered twenty-three and a half people worldwide. When I slowly and reluctantly reached for the cheese, the trap snapped not on my neck to finish me, but on my head that was half in and half out. The out part kept thinking. What follows are that half-head's musings on why I didn't follow my intuition, the whole damn sorry situation we are all in, and what we might do to spring the trap and run free. I don't like this trapped feeling. And, by the way, the cheese was American, which is not exactly real cheese.

In 1960 the sociologist C. Wright Mills said that there was far too much information for people to assimilate and make sense of and that lucid summations were needed. He was echoing Thoreau who in 1854 said, "If you are acquainted with the principle, what do you care for a myriad instances and applications?" Mills said people needed to develop what he called the sociological imagination that would allow them to condense and simplify news and to connect personal and social matters within historical and structural contexts.

That was the long-lost era of newspapers, long-form paper magazines, the reading of books, and minimal television stations. To think that there was far too much information then can only make one laugh, now that the digital revolution has buried us in data, information, and "breaking news" at warp speed, usually contradictory and lacking context. The internet has literally made people crazy, created schizoid or split personalities who don't know whether they are coming or going or what world they are in, physical or virtual. This is the era of social schizophrenia. It is also the era of COVID-19 lockdowns when a far greater online life is promoted as the necessary future.

If people once felt that all the information was too confusing and they were ending up thinking and doing things ass-backwards as a result, back then they might have understood it if you told them that the only way you can do anything is ass-backwards. Today, many would probably greet you with a look of bewilderment as they googled it to see if there was a way to swivel their asses to the front to get adjusted to the way they feel while waiting online for clear directions to emerge. Which way does an ass go?

They will be waiting for a long, long time.

The Internet is a double-bind because we are damned if we do and damned if we don't. News, writing, and information of all sorts is now often not available any other way. The era of paper newspapers is coming to an end. This was meant to be. Other sources of fact and fiction have gradually been eliminated, while the content on the Internet has been dramatically increased and progressively censored. The dream of an open Internet is turning into a nightmare. If you look at the Internet's creation and development by the U.S. military-intelligence-Silicon Valley network as a tool for social control, propaganda, and total spying, if you grasp this nexus and their intentions (see Yasha Levine's *Surveillance Valley: The Secret Military History of the Internet,*) you will come away realizing that the Internet and the total integrated digital world is a dystopian tool designed to make you crazy. To sow confusion and endless contradictory information from minute to minute. To "flood the zone" (see Event 201) with propaganda and disinformation. To give you a headache, keep you agitated, destroy your genuine human experience in the physical world. To put you into a state of frenetic passivity while whispering in your ear that there is no escape, while allowing elements of truth to emerge to keep you addicted.

This is the double-bind. It is what Jacques Ellul in 1964 called the technological society that is ruled by technique in every aspect of its life. Technique is a way of thinking that emphasizes efficiency; it is a way of thinking that emphasizes order and standardized means to a predetermined end. It is rational, deliberate, and focused on results. It is a way of thinking that has penetrated deep into the psychic structures of society and opposes spontaneity and unreflective action. Machines grow out of technical thinking, and today the computer, the internet, and artificial intelligence are the ideal manifestations of such thinking. They are the result, not the cause. As such, digital technology satisfies the technical mindsets that have been created over the decades, which includes regular people who have been gradually softened up to believe these machine dreams. Efficiency, results, practicality, and speed. The human body as a wonderful machine.

We have all been so conditioned, even those of us old enough to have lived before the computer era. Starting particularly in the early 1990s with the rat-a-tat electronic frenzy of the U.S. televised aggressive war against Iraq, euphemistically called The Gulf War and presented live with round-the-clock television coverage by ghoulish announcers more excited than 13-year-old boys with a porn magazine, the speed of everyday life has increased. If you lived through those years and were sensitive to the social drift, you could feel the pace of life pick up year-to-year, as everyone was induced to get in the fast lane. On the information superhighway, it is the only lane. Paul Virilio, a French thinker, has focused on this issue of speed in his studies of dromology—from *dromos*: a race, running. While his language is perhaps too academic, his insights are profound, as with the following point:

> The speed of the new optoelectronic and electroacoustic milieu becomes the final **void** (the void of the quick), a vacuum that no longer depends on the interval between places or things and so on the world's extension, but on the interface of an instantaneous transmission of remote

> appearances, on a geographic and geometric retention
> in which all volume, all relief vanishes.

This is the world of teleconferencing and the online life, existence shorn of physical space and time and people. A haunted world of specters, words, and images that can appear and disappear in a nanosecond. A magic show. A place where, in the words of Charles Manson, you can "get the fear," where fear is king. A locus where, as we sit at home "sheltering in place," we are no longer there.

Things have changed a wee bit since then. But the essence of propaganda and social control remains the same. "All those people who seek to control the behavior of large numbers of other people work on the *experiences* of those other people," wrote R.D. Laing in *The Politics of Experience.* "Once people can be induced to experience a situation in a similar way, they can be expected to behave in similar ways." Mystification takes place when people can be convinced that a social construction—e.g. the Internet and the digital life—is part of "the natural order of things," like the air we breathe. And that life online is real life, better and more real than physical existence.

I believe the digital revolution has gone a long way toward destroying our experience as persons. It is the endless magical mystery tour that goes nowhere. It is the ultimate psychodrama conjured by a satanic magician.

Do I exaggerate? Perhaps. But how else explain the spell this medium has cast on billions of people worldwide? Did the human race suddenly get smart? Or are many more people crazy?

I ask myself this question, and now I ask you. Has the Internet and the devices to access it made your life better or worse?

Has it made the life of humanity better or worse?

Has its essential role in globalization made for a better world?

Obviously, there are pluses to the Internet, just as there are pluses to almost everything. I don't deny that. The plus side of death is that the thought of it reminds you that you are alive. The plus side of television is you don't have to turn it on. Like you, I could rattle off many good things about the Internet (not cell phones, sorry). But on the scale of good and bad, where do you come down? Where do I?

Or is it possible we can't decide because we are too conflicted and caught in a double-bind?

I am of two minds, or more accurately, two half-heads. The upper part, pinned in the trap and dead to my situation, can only answer yes, sir, now that I am trapped, my life is better. I can debate endlessly the minutiae of every issue thrown out like pieces of meat for caged lions. I can check the weather forecast for every hour of every day of the week, even though I know they will probably be wrong. I can get directions even though I know you don't need a director to know which way the roads go. I can research issues quickly and pontificate as if I were an expert on every matter from a to z. I can feel I am informed while feeling deformed by the contradictory information that appears and disappears every few minutes. Essentially, I can feel in touch and worthy of respect from friends and neighbors because I can exchange empty words with them about nothing. I can feel so very normal and rejoice in that. I can feel sane.

On the negative side, well, my lower half-head, the one that's still thinking lead-pencil thoughts, the slow and easy stuff, the calm cool breeze oh what lovely day dreams—you don't really need to hear what it has to bitch about the Internet. You can probably guess.

In a fine article, "Vicious Cycles: Theses on a philosophy of news," in *Harper's Magazine*, Greg Jackson writes the following about our addiction to so-called "news" (the Internet):

> When we turn away from the news, we will confront a startling loneliness. It is the loneliness of life. The loneliness of thinking, of having no one to think for us, and of uncertainty. It is a loneliness that was always there but that was obscured by an illusion, and we will miss the illusion. . . . And we will miss tuning in each day to hear that voice that cuts boredom and loneliness in its solution of the present tense, that like Scheherazade

assures us the story is still unfolding and always will be.
I don't know whether we can give it up.

Nor do I.

Rehearsed Lives and Planned History

"The technical achievement of advanced industrial society, and the effective manipulation of mental and material productivity have brought about a shift in the locus of mystification. . . . the rational rather than the irrational becomes the most effective vehicle of mystification."

—HERBERT MARCUSE, *One-Dimensional Man*

"General, man is very useful.
He can fly and he can kill.
But he has one defect:
He can think."

—BERTOLT BRECHT

Langdon Winner opens his prescient book, *The Whale and the Reactor: A Search for Limits in an Age of High Technology* (1986), with an anecdote about John Glenn and his experience orbiting the earth in 1962 aboard Friendship 7. After long, rigorous training in simulators, Glenn found that when he looked at earth from orbit—only the third man after Soviet pilots Yuri Gagarin and Gherman Titov to do so—he felt as if he had seen it all before. Rather than a sense of awe, he felt that his training exercises had deprived him of true experience. Winner writes, "Synthetic conditions generated in the training center had begun to seem more 'real' than the actual experience."

Glenn's example might seem unusual for the early 1960s, but it is now commonplace, the rule rather than the exception. I think many people today sense, but can't admit, that technology has usurped direct human experience while presumably enhancing it with so-called awe-inspiring, tech-enhanced products. Just as people walk around embalming time with their camera phones, there is something funereal about activities that have been rehearsed, reviewed, and planned on digital screens before they are undertaken. It's as if the hearse doesn't come rolling in soon enough.

I just checked the local weather forecast and "they" say there is a 37.235 % chance of showers on Saturday, six days away. Should I start worrying today since I have planned a picnic for that day? Would I be wrong to wonder when on that future day, if it ever arrives and I am around to greet it, that the 37.235 % chance of showers applies? Day or night, morning or afternoon? The picnic is scheduled for 1–3 PM, so should I play it by the odds and assume those 8.33 % of the 24 hours have a decent chance of avoiding the 37.235 %? Should I live by numbers and computer simulations?

In *The Abolition of Man*, C. S. Lewis, a man not opposed to science, tells us:

> There is something that unites magic and applied science while separating both from the "wisdom" of earlier ages. For the wise men of old the cardinal problem had been how to conform the soul to reality, and the solution had been knowledge, self-discipline, and virtue. For magic and applied science alike the problem is how to subdue reality to the wishes of men: the solution is a technique. . .

Why was Glenn circling the earth anyway?

If the novelty of experience and the real objective value of the outside world have been crippled by the repetitive and predictive nature of technology, it is worth reminding ourselves of the simple truth that technology does not just happen; it is rooted in a philosophical premise of control, the inability to let the earth breathe and to stop trying to control life. This is a human choice.

It is possible to show reverence for nature and our part in it and to use technology for humane goals, not because we are adept at techniques, but because we understand that human beings are emphatically not machines but spiritual and moral beings. This has seldom been the case in modern times. To do so demands asking what are our first principles and what are the ends we are seeking. This requires subordinating science and technology to higher values. All technical decisions are political, and all political decisions are moral.

Most new technologies of the past two hundred years have been touted as "revolutionary," machines that will radically transform life for the better—i.e. leading to less labor, more equality, and the enrichment of human experience. Nowhere has this been truer than with the promotion of the computer and the digital "revolution" with its information superhighway—the Internet—that has been sold as leading to more benefits than the mind can imagine. The result, however, has been the loss of our minds as the nonsense that "information is power" has become a mantra of those controlling the digital information flow, as they promote information as an elixir for democracy. Such a strange sort of democracy it is where more and more power has accrued to the power elites and diversions of data and digital dementia to regular people who have a hard time remembering and forgetting, seemingly an odd couple if ever there were one.

Currently you hear a lot of complaining about artificial intelligence (AI), as if its development is some great surprise. Much of this caviling has been coming from the very people who created AI and continue to develop it. Now these experts are warning that it could get out of control, so we must be careful and take action since we risk "extinction" from AI. Only an idiot wouldn't laugh at such rhetoric. Who are the "we" who need to take action? The fear campaign never stops, while the controls tighten.

Thirty-seven years ago Winner wrote, "Some observers forecast that 'the computer revolution' will eventually be guided by new wonders in artificial intelligence. Its present course is influenced by something more familiar: the absent mind."

And malevolent hubris.

For AI has been the stuff of popular screen and book entertainment for a long time, dress rehearsed in the popular consciousness far in advance of opening night. Now that the hearse has appeared and the identity of its occupants has become cause for wonderment, much chatter has erupted on the Internet. Could we be dead? Where are our controls?

The process of creating dread has been rather smooth, so surprise is an odd reaction. We have been in the simulators far longer that John Glenn was in his, and we too have seen it all before. First they created millions of artificial people drip-by-drip by drugging them with the "magic" of technological devices that were "irresistible," then, when most of "reality" had become unreal and people had downloaded their natural lives into the devices, they roll out the latest fraud about how the machines will inevitably take over from humans, as if people don't have hands and eyes and walk upon the earth; that they can't see the birds in the trees or feel the breeze upon their heads. That they are not free to determine their own lives.

Be afraid, for "you have no freedom" has been the message for decades. This is the repetitious, implicit message of fear used to paralyze people. The AI experts who create the instruments of "control," even as they continue to develop them, then warn of their dangers. Here is their recent one sentence warning:

> Mitigating the risk of extinction from AI should be a global priority alongside other society-scale risks such as pandemics and nuclear war.

Is that so? Our Dr. Frankensteins are so kind to create these monsters only to warn us about them.

Have you heard it all before?

Have you seen it all before?

Is the same-old, same-old getting you down?

Does the news seem like déjà vu all over again?

Does your life seem rehearsed and official history produced in advance?

Has the Weirdness arrived?

I think it's fair to say that wherever people travel these days, it's as if they were already there before they even left. Or at least the pictures they have seen have taken the newness out of the places they are going to in today's simulated lives.

Moving pictures, what they used to call films—how quaint that sounds today when the moving pictures now move in the dinguses in people's pockets wherever people move, on the go to nowhere new. John Glenn would probably understand.

In his concluding chapter, Winner writes:

> More and more, the whole language used to talk about technology and social policy—the language of "risks," "impacts," and "trade-offs"—smacks of betrayal. The excruciating subtleties of measurement and modeling mask embarrassing shortcomings in human judgment. We have become careful with numbers, callous with everything else. Our *methodological rigor is becoming spiritual rigor mortis.* [my emphasis]

This leads me back to the Internet and all the verbal and pictorial information published there. This is where most people now get their "news" and analyses about the "outside" world, where they get much of their official history before it happens. Even when people have learned how to choose sites judiciously, it is still information overload that destroys their ability to think, to remember what is important and forget the inessential.

Paul Virilio, the French scholar of technology and speed (dromology), calls it the "information bomb" (added to the nuclear and genetic bombs), the glut of repetitive information that deranges regular people but is a boon to the elites who think they are in full control of people's minds and the technology they promote. Virilio writes:

> A black hole of Progress into which has now fallen this whole philanoia, this love of madness on the part of the sciences and technologies, which is now seeking to organize the self-extinction of a species that is too slow. . . . Not liberation, but global takeover of humanity by totalitarian multimedia powers, applying intensely to populations that age-old strategy which consists in sowing division everywhere—between peoples, regions, towns, countries, races, religions, sexes, generations, and even within families.

Like John Glenn's loss of awe while in orbit because of his simulator experience, and like the rehearsal for travel and so much else people do through screens—"pre-planning," as the redundant word usage reveals the truth—the Internet has become a place to lose your mind as fast as you can and to make sure your life is devoid of surprises.

And because Internet content is posted so rapidly and in such large quantities, the providers and their readers can't move on from the past because they are repeating it in ways that let them hold onto it without understanding it. There is no "space" for new thoughts. It is analogous to those individuals who have suffered some childhood trauma but because it was so overwhelming, keep unconsciously repeating it in disguised form rather than facing its truth and creating a new future.

Some of the Internet repetition is unconscious and innocent blather, and much of it is the basic method of propaganda. Repeat and repeat lies so that those hearing them can't imagine there could be another truth. And then those hearing them can't forget what they have heard so often because, as Thoreau once said, "It is so hard to forget what it is worse than useless to remember." And of course they can't remember what they never heard since it has been omitted. Propaganda is two-faced.

There is a stuckness to so much on the Internet because the space is unlimited and sites keep posting at rapid-fire speed to keep up with each other. The Internet is like a clogged highway on a Friday evening with hoards fleeing to the same "isolated" getaway. By the time they get there, they wonder why they ever left, or if they did.

If you stop reading or viewing the Internet for a week or more, and then return, you won't miss much.

Take, for example, Russia-gate and the Durham Report. Patrick Lawrence has written an intriguing article about it: "John Durham and the Burying of American History."

Special Counsel Durham's four year investigation, "Report on Matters Related to Intelligence Activities and Investigations Arising Out of the 2016 Presidential Campaigns," is, as Lawrence says, more a confirmation than a revelation. It verifies in its tricky way what some have known for seven years and others continue to deny because the implications are so explosive: that in 2016, Hillary Clinton, the Democratic Party, and the FBI conspired to create the Russia-backed-Trump hoax to smear Donald Trump as a Russian proxy to help Clinton get elected president. The CIA and FBI knew from the start that the claims of a Trump-Russia conspiracy were completely fraudulent.

Once Trump was surprisingly elected, however, the Russia-gate lies were repeated endlessly for years by the conspirators, the mainstream press, and some alternative media. Such propaganda had the effect of fueling hatred for Russia and President Putin, enabling NATO's continuing expansion to Russia's borders and Ukraine's neo-Nazi ongoing attacks on the Donbass, the persecution of Julian Assange as Clinton regularly accused him and Trump of being in cahoots with the Russian government, and eventually, after enough U.S. provocations, led to the present U.S./NATO war against Russia in Ukraine and the growing danger of nuclear war.

The Durham Report lays out some of the conspiracy that led to them, but not these consequences. It doesn't call for criminal prosecutions and is very lacking in many ways; it excludes the central role of CIA Director John Brennan and the false and discredited Clinton claim that Russia interfered in the 2016 election by hacking Democratic party servers to help elect Trump by releasing the material through Wikileaks, etc. No one hacked those emails, as ex-CIA analyst Ray McGovern and Veterans

Intelligence Professionals for Sanity (VIPS) have shown time and again.

It is a limited-hangout, a report so late and lacking that most people will have forgotten what engendered it, and, if that isn't enough, the mainstream media is burying it anyway.

I mention Lawrence's article, not because I agree with all his points—i.e. his historical examples exclude the COVID hoax and he claims that "Watergate was at bottom one man's scandal," which it surely was not—or to analyze the report, but to pick up on points he makes about the burying of history and our faculties of remembering and forgetting. He writes:

> To value history, Nietzsche told us in very different circumstances, is "to understand the meaning of the phrase 'it was.'" But the health of an individual, a people, or of a culture he also said, depended on forgetting, too: It is only when we can forget that we escape the bonds of the past and dare to begin again, to imagine and create, "to perceive as we have never perceived before." Having the certainty of a written history is what makes possible this desirable kind of forgetting.

I think understanding these ideas is necessary for understanding what has become of us in the era of digital simulacra, how we have lost our way while learning to imitate rather than live. Our reactions have become copies of copies. History has become a series of pseudo-debates with fewer and fewer matters factually settled so one can forget and move on. While the Internet provides us with massive amounts of information, some of it very important, its very nature or the method of its delivery of its contents controverts its claim to seriousness. It is hard to remember or forget when one subjects oneself to a steady stream of electronic images that speed through one's mind like flashing lights.

Forgetting is usually considered a failing that happens to you, not something good that one can do. It has come to be associated with ailments such as dementia and Alzheimer's. Rarely is it seen as a necessary art—Nietzsche's "music of forgetting"—that one might practice in order to make "room" for the onrushing future. For we know that the significance of the past depends on its importance for the future and only once one takes a stance toward the past can one create a new future. This is true for individuals and society. Learning to remember the past so as to forget it for the future is central.

Lawrence uses the JFK assassination, which occurred 60 years ago, as an example. The Internet is full of articles that still debate the assassination, as if the facts were not clear long ago. These pseudo-debates encourage readers to forget the *meaning*—that the CIA killed Kennedy—and all its implications for understanding the world that we live in. These pseudo-debates encourage readers to forget the facts—that the CIA killed Kennedy—and that the evidence is readily available if one reads a few scholarly books with impeccable sources, such as James W. Douglass's *JFK and the Unspeakable; Why He Died and Why It Matters.* (Books obviously differ significantly from the Internet.) How long such nonsense will continue is a guessing game, but because the truth is so unsettling, as is Russia-gate, I suspect it will continue for a long time. One is encouraged to remember incidentals, while the core is elided to keep the debate going. It is true, as Lawrence says, that certain lies are too big to fail, for if they did and entered the official histories as truths, they would be preserved, not to be forgotten. Then society could deal with their implications. But as long as matters such as the facts in the Durham Report, the JFK assassination, etc., are buried or endlessly debated, as they are being now, their continuing ramifications in Ukraine, U.S. politics, etc. will be more deadly history planned in advance and nothing will seem new or hopeful. Like John Glenn, we will have seen it all before in our simulated lives.

Only to repeat it as we fly in circles in a country of endless lies.

Bob Cousy, Bob Dylan, and the Art of Playing Well

I never met the great basketball player, Bob Cousy, the man known as "the Houdini of the Hardwood," yet he somehow influenced my life in ways I never knew, or to be more accurate, in ways I didn't reflect upon except in superficial ways.

So much of life passes behind our backs unless we develop full-court vision.

Cousy was the guy who brought professional basketball into the modern era with his bag of fancy tricks that included no-look and behind-the-back passes, uncanny dribbling, and a magical court sense that made the fast break into an exquisite art form. The captain and point-guard of the Boston Celtics from 1950–1963, Cousy led the Celtics to six NBA titles, made thirteen all-star teams, founded the NBA players union, and changed professional basketball from a stodgy, boring, and slow game into a fast-paced spectacle, entertainment as much as sport. He was a wizard with a basketball and set the stage for Guy Rodgers, "Pistol Pete" Maravich, Bob Dylan, Magic Johnson, and Steve Nash, among other tricksters, modern Hermes.

Over the years I have written a great deal on a very wide range of topics, but it wasn't until a friend from high school sent me Gary Pomeranz's fascinating book, *The Last Pass: Cousy, Russell, the Celtics, and What Matters in the End,* that something clicked for me. A few weeks previously, as the weather had turned spring-like, I had started to shoot hoops at our basket in the driveway. The warm air, the feel of a loose flowing freedom as I dribbled and shot, brought me back to the days when I spent so many hours playing in the Bronx schoolyards of my youth, perfecting my skills in what I can only call a fanatical way. Rushing to the schoolyard after school and on Saturday mornings to be the first there, to command the court, to compete with the older guys and beat their asses. Traveling around the city's best basketball neighborhoods to play and make my mark. The endless hours in gyms. The search for perfection. The adrenaline rush, the thrill, the joy of the perfect pass, the sweet swish of the net from a shot you had practiced a thousand times. From the age of eleven until twenty-three, basketball was central to my life and identity. It was my passion.

It was during these recent days shooting around that I started to have almost nightly dreams of my younger years, playing basketball in high school and then in college on a Division I scholarship. They were very vivid dreams, and at the time I didn't understand why I was having them. And they were starting to annoy me, as persistent and weird dreams can do. Begone, dread spirits! Yet I knew they were telling me to heed their tales, told when no one was looking, only this dreamer in the night.

While this was happening, I wrote an article about Bob Dylan and his 2020 release of "Murder Most Foul," his powerful song about the assassination of President Kennedy, wherein he brilliantly accuses elements within the U.S. government and intelligence forces of killing the president in cold blood, while framing Lee Harvey Oswald for the deed.

I had written about Dylan before, loved his music, and found him an intriguing if enigmatic character, a Houdini of song. "Murder Most Foul" seemed to burst out of Dylan after decades of avoiding straightforward political themes. It struck me that with this song he had ripped off the masks he had been wearing for decades, as if he were Odysseus at the end of *The Odyssey*, shrugging off his beggar's rags and announcing to the suitors of his wife Penelope that the jig was up, and they were going down.

It seemed to me that Dylan was coming full circle, as if he were coming home to take revenge on the killers who had scarred his youth as they did mine and so many others'. "Like a musician, like a harper, when/ with quiet hand upon his instrument," Homer tells us, Odysseus lets the arrows sing, while Dylan reaches back to sing:

> The day they blew out the brains of the king
> Thousands were watching, no one saw a thing
> It happened so quickly, so quick, by surprise
> Right there in front of everyone's eyes
> Greatest magic trick ever under the sun
> Perfectly executed, skillfully done

Slowly it dawned on me that everyone's life has a shape, as if it were a drawing or a story or song. And that, if we pay close attention and see through all the snares and temptations meant to divert us from our true paths, we will find our beginnings in our ends and without directions we will find our way home. As T. S. Eliot puts it: "What we call the beginning is often the end/And to make an end is to make a beginning. . . . We shall not cease from exploration/And the end of all our exploring/Will be to arrive where we started/And know the place for the first time."

It is very hard to explain to someone who didn't know you in that time long before you met, how important certain activities were to you, what they meant and still mean in the deepest recesses of your psyche. How they shaped you, or better still, how you used them to bend your life when you strung your bow so effortlessly to hit the target that you aimed for. Or thought you were aiming for. My life in basketball shaped the man that I became, but my wife only knows the aftermath since she met me when I had taken a vacation from basketball, playing the role of a university professor. Like Cousy, sitting and talking with Pomeranz, or Dylan sharpening his arrows and letting them fly in his recent song *False Prophet*, I could say:

> You don't know me darlin'—you never would guess
> I'm nothing like my ghostly appearance would suggest
> I ain't no False Prophet—I just said what I said
> I'm here to bring vengeance on somebody's head

In conversations with Pomeranz, Cousy was hoping to be inspired to understand the journey that has left him, an old man, frightened, alone, and approaching death in a large house in Worcester, Massachusetts, trying to understand, not only his fraught relationship with his black Celtic teammate, Bill Russell, but what his life has been all about: the court wizardry and cheers, the years on the road, the applause and awards, the championships and the price they exacted. He went to the basketball wars and won, came home, but now wonders what home really means. Unlike Odysseus, he only has ghosts to slay. His wife is dead, and no suitors occupy the great house of shades. There is no one to kill except his regrets.

My friend, Wayne, who sent me the book, spent three years in high school with me studying Greek, and over the course of those years, we translated Homer's *The Odyssey* line by line. We were also basketball teammates. Odysseus, of course, was the ultimate trickster, the man of many wiles and disguises, what the nymph Calypso, who held Odysseus captive for seven years on her island Ogygia, called "a rascal."

Like Houdini, Odysseus was able to escape this phantom island with the help of the messenger and trickster, Hermes.

Like Cousy, Odysseus was the Houdini of the ancient world, the hero who could escape any trap and thread an arrow through the smallest space to defeat the enemy.

Cousy's fierceness on the court is legendary; his poker face hid the killer instinct, like Odysseus with his wily habit of standing with downcast eyes to disguise his intent. Cousy could thread a pass between an opponent's eyes without them blinking. They often never knew what hit them.

No doubt JJ Redick, the former NBA player and TV commentator, didn't either, as the 93-year-old Cousy recently lashed him with his fierce and fiery competitor's tongue for saying that Cousy competed against plumbers and firefighters. An old warrior still, despite his melancholic musings on life and games and the strangeness of it all.

Like the rascal he is, Dylan, who is deeply influenced by the Greek and Roman classics, not only possesses the lyrical genius to conjure the past in his words and playing, but to use it to light up the present for those who wish to forget the past's importance for the present. His music is magical. He is our Emerson. His artistic philosophy has always been about movement in space and time through song. Always moving, always restless, always seeking a way back home through song, even when, or perhaps because, there are no directions.

"An artist has got to be careful never to arrive at a place where he thinks he's at somewhere," he's said. "You always have to realize that you are constantly in a state of becoming and as long as you can stay in that realm, you'll be alright."

I was reminded of this as I was rereading bits of Bob Dylan's fascinating and poetic memoir, *Chronicles: Volume I,* and came upon his memory of hearing the news of the death of "Pistol" Pete Maravich, the greatest scorer in college basketball history and a magician without par on the court. Maravich was Cousy's heir, and the blood line connects to Dylan also, a Houdini with words. It was January 5, 1988:

> My aunt was in the kitchen and I sat down with her to talk and drink coffee. The radio was playing and morning news was on. I was startled to hear that Pete Maravich, the basketball player, had collapsed on a basketball court in Pasadena, just fell over and never got up. I'd seen Maravich play in New Orleans once, when the Utah Jazz were the New Orleans Jazz. He was something to see—mop of brown hair, floppy socks—the holy terror of the basketball world—high flyin'—magician of the court. The night I saw him he dribbled the ball with his head, scored a behind the back, no look basket—dribbled the length of the court, threw the ball up off the glass and caught his own pass. He was fantastic. Scored something like thirty-eight points. He could have played blind. Pistol Pete hadn't played professionally for a while, and he was thought of as forgotten. I hadn't forgotten about him, though. Some people seem to fade away but then

when they are truly gone, it's like they didn't fade away at all.

He goes on to write that, after hearing the news of Pistol Pete's sad death playing pickup basketball, he started and completed the song "Dignity" the same day, and in the days that followed, song after song flowed from his pen. The news of one creative spirit's death gave rise to another creative spirit's rebirth. (I am reminded of Shakespeare writing Hamlet after his father's death.)

"It's like I saw the song up in front of me," writes Dylan, "and overtook it, like I saw all the characters in this song and elected to cast my fortunes with them. . . . The wind could never blow it out of my head. This song was a good thing to have. On a song like this, there's no end to things."

No one wants to end, to fade away. To not be recognized. To die and be forgotten. To fail to make their mark. Not Dylan, Cousy, Maravich, me nor you. We all wish to become who we feel we were meant to be. To fulfill the creative dreams we had when young, to stay true to ourselves, and not to waste our lives in trivial pursuits. Years pass and many people often ask with Dylan in "Shooting Star":

Seen a shooting star tonight
And I thought of me
If I was still the same
If I ever became what you wanted me to be
Did I miss the mark or overstep the line
That only you could see?

Yes, many ask and so often realize that they betrayed their best selves for a pot of gold. As Paul Simon puts it in "The Boxer": "I have squandered my resistance for a pocketful of mumbles . . ."

I keep thinking: who is you for you? For me? Who is mumbling to whom?

When I was a young boy, I wanted to stand out, to be exceptional, to be one-of-a-kind, an individual. Basketball became my obsession and Bob Cousy my idol. I wanted to be a shooting star, a dribbling star, a passing star. I watched him on television and live, studying him. His every move inspired me to imitate it. I would spend hours every day practicing behind the back passes, first right-handed, then left, against the wall where I had marked an x in chalk. I worked on my peripheral vision, so I could see the whole court and control the show. In the hidden recesses of my basement, I used tape to mark spots on the floor where I spent hour after hour dribbling behind my back, first this way and then that, past imaginary opponents. I made dribbling glasses with black tape out of my mother's old sunglasses. Worked on circling the ball behind my back either way. Hour after hour, day after day, year after year, I devoted myself to perfecting my basketball skills as a point guard. Being like Bob Cousy. Being the one whose magic feats were the talk of the town the day following the games.

One day, I met and talked with the actor Paul Newman on the street after high school basketball practice. When I was leaving, after talking with him for a few minutes, he called me Fast Eddie, which to my mind added to the mystique I felt as a trickster on the hardwood. I felt fast and loose like Paul's character Eddie Felson in *The Hustler* who said when he was on a roll with his cue stick, "You don't have to look, you just Know. You make shots that nobody has ever made before. I can play that game the way. . . . Nobody's ever played it before." That was my goal and the impetus behind my fanatical devotion to practice. I loved it, there was joy in it, but there was also a driven quality to my quest.

For whom? Only you? Who are we all performing for?

I was easily bored by conventional life and conventional basketball. But the conventional world surrounded me. It was in school, church, the way people talked and walked; it seemed like people were straightjacketed—which they were. Blake's mind-forged manacles. I sensed people were dissemblers, and that lies were the essence of social life. Or as Simon and Garfunkel put it to end "The Boxer": "Lie la lie, lie la lie la lie la lie"

Nowhere was this truer than on the basketball court in high school and college where the coaches had their systems and their rules and discouraged innovation, as if it would reveal them to be artists in disguise, weird, less-than-manly men who couldn't run a tight ship. They always rewarded those who obeyed them and kept within the strict rules of the system. Creativity frightened them. The old ways sufficed. It was just like society, and though Cousy had broken through and been idolized for doing so, he had retired from the Celtics in the spring of 1963, while the high school and college programs were stuck in the past.

I felt imprisoned. I wanted to bust out and play free. Be free. It was like the classics that I studied in high school and college: the lesson was always that the exploits you read about were things of the past, and now we were civilized gentlemen who must learn the rules of the game and play by them. Tradition. But the rules were suffocating me.

The rules of the game had almost brought the world to an end during the Cuban Missile Crisis in October 1962. The rules of the game had created a system of war and racism that was badly broken, resulting in the savage killing not only of a president who had undergone a radical spiritual conversion toward peace-making, but also four little black girls in the 16th Street Baptist Church in Birmingham, Alabama on Sunday September 15, 1963, a year to the day after I started college with my trivial young man's dreams of being the Cousy of college hoops.

The rules of the game would soon be violated by Dylan at the 1964 Newport Folk Festival when he would shock Pete Seeger and other elders with his song, "Mr. Tambourine Man," a radical break with strictly political songs in favor of pure dazzling poetry in song. That was a Cousy moment, poetry in motion, Houdini out of the locked box, dancing "beneath the diamond sky with one hand waving free."

Bob Dylan, whose life and career follows Odysseus' trajectory, ended his 2017 Nobel Award Lecture with the first line of the Odyssey: "Sing in me, oh Muse, and through me tell the story." My friend Wayne and I, together with all our high school classmates, had memorized those lines in Greek. They were ingrained in us for life, as they have been for Dylan. In the end are our beginnings.

But tell what story? For whom? Only you?

Dylan has told so many. Here's one I have for you, one you never heard. Here are the opening lines; let's call it Book I. Not that a Goddess intervened, but it was, in Odysseus' words, the beginning of the end of my "clean-cut game," as Homer put it.

A month after the Cuban Missile Crisis, I played my first college basketball game. In those days, all freshmen were required by the rules of college sports to play one year of freshman basketball before playing varsity. This was the day I had been waiting for since the sixth grade when my dedication to basketball began. My blood was flowing fast, I had no fear and was ready to use all the skills I had spent years honing. The stands were packed. My proud family sat a few rows up behind our bench, my parents and four of my sisters, two of whom were quite young at eight and eleven-years-old.

The game was close, back and forth it went. With about a minute and a half left, we were leading by two points. The other coach called a time out with the ball in their possession. In the huddle, our coach assigned me to guard the opponent's best player, a six-foot-four inch jumping jack who was highly acclaimed and a very good player by the name of Albie Grant. I was five-foot-eleven, and in addition to my offensive skills, was a tough and tenacious, very well-conditioned defender who took pride in sticking to an opponent like glue. They threw the ball in and screened for Grant. He got the ball, and I got in his face. He went up for a jump shot from about 20 feet out, and since I was not going to block his shot, I did what all good defenders do, I got my hand in front of his eyes. But he made the shot anyway, and the referee called a shooting foul on me. But I never touched him. It was a terrible call, but I could do nothing about it.

Behind my back, I could hear my coach cursing me out with every name in the book—you fucking bastard, you shit, etc. He could be heard throughout the arena. The crowd went silent. He kept cursing me out and my already sweaty, red face must have turned purple. I felt on fire. He took me out of the game, a game I had played throughout. He kept cursing at me. I sat away from him on the bench, and he came down and stood over me, calling me every name in his limited vocabulary, you fucking this, you fucking that. I looked at him in rage. The game continued. Grant made the free throw, and we lost by one point. As we walked off the court to the locker room door at the end, he kept screaming invective at me. I could feel my rage swelling. My family was descending from the stands and could hear it all. I noticed others staring in disbelief. To say it was humiliating barely captures what it felt like, but just as I played the game fiercely, I was not one to take such abuse. But I kept telling myself to control myself. It was the coach who was making a fool of himself. Then, when we entered the locker room, he let loose at me again, you fucking idiot, you fucking bastard.... when I snapped and grabbed him by his shirt and tie, my hands around his neck, I threw him up against the wall and let him have it, screaming that I'd had enough of his shit and I would kill him if he ever did it again. All hell broke loose as people were pulling me off him, and my father, who was outside the locker room, came rushing in to intervene.

Years of passionate dedication to becoming the best basketball player I could, came to this. I had reacted in fury to being humiliated "in my own house" in front of my family. I think now of Odysseus when he stood on the broad door sill and killed AntÍnoös, the worst of the suitors of his wife, Penelope. "Odysseus' arrow hit him under the chin/ and punched up to the feathers through his throat." How dare he take revenge and defend his honor, came the shouts from the easily offended but secretly guilty. The other suitors screamed at him: "Foul! To shoot at a man! That was your last shot." It wasn't, of course, for they were next.

It wasn't my last shot either, and after that I became the coach's favorite player and had a great year. It was as if he knew I was right in my anger and respected how I had fought back, for he was a hothead himself. But that is the rest of another story.

My passion changed in the years following college. I no longer tried to imitate other tricksters like Bob Cousy or Bob Dylan, but I slowly turned my attention to the magic of stringing words together, to tell stories in my way, not theirs. To analyze politics and culture logically but never without artistry. And to always remember that beautiful writing is akin to music and playing life is the most important game.

Dylan and Cousy have their own tales to tell. Dylan has fused his themes into an incantatory delivery that casts a moving spell of hope upon the listener. He is nothing if not a spiritual spellbinder; similar in many ways to that other quintessential American—the Beat poet Allen Ginsberg, whose best work was a poetic quest for an inspired salvific poetry.

Cousy is a very smart man, and he knows the sport he played so well is only a game with no ultimate purpose; as such, it is a diversion, an amusement like all sports—the etymology of the word sport comes from the Old French *desporter*, which means to carry away (from serious concerns). It is not a weighty pursuit, except monetarily as a massive business. Yet it's fun to play and watch. But because it is only a game, it can teach us much about life itself. Its rhythms and its magic. How it is all about movement and music when it is played as a team sport. And what we might be moving away from and toward in caring who wins or loses.

Like Cousy, who is aware of the paradoxically frivolous nature of basketball even as he played it so seriously, Dylan is an artist at war with his art. His songs demand that the listener's mind and spirit be moving as the spirit of creative inspiration moved Dylan. A close listening will force one to jump from verse to verse—to shoot the gulf—since there are no bridges to cross, no connecting links. The sound carries you over and keeps you moving forward. If you're not moving, you'll miss the meaning and the beauty of his playing.

So now I play with words in my own way. Playing is always the thing, and not just to catch the conscience of the king.

Like Dylan, who surely deserved the Nobel Prize for Literature for decades of mesmerizing songs, I return once again to Homer who says, "Sing in me, oh Muse, and through me tell the story." Such telling is tricky business. For our stories often pass behind our backs where we can't see them. Not just our personal tales but the political ones.

Dylan's artistic philosophy has always been about movement in space and time through song. Always moving, always restless, always seeking a way back home through song, even when, or perhaps because, there are no directions.

It's the only way to play. Fast Eddie Felson was right: Play it fast and loose like "nobody ever played it before." Like Cousy. Like Dylan.

The End of Reality?

In 1888, the year before he went insane, Fredrich Nietzsche wrote the following in *Twilight of the Idols*:

> We have got rid of the real world: what world is left? The apparent world perhaps? ... But no! *Along with the real world we've done away with the apparent world as well.*

So, if you feel you also may be going insane in the present climate of digital screen life, where real is unreal but realer than real, the apparent is cryptic, and up is down, true is false, and what you see you don't—it has a history. One hundred and thirty-two years ago, Nietzsche added that "something extraordinarily nasty and evil is about to make its debut." We know it did, and the bloody butcher's bench known as the twentieth century was the result. Nihilism stepped onto center stage and has been the star of the show ever since, straight through to 2020. Roberto Calasso puts it this way in *Literature and the Gods*:

> *Here we are*, announces Nietzsche, and it would be hard not to hear a mocking ring in his voice. We thought we were living in a world where the fog had lifted, a disenchanted, ascertainable, verifiable world. And instead everything has gone back to being a "fable" again. How are we to get our bearings.... This is the paralysis, the peculiar uncertainty of modern times, a paralysis that all since have experienced.

Obviously, we haven't gotten our bearings. We are far more adrift today on a stormy electronic sea where the analogical circle of life has been replaced by the digital, and "truths" like numbers click into place continually to lead us in wrong, algorithm-controlled directions. The trap is almost closed. This is the 24/7 Internet life that the brilliant Jonathan Cray dissects in a pair of books: *Scorched Earth: Beyond the Digital Age to a Post-Capitalist World* and *24/7*. He writes: "If there is to be a livable and shared future on our planet, it will be a future off-line, uncoupled from the world-destroying systems and operations of 24/7 capitalism." It is a sentiment I share.

Of course, Nietzsche did not have the Internet, but he lived at the dawn of the electric era, when space-time transformations were occurring at a rapid pace. Inventions such as photography, the phonograph, the telephone, electricity, etc. were contracting space and time and a disembodied "reality" was being born. With today's Internet and digital screen life, the baby is full-grown and completely disembodied. It does nothing but look at its image that is looking back into a lifeless void, whose looking can't figure out what it's seeing.

Take, for example, the phonograph, invented by Thomas Edison in 1878. If you could record a person's voice, and if that person died, were you then listening to the voice of a living person or one who was dead? If the person whose voice was recorded was alive and was miles away, you had also compressed earthly space. The phonograph suppressed absence, conjured ghosts, and seemed to overcome time and death as it captured the flow of time in sound. It allowed a disembodied human voice to inhabit a machine, an early example of downloading.

"Two ruling ambitions in modern technology," writes John Durham Peters in his wonderful book, *Speaking into the Air*, "appear in the phonograph: the creation of artificial life and the conjuring of the dead."

Many people started to hear voices, and these people were not called deluded. Soon, with the arrival of cinema, they would see ghosts as well. Today, speaking ghosts are everywhere, hiding in hand-held devices. It's Halloween all year round as we are surrounded by electronic zombies in a screen culture.

This technological annihilation of space and time that was happening at a frenetic pace was the material background to Nietzsche's thought. His philosophical and epistemological analyses emerged from German intellectual life of his time as well, where theologians and philosophers were discovering that knowledge was relative and had to be understood *in situ*, i.e., within its historical and social place or context.

Without going into abstruse philosophical issues here, suffice it to say, Nietzsche was suggesting that not only was God dead because people killed him, but that knowledge was a fiction that changed over time and was a human construction. All knowledge, not just science, had to be taken "as if" it were true. This was a consoling mental trick but falsely reassuring, for most people could not accept this, since "knowledge" was a protection racket from pain and insanity.

It still is. In other words, not only had people murdered God, but they had slain absolutes as well. This left them in the lurch, not knowing if what they knew and believed were really true, or sort of true—maybe, perhaps. The worm of uncertainty had entered modern thought through modern thought.

While the average person did not delve into these revolutionary ideas, they did, through the inventions that were entering their lives, and the news about Darwin, science, religion, etc., realize, however vaguely, that something very strange and dramatic was under way. Life was passing from substance to shadow because of human ingenuity.

It is similar to what so many feel today: that reality and truth are moving beyond their grasp as technological forces that they voluntarily embrace push everyday life towards some spectral denouement. An inhuman, transhuman, on-line electronic life where everything is a parody of everything that preceded it, like an Andy Warhol copy of a copy of a Campbell's soup can with a canned mocking laugh track that keeps repeating itself. All this follows from the nineteenth century relativization of knowledge, or what at least was taken as such, for to say all knowledge is relative is an absolute statement. That contradiction goes to the heart of our present dilemma.

This old feeling of lostness is perhaps best summarized in a few lines from Matthew Arnold's 19th century poem, "Dover Beach":

> The Sea of Faith
> Was once, too, at the full, and round earth's shore
> Lay like the folds of a bright girdle furled.
> But now I only hear
> Its melancholy, long, withdrawing roar,
> Retreating, to the breath
> Of the night-wind, down the vast edges drear
> And naked shingles of the world.

But that was then. Today, the Joker's sardonic laughter would suffice.

I am sitting outside as I write, sipping a glass of wine before dinner. Although New England fall weather is approaching, a nasty mosquito is buzzing around my head. I hear it. I am in killer mode since these bastards love to bite me. This is real life. If I went into the house and connected to the Internet on the computer screen—news, social media, anything—I would be entering another dimension. Screen life, not real life. The society of the spectacle. No real mosquitos, no wine, no trees swaying in the evening breeze.

In his novel, *The Sun Also Rises*, written between Nietzsche's time and now, Ernest Hemingway, a man who surely lived in the physical world, writes of how Robert Cohn, the boxing champion from Princeton University, wants Jake Barnes, the book's protagonist, to take a trip with him to South America. As they sit and talk in Paris, Barnes says no, and tells Cohn, "All countries look just like the moving pictures."

Whether Hemingway was being ironic or not, or simply visionary, I don't know. For in the 1920s, before passports and massive tourism, there were many places you could only see if you travelled to them and they would never appear in moving pictures, while today there is almost no place that is not available to view beforehand on the internet or television. So why go anywhere if you've already seen it all on a screen? Why travel to nowhere or to where you have already been? Déjà vu all over again, as Yogi Berra put it, and everyone laughed. Now the laugh is on us.

This is neither an argument nor a story. It's real. I am trying to get my bearings in a disorienting situation. Call it a compass, a weathervane, a prayer. You can call me Al or Ishmael. Call me crazy. Perhaps this writing is just an "as if."

About fifteen years ago, I was teaching at a college where most communication was done via email. I was, as they say, out of the loop since I didn't do email. I was often asked why I didn't, and I would repeatedly reply, like Melville's Bartleby, because "I prefer not to." Finally, in order to keep my job, I succumbed and with the laptop computer they provided me, I went "online." There were 6,954.7 emails in my in-box from the past three years. In those three years, I had performed all my duties scrupulously and hadn't missed a beat. Someone showed me how to delete the emails, which I did without reading any, but I had entered the labyrinth. I went electronic. My reality changed, and I am still searching for Ariadne's thread.

But I am not yet a machine and refuse the invitation to become one. It's a very insistent invitation, almost an order. Neil Postman (Oh such a rich surname!) sums it up well in *Technopoly: The Surrender of Culture to Technology:*

> The fundamental metaphorical message of the computer, in short, is that we are machines—thinking machines, to be sure, but machines nonetheless. It is for this reason that the computer is the quintessential, incomparable, near perfect machine for Technopoly. It subordinates the claims of our nature, our biology, our emotions, our spirituality. The computer claims sovereignty over the whole range of human experience, and supports its claim by showing that it "thinks" better than we can. . . . John McCarthy, the inventor of the term "artificial intelligence" . . . claims that "even machines as simple as thermostats can be said to have beliefs" . . . What is significant about this response is that it has redefined the meaning of the word "belief" . . . rejects the view that humans have internal states of mind that are the foundation of belief and argues instead that "belief" means only what someone or something does . . . rejects the idea that the mind is a biological phenomenon. . . . In other words, what we have here is a case of metaphor gone mad.

Postman wrote that in 1992, long before the computer and the internet became ubiquitous and even longer before online living had become de rigueur—before it was being shoved down our throats as it is today under the cover of COVID-19.

There is little doubt that we are being pushed to embrace what Klaus Schwab, the Executive Chairman of the World Economic Forum (WEF), calls COVID-19: The Great Reset, that involves a total acceptance of the electronic, online life. Online learning, online news, online everything—only an idiot (from Greek, *idiotes*, a private person who pays no attention to public affairs) would fail to see what is being promoted. And who controls the electronic life and internet? Not you, not I, but the powers that be, the intelligence agencies and the power elites. Goodbye body, goodbye blood—Let's hope no one ever shakes hands again, as Dr. Anthony Fauci so wisely advised.

Peter Koenig, one of the most astute investigators of this propaganda effort, puts it this way:

> The panacea of the future will be crowned by the Pearl of the Fourth Industrialization—Artificial intelligence (AI). It will be made possible by a 5G electromagnetic field, allowing the Internet of Things (IoT). Schwab and Malleret [Schwab's co-author] won't say, beware, there is opposition. 5G could still be blocked. The 5G existence and further development is necessary for surveillance and control of humanity, by digitizing everything, including human identity and money.
>
> It will be so simple, no more cash, just electronic, digital money—that is way beyond the control of the owner, the truthful earner of the money, as it can be accessed by the Global Government and withheld and / or used for pressuring misbehaving citizens into obeying the norms imposed from above. You don't behave according to our norms, no money to buy food, shelter and health services, we let you starve. No more travel. No more attending public events. You'll be put gradually in your own solitary confinement. The dictatorial and tyrannical global commandeering by digital control of everything is the essence of the 4th Age of Industrialization—highly promoted by the WEF's Great Reset.

Like everything, of course, this push to place life under the aegis of cyberspace has a history, one that deifies the machine and attempts to convince people that they too are machines without existential freedom. Thus, the ongoing meme pumped out for the past three decades has been that we are controlled by our brains and that the brain is a computer and vice versa. Brain research has received massive government funding. Drugs have been offered as the solution to every human problem. So-called diseases and disorders have been created through the Diagnostic and Statistical Manual of Mental Disorders (DSM) and matched to pharmaceutical drugs for scandalous profits. And the mind has been reduced to a figment of deluded imaginations. People are machines

If one wishes an historical example of techno-fascism, there is one from the art world. Back in the 1920s and 1930s there was an art movement known as Futurism. Its leader proponent was an Italian fascist, friend of Mussolini, Filippo Tommaso Marinetti. The futurists claimed that all life revolves around the machine, that the machine was god, that it was beyond human control and had to be obeyed. They extolled war and speed and claimed that humans were no more significant than stones. Patriotism, militarism, strength, method, and the kingdom of experts were their blueprint for a corporate fascist state. The human eye and mind would be re-educated to automatically obey the machine's dictates.

Now we have cyberspace, digital machines, and the internet, an exponential extension of the machine world of the 1930s and the rise of Mussolini, fascism, and Hitler. That this online world is being pushed as the new and future normal by transnational elite forces should not be surprising. If human communication becomes primarily digitally controlled online and on screens, those who control the machines will have achieved the most powerful means of mind control ever invented. That will be MKULTRA on a vast scale.

Yes, there will be places on the internet where truth is and will be told, but as we can see from today's growing censorship across the web, those forces that control the companies that do their bidding will narrow the options for dissenting voices. Such censorship starts slowly, and then when one looks again, it is a fait accompli. The frog in the pan of slowly heating cold water never realizes it is being killed. The purpose of so much internet propaganda is to confuse, obsess, depress, and then repress the population.

The overlords accomplish this by the "peculiar linking together of opposites—knowledge with ignorance, cynicism with fanaticism—[which] is one of the chief distinguishing marks of Oceanic society," writes Orwell in *Nineteen Eighty-Four*. "The official ideology abounds with contradictions even where there is no practical reason for them." One look into one's life will suffice to see how the overlords have set people against each other. It's a classic tactic that few ever wake up to. Divide and conquer. Trump vs. Biden, Democrats vs. Republicans. Pure mind games.

Nietzsche said that along with the real world we have done away with the apparent as well. Digital online life allows the rulers—through the media who are the magicians who serve them—to create fake news and fake videos at will, and to push breaking news items so fast that no one half-way sane could keep up with their magic shows. Nietzsche obviously didn't foresee this technology, but he sensed its birth.

Jesus, Gaza, and the Murder of Useless People

Jesus was a Palestinian Jew born in Bethlehem. He grew up in Nazareth and was executed as a criminal in Jerusalem. It is because of him that we celebrate Christmas. But it is in spite of him that what we celebrate is the opposite of what he stood for.

The different stories of his birth, told by Matthew and Luke in the New Testament, which are the bases for Christmas, are not filled with sugar plum fairies and sleighs filled with useless, unnecessary consumer goods. There's nothing about a Jolly Old St. Nicholas or baked ham or candy canes. No gifts to return in a frenzied rush that replicates their purchase. No credit card bills that come due in the new year. No "Jingle Bell Rock" with Brenda Lee or "White Christmas" with Bing Crosby.

Just a poor child's birth to fulfill a prophecy that out of life would come death and out of death would come life. That hope was improbable but possible with faith.

These birth narratives, which tell of a nativity that concludes with the grown child's suffering, public crucifixion, death, and Resurrection—a story that lives on with the suffering of so many innocents—are, as Gary Wills puts it in *What the Gospels Meant*, ". . . far from feel-good stories. They tell of a family outcast and exiled, hunted and rejected. They tell of children killed, of a sword to pierce the mother's heart, of a judgment on the nations." They are stories of rejection, massacre, and a desperate flight from death at an early age. They are not what most people now consider to be the essence of Christmas since a radical Palestinian Jew's story has been almost totally erased by the glitz and greed of getting and spending to fuel an economy geared for war and killing.

Matthew and Luke's birth narratives are replicated again and again throughout history, presently in Gaza and the West Bank, as the massacre of the innocents continues under today's King Herod, Benjamin Netanyahu, the client king of Washington, not Rome, while U.S. politicians, including Robert F. Kennedy, Jr., who claims to be a defender of children and opposed to U.S. war policies, support this genocide with rhetorical justifications that the Trappist monk Thomas Merton called the unspeakable:

> It is the void that contradicts everything that is spoken even before the words are said; the void that gets into the language of public and official declarations at the very moment when they are pronounced, and makes them ring dead with the hollowness of the abyss. It is the void out of which Eichmann drew the punctilious exactitude of his obedience . . .

To the shock of so many of Kennedy's early supporters, he claims, among other unspeakable assertions, that the Israelis have been the innocent victims of the Palestinians for 75 years, and they "could flatten Gaza" if they chose to, but instead have kindly used high-tech explosives "to avoid civilian casualties"; that they are not committing genocide intentionally. Indeed, his defense of the indefensible Israeli war crimes is widely shared by the compromised political leadership—including Biden and Trump—of both parties in Washinton, D.C., a place Kennedy is hoping to reach as the top of the heap, though he is contradicting all his talk about spiritual renewal and healing the divide, and it is especially galling and hypocritical as we try to celebrate the birth of the Prince of Peace.

While the genocide of Palestinians is being documented every ongoing day now, the Gospel stories are different in that they were written after the fact and were not based on eyewitness testimony but are narratives of deep symbolic faith significance, historically wrong in places, but told to signify religious truths of the early Christian faith community.

Once there was a mother and father with their child on the run to safety in Egypt, today there are millions of Palestinian refugees on a bombed-out unarmed road of flight to nowhere but a dead end.

A few days ago, my wife and I were caring for our son's two dogs. Down the hill as night came on, the town set off fireworks—those bombs bursting in air (Oh how lovely is war!)—to celebrate and encourage people to buy holiday gifts in what can only fairly be described as acquisitive consumer madness that many realize yet have accepted as an essential part of the Christmas message. As the fireworks exploded loudly, the dogs started to quake uncontrollably, and we had to hold them tight to comfort them.

Yes, they are animals, but sentient animals with deep feelings; and yes, they are not children in Gaza quivering in fear as the Israelis bomb them night and day in savage attacks. But as we held those frightened dogs, feeling their hearts beat fast as they gasped for breath, the visceral sense of what those Palestinians must be feeling, as they hold their trembling children who are butchered as useless objects, overwhelmed me. As they are "thinned out," as Netanyahu is reported to have said, I felt sick at heart to be living safely in a country that finances and supports such slaughter. A country in which buying and selling is the real religion, people have become commodities, and Christmas has become the celebration of such grotesqueries.

I keep thinking of the difference between human beings and things; life and death; money and power; acquisitiveness and poverty; and, as Norman O. Brown puts it in *Life Against Death*, "an economy driven by a pure sense of guilt, unmitigated by any sense of redemption."

In his classic study, Brown makes clear that it is erroneous to think that the secular and the sacred are exclusive opposites, as if the secular has replaced the "irrational" beliefs of religion with clean science and logical thinking; has banished irrational superstitions with abstract, objective, quantitative, and impersonal thinking. On the contrary, he argues that the whole modern secular money complex—the spirit of capitalism—is rooted in the psychology of guilt and the secular sacred. He writes:

> The psychological realities here are best grasped in terms of theology, and were already grasped by Luther. Modern secularism, and its companion Protestantism, do not usher in an era in which human consciousness is liberated from supernatural manifestations; the essence of the Protestant (or capitalist) era is that the power over this world has passed from God to God's negation, God's ape, the Devil. And already Luther had seen in money the essence of the secular, and therefore of the demonic. The money complex is the demonic, and the demonic is God's ape; the money complex is therefore the heir to and substitute for the religious complex, an attempt to find God in things.

Just like money, beyond a certain minimum necessary for a simple life of use, things do not, as everyone knows, bring happiness. This is because they are dead—excrement—the Devil's favorite toy.

Take all those useless and superfluous objects people exchange during the holiday season. The disposable gifts that are purchased to ease the guilt of not giving yet receiving. Or such "objects" as an autograph of a famous person, an art work such as Andy Warhol's *Shot Sage Blue Marilyn* that sold at auction last year for $195 million, Babe Ruth's bat, Princess Diana's evening dress ($1,148 million at auction), antlers over a fireplace and trophies of all sorts—the examples are manifold—they serve to confer on their owners a sacred prestige (etymology = deception, illusion) that is pure magic. Like vast piles of money, they are talismanic protectors against death. Their magical properties are irrational and rarely acknowledged, for to do so would reveal the absurdity of their acquisition and the pathetic nihilistic core of their owners. They are outward signs of inward barrenness, yet for those who possess these useless objects they are magic ordure.

The more expensive the objects the more social power they mystically confer, since the message is that the owner can always give it up for a pot of gold but doesn't have to since they are sitting on a lot more gold, which is really a pot of shit. In other words, wealth, its possession and the avid desire for it, signifies power over people and that power includes using them in many ways, including their labor, and killing them if one chooses, quickly or slowly, overtly or deviously, directly or indirectly, for some people are useless objects, inferior people.

Such power is central to politics and warfare, as a quick glance at the wealth of war-promoting politicians will reveal.

It is central to the widespread thinking today that the world is filled with useless people who must be disposed of one way or the other.

It is a fundamental tenet of the World Economic Forum, the Gates-Rockefeller *et al.* crowd, and the racist eugenics promoters of today and yesterday.

It is behind the Defense Advanced Research Projects Agency (DARPA) biological weapons gain-of-function research, the COVID-19 propaganda, and the CIA and Defense Department's distribution of the mRNA countermeasures ("vaccines") under Donald Trump.

It is central to the hideously obscene profits of the medical military-industrial complex and the worldwide arms industry.

It is central to the genocide taking place in Gaza. For the Israeli rulers, the problem is that the Palestinians exist, so they must be exterminated.

It's still the same old story told differently down through the ages.

Hitler enacted it against the Jews.

Once long ago, it was a Palestinian Jewish boy born in a manger destined to make trouble for the rulers of the empire who had to be eliminated one way or another. Today that child of God is any Palestinian child destined, we are told by the rulers of Israel, to grow into a terrorist animal.

Christmas is about a birth, the birth of a boy who would become a man who sided with the outcasts, the poor, the forsaken, the gentle, and the peacemakers. His birth and life was a rebuke to the powerful and the rich who lord it over the innocent, the killers, those who profit at the expense of others, who amass wealth and useless possessions to parade their power, a show of power which, unknown to their self-obsessed minds, is a sign of their spiritual nullity.

I have nothing against Santa. I once sat on his lap, and he seemed nice to my four-year-old mind. He was fat and jolly. He told me I would get what I wanted for Christmas. But he forgot to tell me what Christmas was really about.

That is what I want. To remember.

Alien Minds and the Will to Believe

Once upon a time in my youthful naiveté, I would mock those who said they believed in out-of-space aliens and flying saucers. In my hubris, I even wrote an extensive academic paper saying that the popularity of science fiction and the myth of planetary escape provided by the UFO cults and the media served the function of distracting us from earthly problems connected to the changing social structure of western societies and the concomitant transformation of our symbol systems from the traditionally religious to the scientific and technologically based. I argued that there was something devious in this new narrative, like the story of astronauts playing golf on the moon. Although I didn't then say it, I imagined the next public relations stunt would be ping pong on Mars. But I now know that ping pong is a Chinese dominated sport.

I must confess that I have never seen a space movie like *2001: A Space Odyssey* or *Star Wars* or the television series *Star Trek*; and I have never read any science fiction like *Childhood's End*. I was always repulsed by such fantasies, since figuring out what was going on here on earth was hard enough to grasp. They always seemed like a diversion to me. Of course, I have studied their story lines and know about them, and fiction is fiction, right? The movies and television shows aren't real, right?

Culture, I argued in my youthful academic days, is the higher learning we are all subjected to; and culture rests upon the crystallization of a symbolic order that was then changing. I was writing about the late 1960s and early 1970s when the promotion of esoterica of all kinds was widespread and growing madly. And as Philip Rieff wrote in *The Triumph of the Therapeutic*, "Faith is the compulsive dynamic of culture, channeling obedience to, trust in, and dependence upon authority."

I then sensed we were undergoing a massive symbolic transformation in which the controlling symbolic (from Greek: to throw together) order was being replaced by a diabolic (from Greek: to throw apart) order that controlled in a different way, and new stories were emerging that would not order people's lives but would disorder them as they were offered a pastiche of choices to scramble their brains so "they would never know" for sure. This was all happening at the time of the political assassinations of the 1960s, the war against Vietnam, the drug and sexual revolution, the crisis in traditional religion, the turn to the east especially among the young, women's liberation, etc.

As a sociologist, I was following a tradition of theorizing that tries to describe social change and how culture organizes personality through its symbol systems, in this case the crisis happening between the mainstream faith in science and the counter-cultural reactions and the ways this alleged either/or was being manipulated.

Silly as it now sounds, I argued that as a result of the failure of rational, scientific, and technological culture to replace the traditional religious symbolic plausibility structure it destroyed, resulting in a deep existential void of meaning, an alternative myth about outer space and extraterrestrial life was promulgated to divert people's attention from the creation of our Nazi-run military space program, nuclear weapons, and the military-industrial complex's nihilistic intention to use them. I was so naïve then.

My thesis was that through this symbolic transformation, power over all life and death passed from God to men, and a need arose to provide a story about the gods' continuing existence. Thus the UFO and outer space motifs whereby alien gods—through the technique of *deus ex machina*—might swoop down in flotillas of extraterrestrial spacecraft and swoop up the deserving ones to a beautiful beyond while the rest of the world was incinerated in a nuclear war, a staple story line of science fiction. Of course they might also rape you; but they were the bad aliens who were at odds with the good. *ET* and *The X Files* were still to come.

This myth of outer space was joined to a widespread rise in the promotion of occult phenomena—astrology, the Tarot, alchemy, crystal balls, satanism, witchcraft, spiritualism, etc.—that opened up all kinds of alternative, hypnotic visions of other lives past "death," incredible new visions of inner "realities" and the cosmos, spiritual journeys to worlds unheard of, aided or not by the fuel of psychedelic drugs that were pushed by the CIA. Thus, the gods within were added to the alien gods without, and new faiths were born—or rather, created. It was the New Age. These were mixed in a witches mélange with mainstream science or pseudo-science to create an anti-faith faith in forces that could save or destroy us, whether they be aliens, astronauts, or Indian gurus such as the creator of Transcendental Meditation (TM), Maharishi Mahesh Yogi, whose exotic teachings were married to pseudo-science and promoted as a way to reduce crime and violence and bring peace to earth.

This, I maintained in my youthful ignorance, was not a cultural accident. Mass cultural confusion seemed to have a malign purpose that was setting us up for a reactionary backlash that would return us back to the future. To a time when we could "never really know" but knew what we were meant to know even as we sensed what we were not to know.

That was in my old life as a scholar. I was so much younger then but I'm older than that now. For a few years, I have just been a regular beer-swigging normal dude walking unpaved roads and woodland hikes looking for the wild life. I have dispensed with the books. I have recently had a revelation like Saul on the road to Damascus but without the light or falling down. I heard no voices. It happened inauspiciously.

A while back I learned of a nice, peaceful place to take a walk down by the river across an old, covered bridge down a dirt road where lovely birds could be seen and heard. I was surprised to learn of this place since I have lived here a long time and have sought out every wild country walk I could find. But serendipity happens and epiphanies occur.

Three years ago when I first walked the bridge over water troubled by General Electric's dumping of toxic PCBs into it, the place was deserted. On the other side of the twisting Housatonic River I was surprised to see a large stone monument with an inscription signed by the governor of Massachusetts, Charlie Baker. I knew that Baker, a Republican, like the former governor Mitt Romney, was the type of "mild" Republican that the overwhelmingly Democratic voters generally didn't complain about. The monument commemorated a 1969 UFO event, attesting to it being "the first off-world/UFO case in U.S. history" when a nine-year-old boy named Thomas Reed and his family were said to have encountered a UFO and were taken out of their car by the aliens to a cavernous enclosure with strange lights. Beamed up and out in other words. Then deposited back in their car.

I had mocked such reports before, but this one was endorsed by the mild-mannered and thoroughly establishment Charlie Baker, a former CEO of Harvard Vanguard Medical Associates, and now the president of the National Collegiate Athletic Association (NCAA), and I was shocked. So I read about it and discovered it had been a big event in the area on the night of September 1, 1969 when about 40 others reported seeing a UFO. It made me laugh at people's gullibility since remnants of my intellectual skepticism still clung to my numbskull. The more I learned about it, the less I believed it, despite Baker's endorsement.

When I again returned to the spot a few years later, the monument was gone, and I learned a controversy had ensued, some people had complained, and the town had hauled the monument away. Now there is a smaller round shaped plaque on a metal pole commemorating the event.

It seems the 1969 event caused mass confusion, which would seem appropriate for that time and place, as my youthful writings about culture at large explained. This was two weeks following Woodstock, the height of the Vietnam War, twelve days after the release of the movie, *Alice's Restaurant*, based on the 1967 experience of local resident Arlo Guthrie's famous encounter and song about getting anything you want at Alice's restaurant, a local establishment run by Alice Brock that attracted hippies and counter culturists from all over. Clearly something was happening here, what it was wasn't exactly clear, since you could get anything you wanted in those tumultuous times. And anything and everything was everywhere in the culture.

But things are so different now. We are all older and wiser. We follow the science. We just do what we're told. We read the papers about the new government report about UFOs or what they now call UAPs (Unidentified Aerial Phenomena). There are some things we just don't know but others that we think we do, just like the Defense Department and the intelligence agencies. That's what they say, isn't it, and they wouldn't lie? We follow the science today. The CDC wouldn't lie, would it? We just do what we're told.

Chris Carter, the creator of the television show, *The X-Files*, has a prominent Op Ed guest essay in *The New York Times* to explain why he so desperately wants to believe in aliens and how he actually does so without actually admitting it. Along the way, Carter makes sure to slyly tell us he knows the truth about COVID-19:

> We are living in times of uncertainty, where truth may be unknowable. I don't have to tell you this has bred a universe of rampant conspiracy theories. From the Covid conspiracy documentary *Plandemic* to the idea that we're living in a black hole created by the CERN's Large Hadron Collider when we discovered the Higgs boson.

He follows the science. He thinks truth may be unknowable, a saying that you may have heard before. You know: "We'll never know." Except for certain truths. For he knows all about the pandemic and aliens. And he tells us:

> When we were dressing the original set for Agent Mulder's office on "The X-Files," I came up with the

> poster with a UFO on it that reads "I Want to Believe." And I think that's where most people come down on the whole extraterrestrial business. Not quite there yet, but waiting for a sign.

I'm not waiting. I'm there. I received the sign. I know. I got there just a few days ago when again, in my newfound clarity devoid of my old intellectual perspective, I walked that bridge over troubled waters and saw a large piece of metal lying in a watery ditch right where Thomas Reed described his abduction. It was new and very shiny. Talk about signs! If that isn't science, I don't know what is. Direct observation has brought me to the truth. The aliens came back and lost a bumper. Although you might say that's just circumstantial evidence, I must disagree. It's not a symbol, I know that. I saw it with my "eyes wide shut." I follow the science. Life is not a movie, is it?

I once thought the UFO people were crazy and there was a concerted effort to confuse people. But I was so much younger then. I'm older than that now.

Carter ends his essay by saying, "I want to believe."

I say: Lords, I believe. Help my disbelief.

Death, Money, and the Dueling Frauds: Trump and Biden

When *The New York Times* and *CNN* recently (2020) referred to the staged town hall spectacles of Biden and Trump as dueling events, they inadvertently revealed the truth that U.S. presidential elections are America's favorite movie and that the corporate media is in the entertainment business.

While it is ludicrous to imagine these tottering actors crossing swords in tights, their skirmishes in suits and ties are good for a few laughs, if you have the stomach to watch them. Only people who still believe in professional wrestling would think these clowns don't work for the same bosses—the Umbrella People, those who pretend to shelter people from a hard rain, aka the power elites, the national security state, etc., who own the country and choose their stooges to represent their interests in the White House.

I much prefer Mel Brooks, a genuinely funny guy.

Columnist Russell Baker once said the purpose of such political entertainment is to "provide a manageably small cast for a national sitcom, or soap opera, or docudrama, making it easy for media people to persuade themselves they are covering the news while mostly just entertaining us."

If you were writing this script as part of long-term planning, and average people were getting disgusted from decades of being screwed and were sick of politicians and their lying ways, wouldn't you stop the reruns and create a new show? Come on, this is Hollywood where creative showmen can dazzle our minds with plots so twisted that when you leave the theater you keep wondering what it was all about and arguing with your friends about the ending. So create a throwback film where the good guy versus the bad guy was seemingly very clear, and while the system ground on, keep people at each other's throats over the obvious differences, even though they were fabricated or minor. Another successful replay of the age-old strategy of divide and conquer.

I realize that it is very hard for many to entertain the thought that Trump and Biden are not arch-enemies but are players in a spectacle created to confound at the deepest psychological levels. I am not arguing that the Democrats didn't want Hillary Clinton to win in 2016. I am saying they knew Trump was a better opponent, not only because they could probably defeat him and garner more of the spoils, but because if he possibly won he was easily controlled because he was compromised. By whom? Not the Democrats, but the "Deep State" forces that control Hillary Clinton and all the presidents. A compromised and corrupt lot. The Democrats and Republicans were not in charge in 2016 or in 2020. Their bosses were. The Umbrella people.

As for debates and town hall farces in television prime time, the witty Baker said that "the charm of television entertainment is its ability to bridge the chasm between dinner and bedtime without mental distraction."

Now let's proceed to the dark side, where the sardonic screams of laughter dissolve into tears.

For such entertainment serves a devious distracting purpose: to conceal the nature of social evil and the driving forces behind American politics today. It is not particularly complicated unless the syllogism—All cats die/Socrates is dead/ therefore Socrates is a cat—rings true.

Then it's an impossible conundrum.

We are not cats or Socrates, as far as I know. But like them, we will also die. Everyone knows this, but the thought of death is not particularly "have-a-nice-day-ish," so people deny it as much as possible in a host of ways. Most people prefer life over death, and when death does approach and can no longer be denied, most hope for immortality in some way, shape, or form.

Yes, there are those who assert this isn't true for them, and there is no reason to doubt their sincerity. There are philosophical arguments to support their position, such as that of the Roman poet Lucretius in his famous poem *De rerum natura* (*On the Nature of Things*). But I would maintain with the great psychoanalyst Rollo May that all such naturalistic efforts, including Lucretius's, to explain away human anxiety rooted in death, founder on the human emotions of pity, grief, love, and loneliness. Rational explanations take us only so far. In their efforts to deny the human condition and dismiss the spiritual dimension, the irrational, and the daimonic, they open the door to madness, as is happening today with the push by the world's economic elite to convince people that they are machines and that their machine dreams will conquer death.

For those who love life, it seems axiomatic to me that some form of perpetuation and redemption of an individual's life in the face and fear of death is widely desired. This can take many forms: a literal afterlife, fame, heirs, monuments, money, children, etc. History is quite clear that people have always sought some way of transcending their physical fates.

This was aptly noted by Graham Greene, the English novelist, when, as an old man approaching death, he was asked if he was disappointed at not receiving the Nobel Prize, and he said no, since he was hoping for a greater prize.

In his important book, *The Denial of* Death (Pulitzer Prize 1974 for general non-fiction), the cultural anthropologist, Ernest Becker, puts it succinctly:

> Man is literally split in two: he has an awareness of his own splendid uniqueness in that he sticks out of nature with a towering majesty, and yet goes back into the ground a few feet in order blindly and dumbly to rot and disappear forever.

Faced with such an impossible situation, then, overwhelmed from childhood with a sense of one's own ultimate physical powerlessness but being symbolic creatures as well as physical ones, the normal person learns to repress the terror of death by building various defenses that allow one to believe that he ultimately controls his death. One's natural impotence is then hidden within "the vital lie of character"; one lives within the manageable social world that helps one blot out existential awareness by offering various social games and cultural symbols, agreed forms of madness that narcotize the fear. One learns to adjust. The aim is to cut life down to manageable proportions, domesticate terror, and trust in the cultural and social authorities for protection and reassurance. Obedience is key.

Listen to Big Daddy and he will rescue you, especially when he first tells you that Mr. Pumpkin Head is coming to get you unless you run into his protective embrace.

These days, it's Halloween all year round in the land of the free and the home of the brave, where the fear of death is handed out like poisoned candy and Big Daddy waits at the door disguised as everyone's benevolent grandfather. To be treated, you must be masked. That is his trick. "Stay well," he mutters, after he drops a dollop of sweet fear into your bag and cackles behind his face.

Everywhere you look these days, people are doubly masked. The paper kind and by definition of persons, since the word person, being derived from the Latin, *persona,* means mask, while there is another Latin word, *larva,* that also means mask or ghost or evil spirit. Clearly there is a dance contest underway, a *danse macabre*. And who will win nobody knows.

"Every conflict over truth," wrote the psychoanalyst Otto Rank, "is in the last analysis just the same old struggle over . . . immortality."

This is exactly what is going on now with the fierce disagreements over COVID-19.

Like the attacks of September 11, 2001, the anthrax attacks, the ginning up of terrorism fear with Homeland "Security's" color-coded warning system, the lies about weapons of mass-destruction, and the coronavirus early warning systems, people have adopted positions upon which they stake their psychological lives. To admit you were snookered is a little death that is hard to swallow.

We are being subjected to mind-control on a vast scale, the continual pumping up of the fear of death to control the population. Americans have been living in an atmosphere of dread for almost twenty years. It's so old and so obvious but cuts so deep it works like a charm. "You don't want to die, do you, so come here into Big Daddy's arms."

In *Nineteen Eighty-Four*, George Orwell writes that "The Party seeks power entirely for its own sake." It is a famous quote that is not true when taken out of context. The Umbrella People and their lackeys don't seek power entirely for its own sake. They have a larger agenda: immortality.

If one reads Orwell carefully, one comes upon a key passage that clarifies the previous quote. The evil O'Brien, the torturer and member of the Inner Party who poses as a member of the resistance to Big Brother (sound familiar?), asks his victim Winston Smith to reverse the slogan from "Freedom is Slavery" to Slavery is Freedom:

> Alone—free—the human being is always defeated. It must be so, because every human being is destined to die, which is the greatest of all failures. But if he can make complete, utter submission, if he can escape from his identity, if he can merge himself in the Party so that he *is* the Party, then he will be all-powerful and immortal. The second thing for you to realize is that power is power over human beings. Over the body—but, above all, over the mind. Power over matter—external reality as you would call it—is not important. Already our control over matter is absolute.

All power is fundamentally power to deny mortality. This is true whether it is the power of the state or church. And it is always sacred power.

Many often ask why do the super-rich and powerful always want more. It's simple. They wish to transcend human mortality and become gods—immortals. They stupidly believe that if they can lord it over others, kill, dominate, achieve status, become billionaires, presidents, magnates, celebrities, etc., they will somehow live in some weird forever.

In a process that has spanned at least a hundred and fifty years or so, our traditional cultural/religious symbol systems have been radically undermined, most momentously by the Faustian creation of Lord Nuke. All forms of symbolic immortality (theological, biological, creative, natural, and experiential) that formerly provided a sense of continuity have been severely threatened. This is the haunting specter lurking in the background of life today.

What is death? How to defeat or transcend it? How to affirm life in the face of death?

One paradoxical way that political leaders do this is by killing. Followers who accede to such killing join their leaders, not simply to see others dead, but to acquire power over death itself—to kill their own deaths. It is perverse, of course, and is summed up in the prescription saying to love the bomb joyously, to experience the nightmare of oblivion as ecstasy. Isn't this what the philosophy of voting for the lesser of two evils is about? At least he will be our killer. Our evil killer, but not as bad as yours. You lose.

I have read that there is a painting still visible at the entrance to a house in ruined Pompeii that tells us much about power and wealth. It perfectly symbolizes the meaning of the economic gap between the super-rich—e.g. those behind the World Economic Forum, the CIA, the presidential candidates, the corporate media—and the rest of us. It pictures a man weighing his penis on a scale of gold coins. Gold, God, wealth, and power. It's an old story.

Today, however, there is a difference, for the spirit of nihilism has grown as belief in the spiritual dimension and God has diminished dramatically. Money or gold, wealth in all its forms, is today's foremost immortality symbol, a sign that one is powerful and can conquer death. What else are Trump's gold-emblazoned Tower and hair, and Biden's boastfully admitted threat to withhold one billion dollars from Ukraine unless they fire the prosecutor investigating his son, Hunter. The greasing of palms, bribery, tax theft, etc.—par for the course in a corrupt society run by thieves and criminals.

Becker says of this wealth obsession:

> The only hint we get of the cultural repression seeping through is that even dedicated financiers wash their hands after handling money. The victory over death is a fantasy that cannot be fully believed in; money doesn't entirely banish feces [decay and death that is of course defeated with toilet paper as COVID-19 has proven], and so the threat of germs and vulnerability in the very process of securing immortality.

Pseudo immortality.

Enter COVID-19. Like the attacks of September 11, 2001, it is death writ large. An insidious terrorist threat. Invisible, sneaky, ready to pounce. Fear and trembling. So-called surprise attacks that were preceded by simulations and live drills. Numerous parallels, too many to mention. Let's not. Have a nice day! Stay safe!

So what do the super-rich controllers want now? What are the World Economic Forum's Claus Schwab, Google and the Defense Department's Eric Schmidt, Bill Gates, Ray Kurzweil of Google and "The Singularity," et al. pushing now that COVID-19 has so many cowering in fear?

These people have realized that the thing that their money and power must do is to create a world where transhumanism must triumph, and people of flesh and blood must be induced and forced to become the machines they have been told they are. If you doubt this is underway, research the World Economic Forum's agenda, see what the Great Reset is about, the Build Back Better slogans, the massive push to create online existence for everyone, etc. As a recent ad I saw says: "The world is going digital."

The goal of these mad technocratic elites is to create a fabricated reality where the visible world becomes nearly meaningless once the screen world becomes people's "window on the world." An electronic nothingness to replace reality as people in the industrialized countries gleefully embrace digital wraparound apparitions and the poor and vulnerable of this world suffer and die out of sight and out of mind. It is the fundamental seismic shift of our era and perhaps the greatest propaganda operation ever undertaken. A sort of end-times desperate gambit.

And "it just so happens" to revolve around the use of death fear to accomplish its goals. Just as so much else just so happens.

But for the elites, there will be no death. For having realized that their stolen wealth and power can only take them so far, and they too will become food for worms, they have commandeered science and medicine to undertake their immortality projects. If medicine fails to find for them the secret of immortality, then computer science and Artificial Intelligence will, and they will be uploaded into computers and live forever in their beloved cyberspace. Digital immortality is not a joke for these people—see "The Singularity" put forward by Kuzweil, the director of engineering at Google, etc.—for they are actually insane but hold key positions throughout the computer and biotechnology industries. Check where the super-rich invest their money to confirm this. None of it is secret.

Having heeded Russell Baker's words about television offering no mental distraction between dinner and bedtime, I took to my crib early, knowing Tweedledee and Tweedledum would be dueling again, this time in what they humorously called a debate. I was surrounded by my stuffed animals that protected me and I slept safe and sound.

Upon awakening, I read that the gladiators had exchanged blows but that both were left standing for the big showdown on November 3. I also noticed that each had used the words "dark winter" in reference to COVID-19. Biden said one was coming and Trump said he didn't know.

Neither, of course, spoke of the Dark Winter Exercise, a senior level war game conducted on June 22–23, 2001, about a biological attack, a smallpox outbreak, the public health response, the lack of vaccines, the need for quarantine and isolation, the restriction of civil liberties, and the role of the Defense Department and the military in the response. Nor did they speak of anthrax attacks, but the book by Canadian researcher, Graeme MacQueen, *The 2001 Anthrax Deception,* will fill you in on both, in case you don't know. Maybe the boys just forgot.

I am sure they didn't talk about the elements of Trump's "Operation Warp Speed," but if you wish to understand how we are being gamed, the journalist Whitney Webb will tell you.

Was there any mention of the Russians? I haven't heard. They are always a kind of a solution. As my friend Joe Green has said:

> All dissenting opinions are Russian. I think Socrates said that. I'm paraphrasing.

Death's Secretary Tries to Forget

We have come to Cape Cod for a few days to forget the manmade world that is too much with us. I have asked my forgettery to get to work. As my childhood friends used to say to me, "Eddy spaghetti, use your forgetty." The adults had no idea what they meant. Many still do not.

Here slowness reigns and forgetting seems possible, even if for just a few days. In mid-May, the beaches are deserted except for the swooping gulls, the sandpipers prancing across the sand, and a few seals eyeing you from just offshore. An occasional frigate bird glides past. The wind rushes through your ears, making conversation almost impossible.

But no words are needed here, for the ocean speaks its own language and the tales it tells are deep. You can only hear them if you shut up and listen. It utters reminders of the immensity of creation and the puniness of human aspirations. The sea dismisses with a roar the pretensions to power of the Lilliputians.

One minute it glistens in the bright blue sunshine and says all is well; then suddenly, as now, the sky and sea turn very dark and foreboding, the increased wind whipping the whitecaps into a maniacal threat. There are limits, it wails, and do not try to exceed them, for if, in your hubris, you attempt it, you will discover that when you think you're on the top, you will be heading for the bottom.

As the Greeks knew so well, Nemesis awaits your response.

If you stand on the forty-mile-long strand of the sandy outer beach and look out to sea, you realize that no matter how well you sail through life, and how deftly you tack your boat, you are not ultimately in control. Those who seek to control others lack the spirit of the wind, the unseen mystery through which we move.

Henry David Thoreau stood on this beach looking out to sea and wrote, "A man may stand there and put all America behind him."

I wish it were so simple. To forget the manmade world that is too much with us isn't easy. Ironically, it can only be briefly forgotten, for when we come to a beautiful and wild seashore like Cape Cod when rarely a soul is around, the contemplation of its majesty implicitly draws us to compare it to human endeavors. I look out across the wide Atlantic and see not just its wild power but the feeble pretensions of the Atlanticist countries that think they can still control the world. Their illusions die hard as their sandcastle empire crumbles before the incoming wave.

And here on this long stretch between bay and ocean, it's hard to forget that many years before the Pilgrims came ashore, the native peoples lived here and were eventually driven from their land. Not far from where I stand sits the Nauset Light house, named for the Nauset tribe that once lived here. You can travel all across the United States and even if you wish to forget, there are constant reminders of the genocide of the native peoples by the European settlers. You bow your head in shameful remembrance.

Of course, in order to forget, it is crucial to remember to try to forget, and in doing so you are caught in the human web of thought.

We tell ourselves, let us go then, you and I, to contemplate the sea and sky, to let go of all the world's woes and pack up our sorrows and give them to the elements as we vacate our minds. Then—ouch!—we are jerked back by the sight of a dead sea gull on the sand or a plaque informing you that the long stretch of outer beach you walk with the ghost of Thoreau was preserved as the Cape Cod National Seashore by President Kennedy in 1961. You find yourself walking with many ghosts: dead writers, sailors drowned in shipwrecks, ancient dead horseshoe crabs along the strand, and an assassinated president who loved this sea and land. You realize that nature, while beautifully majestic, is also a cruel taskmaster, but not as cruel as humans, so many of whom seem to revel in killing.

You struggle to dismiss the thoughts associated with these aperçus, yet you immediately wonder if they are auguries of past events or harbingers of something else. You feel you have been ambushed by another reality. You hear Billie Joel's words from his historical song, *We Didn't Start the Fire*, "JFK blown away, what else do I have to say."

You is I, of course, and although these words are addressed to those who might read them, I am also writing for myself, and I sense my word usage was a way to distance myself from what I sometimes find hard to accept: that for some reason of character or experience or both, it is my fate to be unable to escape for long from what my perceptions suggest to me. Wherever I have gone on that strange word "vacation," I have been trailed by thoughts that others may consider inappropriate for the occasion. Un-vacation thoughts. Wherever I have traveled I have always felt like William Blake as he wandered through each chartered street of London:

> In every cry of every Man,
> In every Infants cry of fear,
> In every voice: in every ban,
> The mind-forg'd manacles I hear

Is it a blessing or curse? I don't know. Such knowing is overrated. My father, an eloquent and brilliant man with deep religious faith, used to end his letters to me with the words: *quién sabe* (who knows)?

There is, however, another form of knowing that is vastly underrated; it is historical, a knowledge of history that illuminates the present. I mentioned the Nauset people who lived on Cape Cod when the pilgrims first temporarily dropped anchor in what is now called Provincetown Harbor. The Nauset people's story, like those of the other native peoples across the United States, is tied to the U.S. history of empire in significant ways.

This country was conceived in the blood of all the native peoples who lived here for eons. They were massacred to make way for the white technologists who sent their iron horses west as they slaughtered the horse-riding natives—including the Pueblo, Pawnee, Comanche and Lakota nations—and other natives who went by shanks mare.

This history is crucial knowledge, for without it one cannot grasp the demonic nature of today's U.S. wars throughout the world. That history has always been demonic. Nemesis is surely watching now, for what began in the blood of others, has a tendency to blow back on those who first unleashed the fire. Those of us alive today might not have started the fire, but if we don't know and recognize its long-term spiritual effects, we can't understand today's U.S. provoked war against Russia via Ukraine or much else.

If you wish to praise the American Revolution, you should be sure to emphasize its demonic side. The mythology of the shining city on the hill needs to be abandoned. American exceptionalism needs to be jettisoned together with reminders of Washington and Jefferson, both rich slave holders. There are no exceptional countries. The Declaration of Independence and the U.S. Constitution read beautifully on paper as ideals, but those who promoted them were far from it.

Is it exceptional to massacre the native peoples and steal their land?

Is it exceptional to have built an economy on the backs of slaves kidnapped from Africa?

Is it exceptional to plunder foreign lands and make them part of your own?

Is it exceptional to wage endless foreign wars, assassinate at will, and steal the resources of other people to fuel a deranged consumer society?

Is it exceptional to grant full freedom to criminal corporations to pollute the land and water?

Is it exceptional to create endless crises and use propaganda to transfer vast sums of wealth from regular people to the super rich?

Exceptional perhaps, but only in the sense that other past empires considered themselves god-like and immune to Nemesis's warning of retribution for such crimes?

A dark wind is blowing across the beach now. The sand stings. I see a storm coming, so we will leave for now and go to the nearest restaurant where we will order a dozen oysters for a buck a piece and drink some wine to enjoy our last day here. When the dozen are gone, perhaps another dozen will taste even better. All will be well for a small slice of time. I will remember to forget.

I might later remember a photo of Gabriel García Márquez's face, the look of a bon vivant who told stories to preserve the mystery of our ordinary, extraordinary lives. The fierce journalist who exposed the mystifications that are used by the powerful to deny regular people their democratic rights. A man who could enjoy life and oppose oppression.

If you can believe it, I will remember that he spoke of "the mission assigned to us by fate." And that the great English essayist John Berger says of him, when comparing his face to that of Rembrandt's blind Homer:

> There is nothing pretentious in this comparison: we, Death's secretaries, all carry the same sense of duties, the same oblique shame (as we have survived, the best have departed) and the same obscure pride which belongs to us personally no more than the stories we tell.

Berger adds that Death's secretaries are handed a file by Death that is filled with sheets of black paper which they can somehow read and out of which they make stories for the living. No matter how fantastic they may seem, only one's incredulity blocks one from entering their truths.

JFK had a secretary named Lincoln, Evelyn Lincoln, who late one night when tidying up his desk, found a slip of paper in his handwriting on the floor. It wasn't black. On it was written a prayer Kennedy loved. It was a message from Lincoln, Abraham

Lincoln: "I know there is a God—and I see a storm coming. If he has a place for me, I believe that I am ready."

It's worth remembering that that was soon after the Bay of Pigs when Kennedy said he wanted "to splinter the CIA in a thousand pieces and scatter it to the winds," and he had just returned from a meeting with Nikita Khruschev where he was shocked by Khruschev's apparent insouciance to an accelerating threat of nuclear war.

Death's secretary can't forget.

And yet those oysters. Their taste upon the tongue! So exquisite! The sea's sweetness in every swallow.

From Terrorists to Viruses

For anyone old enough to have been alive and aware of the attacks of September 11, 2001 and of so-called COVID-19 in 2020, memory may serve to remind one of an eerie parallel between the two operations. However, if memory has been expunged by the work of one's forgettery or deleted by the corporate media flushing it down the memory hole, or if knowledge is lacking, or maybe fear or cognitive dissonance is blocking awareness, I would like to point out some similarities that might perk one up to consider some parallels and connections between these two operations.

The fundamental tie that binds them is that both events aroused the human fear of death. Underlying all fears is the fear of death. A fear that has both biological and cultural roots. On the biological level, we all react to death threats in a fight or flight manner. Culturally, there are multiple ways that fear can be allayed or exacerbated, purposely or not. Usually, culture serves to ease the fear of death, which can traumatize people, through its symbols and myths. Religion has for a long time served that purpose, but when religion loses its hold on people's imaginations, especially in regard to the belief in immortality, as Orwell pointed out in the mid-1940s, a huge void is left. Without that consolation, fear is usually tranquilized by trivial pursuits.

In the cases of the attacks of September 11, 2001 and the current corona virus operation, the fear of death has been used by the power elites in order to control populations and institute long-planned agendas. There is a red thread that connects the two events.

Both events were clearly anticipated and planned.

In the case of September 11, 2001, as I have argued before, linguistic mind-control was carefully crafted in advance to conjure fear at the deepest levels with the use of such repeated terms as Pearl Harbor, Homeland, Ground Zero, the Unthinkable, and 9/11.

Both the events of September 11, 2001 and COVID-19 in their turns served to raise the fear level dramatically. Each drew on past meetings, documents, events, speeches, and deep associations of dread. This language was conjured from the chief sorcerer's playbook, not from that of an apprentice out of control.

And as David Ray Griffin, the seminal 9/11 researcher (and others), has pointed out in a dozen meticulously argued and documented books, the events of that day had to be carefully planned in advance, and the post hoc official explanations can only be described as scientific miracles, not scientific explanations. These miracles include: massive steel-framed high-rise buildings for the first time in history coming down without explosives or incendiaries in free fall speed; one of them being WTC-7 that was not even hit by a plane; an alleged hijacker pilot, Hani Hanjour, who could barely fly a Piper Cub, flying a massive Boeing 757 in a most difficult maneuver into the Pentagon; airport security at four airports failing at the same moment on the same day; all sixteen U.S. intelligence agencies failing, air traffic control failing, etc. The list goes on and on. And all this controlled by Osama bin Laden. It's a fairy tale.

Then we had the crucially important anthrax attacks that are linked to 9/11. Graeme MacQueen, in *The 2001 Anthrax Deception*, brilliantly shows that these too were a domestic conspiracy.

These planned events led to the invasion of Afghanistan, the PATRIOT Act, the U.S. withdrawal from the ABM Treaty, the invasion of Iraq, the ongoing war on terror, etc.

Let us not forget years of those fraudulent color-coded warnings of the terrorist levels and the government admonition to use duct tape around your windows to protect against a massive chemical and biological attack.

Jump to 2020. Let me start in reverse while color-coded designs are fresh in our minds. As the COVID-19 lockdowns were under way, a funny thing happened as people were wishing that life could return to normal and they could be let out of their cages. Similar color-coded designs popped up everywhere at the same time. They showed the step-by-step schedule of possible loosening of government controls if things went according to plan. Red to yellow to green. Eye catching. Red orange yellow blue green. As with the terrorist warnings following September 11, 2001. In Massachusetts, a so-called blue state where I live, its color chart ends in blue, not green, with Phase 4 blue termed "the new normal: Development of vaccines and/or treatments enable the resumption of 'the new normal.'" Interesting wording. A resumption that takes us back to the future.

As with the duct tape admonitions after 9/11, now everyone is advised to wear a mask. It's interesting to note that the 3 M Company, a major seller of duct tape, is also one of the world's major sellers of face masks. The company was expected to be producing 50 million N95 respirator masks per month by June 2020 and 2 billion globally within the coming year. Then there is 3 M's masking tape.... but this is a sticky topic.

After the attacks of September 11, 2001, we were told repeatedly that the world was changed forever. Now we are told that after COVID-19, life will never be the same. This is now the "new normal," so the post-9/11–pre-COVID-19 world must have been the old new normal. So everything is different but normal also. So as the Massachusetts government website puts it, in the days to come we may be enabled to enact "the resumption of 'the new normal.'" This new old normal will no doubt be a form of techno-fascist transhumanism enacted for our own good.

As with 9/11, there is ample evidence that the corona virus outbreak was expected and planned; that people have been the victims of a propaganda campaign to use an invisible virus to scare us into submission and shut down the world's economy for the global elites. It is a clear case, as Peter Koenig tells Michel Chossudovsky in an interview, not a conspiracy theory but a blatant factual plan spelled out in the 2010 Rockefeller Report, the October 18, 2019 Event 201, and Agenda 21, among other places.

Like amorphous terrorists and a war against "terrorism," which is a tactic and therefore not something you can fight, a virus is invisible except when the media presents it as a pale, orange-spiked bunch of floating weird balls that are everywhere and nowhere. Watch your back, watch your face, mask up, wash your hands, keep your distance—you never know when those orange spiked balls may get you.

As with 9/11, whenever anyone questions the official narrative of COVID-19, the official statistics, the validity of the tests, the effectiveness of masks, the powers behind the heralded vaccine to come, and the horrible consequences of the lockdowns that are destroying economies, killing people, forcing people to despair and to commit suicide, creating traumatized children, bankrupting small and middle-sized businesses for the sake of enriching the richest, etc., the corporate media mock the dissidents as conspiracy nuts, aiding the viral enemy. This is so even when the dissenters are highly respected doctors, scientists, intellectuals, et al., who are regularly disappeared from the internet.

With September 11, there were initially far fewer dissenters than now, and so the censorship of opposing viewpoints didn't need the blatant censorship that is now growing daily. This censorship happens all across the internet now, quickly and stealthily, the same internet that is being forced on everyone as the new normal as presented in the Great Global Reset, the digital lie, where, as Anthony Fauci put it, no one should ever shake hands again. A world of abstract images and beings in which, as Arthur Jensen tells Howard Beal in the film, *Network*, "All necessities [will be] provided, all anxieties tranquilized, all boredom amused." A digital dystopia that is fast approaching as perhaps the end of that red thread that runs from 9/11 to today.

Heidi Evens and Thomas Hackett write in the *New York Daily News*:

> With the nation's illusion of safety and security in ruins, Americans begin the slow and fitful process of healing from a trauma that feels deeply, cruelly personal . . .

> leaving citizens throughout the country with the frightening knowledge of their vulnerability.

That was written on September 12, 2001.

Chasing the Light by Oliver Stone

– A BOOK REVIEW –

Like the wandering and rascally Odysseus upon whom he models his life, Oliver Stone is "double-minded" in the most profound and illuminating ways. The title of his fantastic new memoir is a case in point. "One of the first basic lessons in filming," he writes, "is chasing the light. Without it, you have nothing—no exposure that can be seen; even what you see with your naked eye needs to be shaped and enhanced by the light."

For as a true artist living out a marriage between his writing and his filmmaking, his father and his mother, the warrior and the peacemaker, the domesticated and the wild man, he has chosen a title that has a double meaning that is subtly woven like a thread through this labyrinthine tale. It takes the reader from his childhood through his service in Vietnam and his struggles as a writer and filmmaker up to 1987 and his great success with his powerful autobiographical film, *Platoon,* for which he received Oscars for Best Film and Best Director, among others.

Driven by a youthful urge to escape his internal demons first brought on by his mismatched parents' divorce when he was fifteen, Stone dropped out of Yale, his father's alma mater, where he had enrolled to fulfill his stockbroker father's dream. He accepted an offer from a Catholic Church group to teach English-speaking high school students in Chalon, a suburb of Saigon, which he did for six months before traveling around southeast Asia. Back in Saigon, he joined the merchant marine and worked his way back to the States cleaning boilers, the lowest and dirtiest job on the ship. After a storm-tossed 37 days journey, he was cured of his desire to go to sea, a romantic fascination he had acquired from literature.

The lesson: Books are not life, nor are movies—they are ways to shape and illuminate it.

Back in the states he threw himself into writing, his first love and the place where his "anxieties could be relieved" and where he felt he could confirm his independent existence separate from his parents. Through writing he could control his story. He wrote a novel called, *A Child's Night Dream.*

He reentered Yale but only lasted a few months since his heart was not in the placid life of academia, having already had a taste of the wandering life. He then quit Yale for good, to his father's great disappointment. Lou Stone thought Oliver might turn into a "bum," a painful refrain in this memoir. This twisted parental inculcation of shame and fear cast a deep shadow on Oliver's soul and became one of the ghosts that he spent years trying to outrun by becoming a workaholic desperate for success. His novel was subsequently rejected, and he fell into a deep depression and self-loathing.

Suicidal at nineteen, he volunteered to serve in the U.S. Army in Vietnam to expiate his guilt, shame, and self-loathing, thinking that perhaps God would take his life for him.

"Odysseus thought he would return home when he left Ithaca," he writes, "I wasn't sure of anything. . . ."

It was in Vietnam on January 1–2, 1968, after a terrifying night battle along the Cambodia border where his unit was in a hot zone interdicting North Vietnamese Army troops coming through Laos and Cambodia toward Saigon, when he experienced a profound light experience very different from the type he would later chase while making films.

The battle raged throughout the dark jungle night where confusion and terror reigned. It was impossible to hear or see, and although 25 Americans and 400 North Vietnamese were killed, Stone "hadn't seen a single one of them [Vietnamese]," although he performed bravely. Here is his brilliantly disturbing and revealing description of what ensued.

> Full daylight revealed charred bodies, dusty napalm, and gray trees. Men who died grimacing, in frozen positions, some of them still standing or kneeling in rigor mortis, white chemical death on their faces. Dead, so dead. Some covered with white ash, some burned black. Their expressions, if they could still be seen, were overtaken with anguish or horror. How do you die like this? Charging forward in a hailstorm of death into these bombs and artillery. Why? Were you terrified, or were you jacked out of your fucking mind? What kind of death did you achieve? It was frightening to contemplate, and yet, I wasn't scared. It was exciting. It was as if I passed from this world and was somewhere *where the light was being specially displayed to me in a preview of another life.* Soldiers might say it was hell, but I saw it as divine; the closest man would ever come to the Holy Spirit was to witness and survive this great, destructive energy. [emphasis added by author]

So after fifty years in another life, the survivor remembers in that odd mixture that memory is, a shaping force that relies on the light of experience to enhance the existential marriage of hope lost and found, fact and fiction joined to find the truth of an epiphany. He continues:

> No person should ever have to witness so much death. I really was too young to understand, and thus I erased much of it, remembering it in this strange way as a stunningly beautiful night full of fireworks, in which I hadn't seen a single enemy, been fired on, or fired at anyone. It'd been like a dream through which I'd walked unharmed, grateful of course, but numb and puzzled by it all. It reminded me of passages in Homer of gods and goddesses coming down from Mount Olympus to the bloody battlefields at Troy to help their favorites, wrapping a mist or cloak around them and winging them to safety.

These passages appear early in the book, and I quote them not just to point out the dual nature of the book's title—only something a truly creative writer would conceive—but because the dual theme of chasing and being chased by the light is central to Oliver's life story. It is a tale of a split-soul, the twice wounded warrior who receives a Bronze Star for heroism but who hates war and journeys to get back home where he can rest with his family by the hearth and feel at peace, and the wild, restless, tormented free pirate sailing for adventure and new discoveries. Of course, getting back home is no simple matter, especially when you left because home had set the conflict in your heart in the first place, as it did for Stone.

Home is a country as much as a family, and this personal tale is also a guidebook through modern American history, a country badly riven since the 1960s. A country that's been feeding on lies that had "infected everything, and I was still numb from it. Because I'd basically never woken up."

But there are epiphanies along the way that wake Stone up, intuitions, hunches, risks he takes, and there are luminescent passages throughout this book to crack open the reader's consciousness to a second reality. *Chasing the Light* is not a superficial trip down memory lane like so many memoirs by famous people. Stone is a wonderful writer, and as with his films, he takes you deep to places you may wish to avoid but are essential for true sanity. The great thing about this memoir is his passion for truth and life that courses through its pages. He seizes the reader by the throat and shouts: Consciousness! Wake up! Don't let sleep and forgetfulness make you into one of the living-dead! A lesson he learned fortuitously at NYU when he took a course in classical drama and his professor, Tim Leahy, raged about the fate of Odysseus and how he was the only one of his crew to get back home because he dared to keep his eyes and ears open to both the dark and light forces whirling all around him. He refused "LETHE"—sleep and forgetfulness.

But as the fates decreed, when the desperately poor warrior Stone came back from Vietnam to NYC and was still struggling to find his way back to a true home he couldn't envision, writing to make sense of his life, he encountered his Calypso, as did Odysseus along his wandering journey to get home to Ithaca. Her name was Najwa Sarkis, an older Lebanese woman who worked at the United Nations. They fell together and for five years Najwa gave Oliver shelter from the storm in her apartment in the East 50s. The sex was passionate and the living conditions in Calypso's cave comfortable, and although they married at her insistence, it was like his parents' marriage, built on a lie. "I can't say the marriage, from my side," he writes, "was built on love, but rather on comfort and caring for each other." Tempted to stay by the thought of comfort, as Odysseus was by the promise of immortality, Stone finally admits the truth to Najwa and himself, packs his bags and leaves "his goddess." He knew he wasn't home yet and had to risk much more to try to get there. "The flaw was that I hadn't grown into my own man. This I knew in my gut—that I hadn't yet been successful as a writer because I'd failed to complete the journey I started when I went to Vietnam." So Odysseus heads to the uptown subway with his two suitcases.

Vietnam haunts him. He starts to write what eventually will become the script for *Platoon*, using Odysseus as his template and example of conscious behavior to expose all the lies of the Vietnam war and the insidious hypocrisy of American life. As in Tennyson's poem about the older Odysseus, still wanting "to seek, to find, and not to yield," the memoirist, himself now not young, says, "In my seventy-plus years from 1946 to now, the chorus of fear-mongering bullshit has never ceased—only grown louder. The joke is on us. Ha Ha Ha."

Throughout this book, Stone is very hard on himself as well as the country:

> I had my story, I realized. I was no hero. I slept on my consciousness. My whole country, our society had. But at the least—If I could tell the truth of what I'd seen—it was better than . . . what? Nothing—the void of a meaningless war and waste of life while our society was stuffing its ears with wax. Odysseus, lashing himself to his mast to preserve his sanity, had insisted on

> hearing the Sirens, and remembering it. Whereas I was honored for my service to my country, the truth was I soiled myself when I could've resisted, exiled myself, gone to jail for it like the Berrigans, the Spocks, and some 200,000 others. I was young, yes, and I can say that I didn't know better, that I was part of the unconsciousness of my country.

He tells us he didn't wake up until he was nearly thirty years old—in 1976.

Ever since he has devoted his life to the art of waking up his fellow Americans through writing and filmmaking, which he had the great good fortune to learn at NYU film school from that other passionate New York filmmaker, Martin Scorsese, who was his professor. Scorsese shone a light on Oliver after he had made a short film without dialogue called *Last Year in Vietnam*. It was shown to the class, a tough group of critics, but before anyone had spoken, Scorsese said, "Well—this is a filmmaker." It was an epiphany that Stone says he will never forget. A pure gift that set him on his way to eventually make his great films.

But the journey was hard and took years to complete.

Stone's mother, Jacqueline Pauline Cézarine Goddet, and his father, Louis Stone (born Abraham Louis Silverstein), were married in Paris as World War II ended. He was an U.S. Army officer and she, a "peasant" French girl, were mismatched from the start. They "made possibly the greatest mistake of their lives—to which I owe my existence," he tells us. Oliver became very close to his French grandparents, especially his Mémé. As he was struggling to write successful screenplays and break into filmmaking, his beloved grandmother dies and he goes to France for her funeral. There is a scene in this memoir—I almost said movie—where he arrives alone in a suburb of Paris where she is laid out in her musty apartment in an old apartment building. He felt the dead were calling to him from the past—Vietnam, France. So much death, so many lies, betrayals. He writes:

> I thought about how Odysseus went to the Underworld to find Tiresias for a prophecy about when and how he'd return home to Ithaca. And once in the Underworld, he recognized his mother, Anticlea, who, like the other shades, had come to him to slake herself at the pool of sheep's blood he had sacrificed to get there.

For Oliver, his Mémé was like a mother to him, and with her forty-year marriage to her beloved Pépé, who had predeceased her, was a symbol of what family life should be all about, the family Oliver had lost and desperately wished for. Home as love and commitment. "Without a family, we one and all suffer," he says.

In less than four pages, his description of this encounter with his grandmother illuminates the heart of this memoir and is an exquisite example of a great artist at work. An artist who uses words to touch your soul, heart-breaking, tender, and hopeful in turns, far different from the often-popular image of Stone. I would buy this book for these four pages alone. Listen:

> I drew up my chair closer to be with her, like we'd been when I was young, cuddled in her big bed as she told me the stories of the wolves in Paris who'd come down the chimneys to snatch the children who'd been bad.... There was the silence of "la mort," and then the October light began to drop. No one else knocked or visited. Just me. And you, Mémé—and that something listening between us. Not long ago I'd been twenty-three. You were so happy when I'd returned in one piece from over there. I'd tried to pay my debt to society. We all have one, we don't only live for ourselves. But I still felt uneasy and Mémé did too. What did Vietnam have to do with saving our civilization when it only made the world more callous? You never asked me for an explanation. Three wars in your life time... I'd done nothing. I'd achieved nothing. Therefore I was nothing. ... I was crying but didn't know I was until I felt the tears. I hadn't cried in so any years—I was a hard boy. I had to be, I felt, to

survive. I was raised to believe men don't cry. But this time it feels fresh, like a rain. But who am I crying to? Not you, Mémé—you're not the one judging me. You never have. Is it my self I'm crying to? My self, but *who* was that? I could not see myself. I was ugly, hiding. I could cry myself dry with self-pity. All this pain, so much pain. Yes, I feel it now—feel sorry for myself, it's okay—so raw, all my lies, my embarrassment naked for the dead to see, naked to the whole world! No one loves me, no one will ever love me. Because I can't love anyone—except you, Mémé, and you're gone now. Can I . . . can I learn to love? How can I start? By just being kind like you were? Can I be kind—to myself? In my mind, I heard Mémé reply: "Try—you're a man now. You're no longer seventeen sitting on the sidelines of your life, judging. You've seen this world, tasted its tears. Now's the time to recognize this, Oliver, Oliver, Oliver"—my name, invoked three times to rouse myself, to wake myself from this long slumber. Do something with your life, I demanded, all this energy bottled up for years, hopeless dreaming and writing, no excuse, you can do better. Stop fucking around . . . Mémé continued speaking to me so gently. That soft voice: "Mon chéri, mon p'tit Oliverre, te fais pas de soucis pour rien . . . Fais ta vie. Fais ce que tu veux faire. C'est tout ce quil y a. Je t'embrasse, je t'adore." (My darling, my little Oliver, don't be miserable for nothing. . . . Make your life. Do what you have to do. That's all there is. I embrace you, I adore you.) . . . The other shades were approaching now, smelling the blood, so many young men groaning . . . faces distorted in death. There was whispering, many voices. "Stone, hey man, don't forget me! Where you goin'? Gimme some! Hey, tell my girl you saw me, will ya? Remember me, will ya? You got a joint?" Mémé wanted me to go—quickly, before it was too late. I couldn't hear, but it was clear what the shades were saying: We, the dead, are telling

> you—your lifespan is short. Make of it everything you can. Before you're one of us. I rose and kissed Mémé's face one last time. . . ." Au revoir, ma belle Mémé. And I walked out—as she looked away and began slaking her thirst with the others. . . . I walked the silent streets to the Metro. Like in a dreamscape, there were no living people. Maybe that's the reason we die. It makes us want to live again.

Oliver does exactly that. Reborn, determined, he returns to the U.S. and makes his life by making the illuminating movies that have made his reputation. He does the opposite of what his father advised him. "People don't want to know the truth," his father told him. "Reality is too tough. They go to the movies to get away from all that." He knew his "very nature was unacceptable to the fantasy world of moviegoers," but he wasn't home yet and pushes on, getting in lots of trouble for telling truths people don't want to hear, except perhaps the dead.

But making those films was far from smooth sailing. It was another form of warfare, treacherous, filled with betrayals, drugs, Hollywood a place where you had to watch your back. Just when the battle seemed over and you had won, another rocket would explode at your feet, throwing you for a loop. It would take another toll on Stone. So often, when he would think his screenplay or deal to direct a film was secured—that the stone he had rolled to the top of the hill was set—back it would roll. He would find that often what seemed to be up was down and that when he thought he was at the top, he was soon on the bottom. The years that followed were a roller coaster ride.

He writes truthfully about his need to quell his anxiety with a host of drugs that fueled his days and nights and led to addiction, his guilt and confusion, his partying like his glamorous party-loving mother, who "was *there* for me, and yet she wasn't; it was more like she was on display." He tells us how he was always running from something, writing, hustling, trying to justify himself as he traveled toward a home called success, the bitch-goddess Success, the pipe dream nurtured in Hollywood.

In numerous chapters, a reader fascinated with the nuts and bolts of filmmaking, from the screenplay through directing, financing, casting, editing, distributing, etc., will delight in his detailed description of the movie game. *Midnight Express, Scarface, Salvador, Platoon* are explored in depth. If you want to know about Al Pacino, Charlie Sheen, Michael Cimino, James Woods, Dino De Laurentiis, the wild Richard Boyle, et al., it's all here. The good, bad, and the ugly. Gossip or insights, call it what you will. It's all interesting.

Stone writes about his second wife, Elizabeth, the joy that the birth of their son, his first child, Sean, brought him, the conflicts that developed as he's torn between home life and the mad pursuit of filmmaking, "even if it's leading you off a cliff." He wrote in his diary:

> What have I become? A Macbeth of workaholics. I've worked straight 17 years, two scripts a year, etc., and what has it brought me? Never been able to relax, but must. I'm always running like a mad rabbit down an Alice in Wonderland hole, always getting bigger or smaller and never knowing what will happen next.

By the end of the book, Oliver, now forty-years-old in 1987, is on the top of the world when he wins Oscars for *Platoon*, and although he revels in this victory, something continues to eat at him, as if he hadn't really reached Ithaca, but was still on the journey. "So I'd come to this moment in time," he writes. "Success was a beautiful goddess, yes, but was I being seduced by this vindication, this proving myself to my father; was it the acceptance, the power? What did I really believe?"

The double-minded rascal was still alive and at sea, despite saying that "And truthfully, I don't think I'd ever been happier." He had finally achieved great film success, had a lovely wife and child, a garden, his books, a pool to jump in. Tranquility.

No. He tells us:

> Mine was a free man's life, without a home, really, except for the wenches in the local ports, like Sabatini's Captain Blood, who "was born with a gift for laughter and the sense that the world was mad." Thus it remains a split in my soul—the home, the hearth, and then out into the wind with your crew—Odysseus's "I am become a name." Could this be? Could I live two different lives? Like those hard men I'd worked with in the merchant marine twenty years before—six months on land, six at sea; unsettled, eccentric men who remained free in their souls yet tormented. In the next years, I'd live out this split in my nature to the fullest.

The reader will have to await a sequel to *Chasing the Light* to see if Odysseus ever finds his way to his true home.

In the meantime, Charlie Sheen's words at the end of *Platoon* will have to suffice:

"Those of us who did make it have an obligation to build again, to teach to others what we know, and to try with what's left of our lives to find a goodness and meaning to this life."

If the Wars Go On

I suppose my title could have been couched in the singular form, as Hermann Hesse, the Nobel Prize winning German/Swiss author, did with his collection of anti-war essays about World War I (the war to end all wars that didn't), *If The War Goes On . . .*

Or more appropriately, I might have eliminated that conditional "If" since it seems Pollyannish.

It's a long hard road, this anti-war business. During the first Cold War and the 1962 Cuban Missile Crisis in the early sixties when Kennedy and Khrushchev narrowly avoided blowing the world to smithereens.

Indeed, there is a system of war that guarantees that the various wars go on and on, ad infinitum, and they are linked. It is why the warfare state has killed our anti-war leaders, first and foremost JFK for turning against war in the last year of his presidency. Then in 1968, Martin Luther King, Jr. and Bobby Kennedy in quick succession. It is why if you dare to look around the world today, you will see that there is a series of wars happening, not only in the obvious places like Ukraine and Gaza, but in places that you may never have heard of, and if you peek a bit further into their causes, you will discover that a familiar culprit with more than 750 military bases around the world has its hand in most of them—the United Staes of America.

These wars have their cold and hot phases. There are days when the corporate media let them sleep and other times when the same media wake them a bit, but never enough to wake their readers up to the reality of the deadly game. That is the media's job as stenographers for the warfare state. Wars being essentially the health of the state, as Randolph Bourne wrote long ago, they provide vast profits for the military-industrial complex/Wall St., whether they are in preparation or in operation, awake or asleep, hot or cold. Ray McGovern, the former CIA analyst with a moral conscience, has aptly named this vast interlocking propaganda apparatus the military-industrial-congressional-intelligence-media-academia-think-tank complex, MICIMATT. It is a complex that blatantly serves the interests of the masters of war who "ain't worth the blood/that runs in [their] your veins," in Dylan's words.

The preparation for war is war. What is prepared must be used up, so other weapons can be prepared to be used up, so other weapons can be prepared to be used up, and on and on until one day no one is left to use anything, for the world will be used up in a nuclear conflagration. These weapons are produced in nice clean factories that pay good wages to people who take their pay and go their way, giving their souls to the killers. For the U.S. economy is built on the waging of wars so continuous that it is nearly impossible to find a break between its hot and cold phases, or what seems like decent employment and the diabolic. They are so intertwined. It is a system of capitalistic finance, a revolutionary system that builds to destroy.

The U.S spends nearly $900 billion dollars annually on "defense" spending; this is more than China, Russia, India, Saudi Arabia, the U.K., Germany, France, South Korea, and Japan combined. The U.S.A. is a warfare state; it's as simple as that. And whether they choose to be aware of it or not, the vast majority of Americans support this killing machine by their insouciance and silence. That their country is spending up to 2 trillion dollars on modernizing its nuclear weapons disturbs them not. It is a death cult. Some—as I myself have done mistakenly—write about the "deep state" or some other deceptive phrase that conceals the truth that the official state is the "deep state." It stares us in the face, but many refuse to stare it back down. It is too obvious, standing, as it does, in the way of a life of illusions.

And what is equally apparent today—or should be if one is not asleep—is that because of the war policies of the U.S., the chances of another world war and the use of nuclear weapons is rising by the day.

Day by day, our masters of war are pushing us toward a nuclear abyss.

In a perceptive article (5/25/24), "Russia and China Have Had Enough," Pepe Escobar writes truths many prefer not to hear. That there is no split between Russia and China but the opposite—a rock solid Russia-China strategic partnership and a determination to oppose and defeat the U.S./UK/NATO hybrid war tactics across Eurasia and the Middle East. That the more these U.S.-led forces attempt to destroy Russia, the more the expanding alliances involved in the Shanghai Cooperative Agreement (SCO) and the expanding BRICS partnerships of emerging economies (originally just Brazil, Russia, India, China, and then South Africa; now also Egypt, Ethiopia, Iran, United Arab Emirates, with many more countries waiting to join) will gain in power. In Escobar's words, ". . . the Global Majority is on the move: Russia is closely cooperating, increasingly, with scores of nations in West Asia, wider Asia, Africa and Latin America."

Despite this fact, the United States and its allies blithely continue as if their control of the world order is secure. As if they can still butcher and badger the world into submission. The insane are usually deluded, but when they control nuclear weapons, the people of the world need to awaken.

Ray McGovern, a Russia expert, has echoed Escobar on the absurdity of the claim of a Russian China split; has emphasized how Israel's genocide of the Palestinians has made it an isolated but desperate pariah state, and how the U.S. war against Russia in Ukraine is leading to the increased use of U.S. tactical nuclear weapons that could lead to full-scale nuclear war. He is not alone in this warning.

There are many signs that we are moving toward a nuclear war with calls for U.S./NATO to support more strikes *inside* Russia, crossing a very dangerous Russian red line. Russia has made it very clear they will respond. As politicians of various stripes—French President Macron, NATO Secretary General Stoltenberg, German Chancellor Olaf Scholz, et al.—have ecstatically been urging the Biden administration, which needs no urging, to escalate the war in Ukraine by attacking Russia proper ("The time has come for allies to consider whether they should lift some of the restrictions they have put on the use of weapons they have donated to Ukraine," Stoltenberg told *The Economist*). Mike Whitney has written about a recent such attack that should send chills down everyone's spines—"Washington Attacks Key Elements of Rusia's Nuclear Umbrella Threatening Entire Nuclear Security Agreement"—but since the corporate media ignore it, most will dream away and get their barbecues ready for Fourth of July celebrations. They and the flag-dressed Dolly Parton can sing all they want about when Johnny comes marching home again, but Dolly and no one will be jolly if there are no homes to march to, no Johnnies marching anywhere but to death, no anything. Just a wasteland.

Scott Ritter, Michel Chossudovsky, Ray McGovern, Eva Bartlett, Craig Murray, Patrick Lawrence, Vanessa Beeley, Pepe Escobar, Oliver Stone, Andrew Napolitano, Paul Craig Roberts, Chris Hedges, Alastair Crooke, Caitlin Johnstone, Peter Koenig, Finian Cunningham, Diana Johnstone, Lew Rockwell, and so many other sane but marginalized writers whose names I am omitting as I write quickly, are warning us of our closeness to nuclear annihilation. Cassandras all, I fear. Marginalized prophets such as writer and antinuclear activist James W. Douglass have been issuing such warnings for decades. It is understandable that so many turn away from such warnings, for the thought of a nuclear war induces deep anxiety hard to control. But unless the vast majority can break through such reticence and see through the official propaganda, the world will be destroyed by madmen sooner or later. The signs today all point to sooner, for we are on the edge of the abyss.

Former British diplomat Alistair Crooke, in a recent article—"The Brink of Dissolution: Neurosis in the West as the levee breaks"—writes about how the Biden administration's policy toward Russia-China, not to say Israel-Palestine being nothing more than more of the same, is stupid, self-defeating, and very dangerous. Rather than accepting that its proxy war against Russia in Ukraine is a disaster, the U.S. is escalating the conflict to a terrifying level. Rather than accepting the obvious deep alliance between China and Russia exemplified in the recent hug between Putin and Xi and their joint 8,000 word joint statement, Biden has said, *"Russia is in a very, very difficult spot right now. They are being squeezed by China."* It doesn't get any stupider. But when more of the same doesn't work and you can't accept the reality of a changing world order, you do more of the same. Crooke writes:

> The paradox is that Team Biden—wholly inadvertently—is midwifing the birth of a "new world." It is doing so by dint of its crude opposition to parturition. The more the western élites push against the birthing—through "saving Zionism"; "saving *European* Ukraine" and by crushing dissent—perversely they accelerate the foundering of Leviathan.
>
> President Xi's double farewell hug for President Putin following their 16–17 May summit nonetheless sealed the birth—even the *New York Times,* with customary self-absorption, termed the warm embrace by Xi as "defiance of the West."
>
> The root of the coming dissolution stems precisely from the shortcoming that the *NY Times* headline encapsulates in its disdainful labelling of the seismic shift as base anti-westernism.

More of the same, yes, that is Biden's approach, inflamed regularly by the anti-Russian hatred spewed by *The New York Times* and its ilk. It is an obsession bordering on full-fledged madness, yet it is integral to the belief that the U.S. is an empire and will remain one while the rest of the world can go to hell. Such a mindset is behind the U.S.'s abrogating all the nuclear weapons treaties that provided a semblance of security that nuclear weapons would not be used.

Crooke ends his piece with these sobering words:

> Put plainly, with the U.S. unable to exit or to moderate its determination to preserve its hegemony, Lavrov [Sergey Lavrov, Russian Foreign Minister] sees the prospect for increased western weapons provision for Ukraine. The discourse of military escalation is in fashion in Europe (of that there is no doubt); but both in the Middle East and Ukraine, western policy is in deep trouble. There must be doubts whether the West has either the political will, or the internal unity, to pursue this aggressive course. Dragging wars are not traditionally thought to be "voter friendly" when campaigning reaches its peak.

Let me repeat that last understated sentence: *"Dragging wars are not traditionally thought to be 'voter friendly' when campaigning reaches its peak."* And so? More of the same?

Ray McGovern suggests what is more likely:

> Israel [is] becoming a dangerous pariah; Ukraine/U.S./ NATO a dangerous loser. As Israel defies the UN, and as the "exceptional" geniuses around Biden ignore Kremlin warnings regarding provocations re Ukraine, the likelihood increases for U.S. use of tactical nukes.

Desperadoes do desperate things. In Biden and Netanyahu, we have two blood-thirsty nihilists at the end of their ropes. These masters of war make me think that a better title for this piece would have been:

If the World Goes On

And now Trump will take another turn.

If you were writing this script as part of long-term planning, and average people were getting disgusted from decades of being screwed and were sick of politicians and their lying ways, wouldn't you stop the reruns and create a new show?

Come on, this is Hollywood where creative showmen can dazzle our minds with plots so twisted that when you leave the theater you keep wondering what it was all about and arguing with your friends about the ending. So create a throwback film where the good guy versus the bad guy was seemingly very clear, and while the system ground on, keep people at each other's throats over the obvious differences, even though they were fabricated or minor. Another successful replay of the age-old strategy of divide and conquer

I realize that it is very hard for many to entertain the thought that Trump and Biden are not arch-enemies but are players in a spectacle created to confound at the deepest psychological levels. I am not arguing that the Democrats didn't want Hillary Clinton to win in 2016. I am saying they knew Trump was a better opponent, not only because they could probably defeat him and garner more of the spoils, but because if he possibly won he was easily controlled because he was compromised. By whom? Not the Democrats, but the "Deep State" forces that control Hillary Clinton and all the presidents. A compromised and corrupt lot.

The Democrats and Republicans were not in charge in 2016 or in 2020. Their bosses were. They are not in charge now.

The Hidden Messages of the Power Elite's Cultural Apparatus

To be crucified is to suffer and die slowly and agonizingly. It was a common form of execution in the ancient world. It is generally associated with Rome's killing of Jesus and carries profound symbolic spiritual meaning for Christians. In its figurative sense, it refers to many types of suffering and death inflicted on the weak by the strong, such as the ongoing genocidal slaughter of Palestinians by the Israeli government.

Twenty or so years ago when the wearing of crosses by all types of people was the cultural rage, a woman I know said she was thinking of getting one. When I asked her why, since she was Jewish, she said it was because she thought they were beautiful. She seemed oblivious to the fact that to Christians they were gruesome but revelatory spiritual symbols, the equivalent of the electric chair or a noose, but linked to the Easter Resurrection and the nonviolent triumph over death that is at the core of Christianity.

Her focus on beauty forcibly struck me that secular culture had triumphed in its establishment of an anti-creed creed wherein the pursuit of a sense of well-being and aesthetic tranquility had trumped traditional belief, while it used all faiths in its pursuit of a self-centered nihilism through a faux-spirituality linked to a precious aesthetic of beauty.

Philip Rieff noticed this in the mid-1960s when he wrote in *The Triumph of the Therapeutic*:

> To raise the question of nihilism, as sociologists since Auguste Comte have done, demonstrates a major change in tone: the note of apprehension has gone out of the asking. We believe that we know something our predecessors did not: that we can live freely at last, enjoying all our senses—except the sense of the past—as unremembering, honest, and friendly barbarians all, in a technological Eden. . . . this culture, which once imagined itself inside a church, feels trapped in something like a zoo of separate cages. Modern men are like Rilke's panther, forever looking out of one cage into another.

While today those cages would better be described as cells—as in cell phones—Rieff's point was prescient in the extreme, echoing in its way Max Weber's 1905 prophecy in *The Protestant Ethic and the Spirit of Capitalism* of the coming "iron cage."

I recently saw a large crucifix foregrounded before the apse of the Medieval Spanish church of San Martin at Fuentidueña. Although one would expect this was in the church, it was not, except if you realize that museums have become the modern churches, where people flock to revere art for art's sake and perhaps to find some consolation they have lost at a deeper level. I was at The Cloisters museum in New York City. The church no longer exists.

Museums have been built and maintained by the very rich to serve as their own churches to the glory of mammon and their own self-deluded immortalization.

Mammon that has been built on the backs of the poor and working class, just as these edifices have.

Beneath all high cultural institutions such as museums and arts venues like The Metropolitan Museum of Art, the Louvre, the Museum of Modern Art, Lincoln Center in New York, etc., lies the expropriated labor and land of the lower classes, the same classes whose sweat and blood was exploited throughout capital's historical transmutations from commercial to industrial to financial to create the immense wealth of the super-rich.

There is a simple reason the nineteenth-century American industrialists such as Vanderbilt, Mellon, Carnegie, Rockefeller, et al. were called "The Robber Barons." They were crooks. They are still with us, of course, aided and abetted by today's latest billionaire class. They build and finance the aforementioned cultural institutions as well as own and operate the major institutions of mass communication and entertainment, such as newspapers, television networks, telecommunication corporations, film studios, etc.—the entertainment industrial complex. In this direct communication capacity, they control the mediation of "reality" to the general population. They serve the interests of what the great crusading sociologist C. Wright Mills called the power elite in and out of government, of which they are an interlocking part, and through which they move smoothly in a game of revolving chairs. They operate the great Spectacle for the general population while moving the levers of power backstage.

When he died, Mills was working on a massive book exploring what he provisionally titled *The Cultural Apparatus*. He defined this complex as follows:

> The cultural apparatus is composed of all the organizations and milieux in which artistic, intellectual, and scientific work goes on and of the means by which such work is made available . . . it contains an elaborate set of institutions: of schools and theaters, newspapers and census bureaus, studios, laboratories, museums, little magazines and radio networks. . . Inside this network, standing between men and events, the images, meanings, and slogans that define the worlds in which [we] live are organized and compared, maintained and revised, lost and cherished, hidden, debunked, celebrated. Taken as a whole the cultural apparatus is the lens of mankind through which men see; the medium by which they report and interpret what they see.

Columbia University, where he taught and is today in the news headlines for its police crackdown on student dissent for their pro-Palestinian protest, is one of those elite cultural institutions, a place Mills was never comfortable at and whose colleagues looked at him askance for his critique of the power elite's warfare state.

Columbia, with its racist history evident as it saw its elite status threatened by the growth of the neighboring black community in Harlem in the 1920s and 1930s, and Columbia's further expansion into these neighborhoods since.

Columbia, like all elite cultural institutions, born in its own mind *sui generis* and raised to the heights in purity and innocence, but whose foundation is rotten with dirty money.

Yet, as Terry Eagleton recently wrote in the *London Review of Books,* "This is not the way culture generally likes to see itself. Like the Oedipal child, it tends to disavow its lowly parentage and fantasise that it sprang from its own loins, self-generating and self-fashioning." Like Columbia and all the elite universities of "higher learning"— Harvard, Oxford, Yale, Princeton, Stanford, etc.—that serve as legitimating tools for the power elite and their mendaciousness, the museums and other well-known arts institutions exert an enormous influence, not only over culture in the high cultural sense, but over the transformation of society as a whole, often in ways that go unnoticed. Eagleton again:

> There's an irony here, since few things bind art so closely to its material context as its claim to stand free of that context. This is because the work of art as autonomous and self-determining, an idea born sometime in the late 18th century, is the model of a version of the human subject that has been rapidly gaining ground in actual life. Men and women are now seen as authors of themselves . . .

The Cloisters in upper Manhattan is where ghosts of dead religious beliefs prowl about the rooms. It is meant to present a "chapel-like gallery." The Cloisters is a museum owned by the Metropolitan Museum of Art and is now known as The Met Cloisters. It, and the beautiful 67-acre Fort Tryon Park upon which it sits, was created and financed by John D. Rockefeller, Jr. who, according to The Met's website, was fascinated with the past. "The expert artistry of medieval art as well as its innate spirituality strongly appealed to this philanthropist and collector," we are told.

Spirituality from the Middle Ages that, I will amend, once it had been transported to the museum, was devoid of its living context and could be presented as a gift from a Robber Baron family to the people of NYC who needed to be uplifted by the noblesse oblige kindness of the Rockefellers. Dead spirits devoid of a living sense of the sacred who smuggle secret messages to a public hungry for meaning.

Like my Jewish friend who considered getting a cross, Rockefeller no doubt found the crucifix and apse that frames it quite beautiful and spiritually uplifting, but not the living spirituality of the criminal Jesus whose message about wealth never informed the Rockefellers' ruthless exploitation of others on their rise to power.

In years long past, when I first visited The Cloisters, being a native Bronx New Yorker, it was known simply as The Cloisters, even though The Met owned it since its inception in the 1930s. Before I visited it as a young man, I had the impression it had some religious significance, as the name cloister suggests (early 13c., *cloystre*, "a monastery or convent, a place of religious retirement or seclusion").

But I was wrong; it is a museum, a beautiful museum built with stones from European monasteries, churches, and convents transported long ago across the Atlantic and reconstructed on the heights above the Hudson River. It is filled with medieval art collected by Rockefeller, George Gray Barnard, and other wealthy art collectors. For those so disposed to wondering what royalty prayed for in medieval days—was it to slaughter as many Muslims as possible in the Crusades?—one can view the tiny prayer book once owned by the Queen of France—and imagine. Such imagining might cause one to realize how little things have changed and how little things mean a lot. The trick is to notice them.

Political power needs cultural power to operate effectively. The elites can't just slam people around and expect no response. They need to worm their ideological messages into the public consciousness in pleasing ways. Writing of Edmund Burke, Eagleton says, "Instead, he recognises that culture in the anthropological sense is the place where power has to bed itself down if it is to be effective. If the political doesn't find a home in the cultural, its sovereignty won't take hold."

Thus, for an example from Hollywood and the pop-cultural realm, we might notice how many movies and TV shows were secretly co-written by the Pentagon.

Another name for this is propaganda, popular culture as propaganda.

Cultural messaging is where the power elite need to seduce regular people to believe that power is being exercised for their own good and everyone is in bed together. Soft power. Nice power. Power that is disguised as beneficial for all. Beautiful power. "Spiritual" power.

As I said, Fort Tryon Park (designed by the Olmsted brothers, sons of the Central Park designer, Frederick Law Olmsted) and The Cloisters are spectacularly beautiful. Walking through the park on a sunny spring day to reach the museum on its northern end—the flowers and cherry blossom trees dazzling and the Hudson River glistening below—one is overwhelmed by the beauty and grateful to its human gift giver—John D. Rockefeller, Jr. It takes a little mental stretching to grasp the paradox or the delusional dream of such thankfulness. But it cuts to the heart of the power of the cultural complex and the ways it works to soften the ruthlessness of its ultra-rich capitalistic controllers.

First they rob you, then they gift you with a walk in the park.

And when you step inside their institutions, you are provided with opportunities to think within controlled parameters, while also getting a whiff of the theatrical nature of your experience. The whiff is as important as the thinking, for it is a reminder to keep your mouth shut and you too will flourish. The fraudulence of the cultural entertainment-educational complex can dawn on some who have been invited into the inner sanctums of power and prestige, as it has done presently for many college students (and some faculty) whose consciences do not allow them to sit still while Palestinians are slaughtered. But if you dare to act upon your sense of being taken for a ride, watch out! You will be banned from the pleasures that are offered for your acquiescence, as these students are now finding out.

They have rejected that part of the learning experience that George Orwell called *Crimestop*:

> . . . [it] means the faculty of stopping short, as though by instinct, at the threshold of any dangerous thought. It includes the power of not grasping analogies, of failing to perceive logical errors, of misunderstanding the simplest arguments if they are inimical to Ingsoc, and of being bored or repelled by any train of thought which is capable of leading in a heretical direction. *Crimestop*, in short, means protective stupidity.

Sometimes real thinking and conscience win the day, for the power of the elite's cultural institutions is not omnipotent. Everyone is not for sale, even those invited into the banquet. Teach people to think and meditate on history and they just might think outside the cage of your expectations.

While the genocide of the Palestinians is transparent for everyone to see, the leaders of these elite universities, unlike the rebellious students, turn a blind eye to the obvious. They follow the script they were handed when they accepted their prestigious positions of power, living up to Julian Benda's famous appellation—*The Treason of the Intellectuals*.

But "beautiful" power becomes the iron fist when the plebes get too uppity and actually take seriously their studies and rebel as human beings with consciences. This is the flip side to the hidden messages of the elite cultural institutions.

This two-sided process of hidden and obvious messages operates also in the media complex. While the so-called liberal and conservative media—all stenographers for the intelligence agencies—pour forth the most blatant propaganda about Palestine,

Israel, Russia and Ukraine, etc. that is so conspicuous that it is comedic if it weren't so dangerous, the self-depicted cognoscenti also ingest subtler messages, often from the alternative media and from people they consider dissidents. They are like little seeds slipped in as if no one will notice; they work their magic nearly unconsciously. Few notice them, for they are often imperceptible. But they have their effects and are cumulative and are far more powerful over time than blatant statements that will turn people off, especially those who think propaganda doesn't work on them. This is the power of successful propaganda, whether purposeful or not. It particularly works well on "intellectual" and highly schooled people.

Some people think that if you see more than is apparent when visiting sites such as The Cloisters in Fort Tryon Park, you are incapable of enjoying the beauty of these "gifts." This is not true. They are not mutually exclusive. The great African American scholar W. E. B. DuBois coined the term double-consciousness, which I think can be used in this context to describe some people's experience, not just that of African Americans. They see at least two truths simultaneously. Their unreconciled double-consciousness prevents them from single vision when visiting the power elite's beautiful creations. William Blake's words—"May God us keep from single vision and Newton's sleep!—inform their perspective.

On the same trip to The Cloisters, my wife and I walked extensively through Central Park, surely one of the most beautiful parks in the world. It was spectacularly aflame with Cherry Blossom trees and people from all over the world enjoying its pleasures, as did we. I, however, when entering and exiting this paradise, couldn't help thinking that this park was caged in by the massive apartment complexes of the super-rich elite class, as if to say to the park's visitors: you can visit but not stay. We oversee your pleasures.

Max Weber said it well a century ago:

> No one knows who will live in this cage in the future, or at the end of this tremendous development entirely new

prophets will arise, or there will be a great rebirth of old ideas and ideals, or, if neither, mechanized petrification, embellished with a sort of convulsive self-importance. For of the last stage of this cultural development, it might be said: "Specialists without spirit, sensualists without heart; this nullity imagines that it has attained a level of civilization never before achieved."

The Etymological Animal Must Slip Out of the Cage of Habit to Grasp Truth

Life is full of slips.

Words slip out of our mouths to surprise us. Thoughts slip into our minds to shock us. Dreams slip into our nights to sometimes slip into our waking thoughts to startle us. And, as the wonderful singer/songwriter Paul Simon, sings, we are always "slip sliding away," a reminder that can be a spur to courage and freedom or an inducement to fear and what Kierkegaard called "shut-upness."

Slips are double-edged.

It is obvious that since September 11, 2001, and more so since the corona virus lockdowns and the World Economic Forum's push for a Fourth Industrial Revolution that will lead to the marriage of artificial intelligence, cyborgs, digital technology, and biology, that the USA and other countries have been slipping into a new form of fascist control. Or at least it should be obvious, especially since this push has been accompanied by massive censorship by technology companies of dissenting voices and government crackdowns on what they term "domestic terrorists." Dissent has become unpatriotic and worse—treasonous.

Unless people wake up and rebel in greater numbers, the gates of this electronic iron cage will quietly be shut.

In the name of teleological efficiency and reason, as Max Weber noted more than a century ago in *The Protestant Ethic and the Spirit of Capitalism,* capitalist elites, operating from within the shadows of bureaucratic castles such as The World Economic Forum (WEF), the World Health Organization (WHO), the International Monetary Fund (IMF), The World Bank (WB), The U.S. Centers for Disease Control and Prevention (CDC), Google, Facebook, the National Security Agency (NSA), the CIA, etc.—run by people whose faces are always well hidden—have been using digital technology to exert increasing control over the thoughts and actions of people worldwide. They have been doing this not only by diktats but by manufacturing social habits—customary usages—through which they exert their social power over populations. This linguistic and ideational propaganda is continually slipped into the daily "news" by their mainstream media partners in crime. They become social habits that occupy people's minds and lead to certain forms of behavior. Ideas have consequences but also histories because humans are etymological animals—that is, their ideas, beliefs, and behaviors have histories. It is not just words that have etymologies.

When Weber said "a polar night of icy darkness" was coming in the future, he was referring to what is happening today. Fascism usually comes on slowly as history has shown. It slips in when people are asleep.

John Berger, commenting on the ghostly life of our received ideas whose etymology is so often lost on us, aptly said:

> Our totalitarianism begins with our teleology.

And the teleology in use today is digital technology controlled by wealthy elites and governments for social control. For years they have been creating certain dispositions in the general public, as Jacques Ellul has said, "by working spells upon them and exercising a kind of fascination" that makes the public receptive to the digital life. This is accomplished slowly in increments, as permanent dispositions are established by slipping in regular reminders of how wonderful the new technology is and how its magical possibilities will make life so free and easy. Efficient. Happiness machines. A close study of the past twenty-five years would no doubt reveal the specifics of this campaign. In *The Technological Society,* Ellul writes:

> The use of certain propaganda techniques is not meant to entail immediate and definite adhesion to a given formula, but rather to bring about a long-range vacuity of the individual. The individual, his soul massaged, emptied of his natural tendencies, and thoroughly assimilated to the group, is ready for anything. Propaganda's chief requirement is not so much to be rational, well-grounded, and powerful as it is to produce individuals especially open to suggestion who can easily be set into motion.

Once this softening up has made people "available," the stage is set to get them to act impulsively. Ellul again:

> It operates by simple pressure and is often contradictory (since contradictory mass movements are sometimes necessary). Of course, this dissociation can be effective only after the propaganda technique has been fused with the popular mores and has become indispensable to the population. This stage may be reached quickly, as, for example, in Germany in 1942, after only ten years of psychic manipulation.

The end result, he argues, is the establishment of an abstract universe, in which reality is completely recreated in people's minds. This fake reality is truer than reality as the news is faked and people are formed rather than informed.

In today's computer-driven world, one thing that people have been told for decades is to be vigilant so that their computers do not become infected with viruses. This meme was slipped regularly into popular consciousness. To avoid infection, everyone was advised to make sure to have virus protection by downloading protection or using that provided by their operating systems, despite all the back doors built in, of which most have been unaware.

Now that another incredible "machine"—the human body—can get virus "protection" by getting what the vaccine maker Moderna says is its messenger RNA (mRNA) non-vaccine "vaccine" that "functions like an operation system on a computer." First people must be softened up and made available and then "set in motion" to accept the solution to the fearful problem built in from the start by the same people creating the problem. A slippery slope indeed.

But slipping is also good, especially when repetition and conventional thought rule people's lives as they do today in a digital screen life world where algorithms often prevent creative breakthroughs, and the checking of hourly weather reports from cells is a commonplace fix to ease the anxiety of being trapped in a seemingly uncontrollable nightmare. It seems you now do need computer generated weather reports to know which way the wind blows.

In our culture of the copy, new thoughts are difficult and so the problems that plague society persist and get rehashed ad infinitum. I think most people realize at some level of feeling if not articulation that they are caught in a repetitive cycle of social stasis that is akin to addiction, one that has been imposed on them by elite forces they sense but don't fully comprehend since they have bought into this circular trap that they love and hate simultaneously. The cell phone is its symbol and the worldwide lockdowns its reality. Even right now as the authorities grant a tactical reprieve from their cruel lockdowns if you obey and get experimentally shot with a non-vaccine vaccine, there is an anxious sense that another shoe will drop when we least expect it. And it will. But don't say this out loud.

So repetition and constant change, seemingly opposites, suffuse society these days. The sagacious playwright John Steppling captures this brilliantly in a recent article:

> So ubiquitous are the metaphors and myths of AI, post humanism, transhumanism, et al. that they infuse daily

> discourse and pass barely noticed. And there is a quality of incoherence in a lot of this post humanist discourse, a kind of default setting for obfuscation.... The techno and cyber vocabulary now meets the language of World Banking. Bourgeois economics provides the structural underpinning for enormous amounts of political rhetoric, and increasingly of cultural expression. . . . This new incoherence is both intentional, and unintentional. The so called "Great Reset" is operationally effective, and it is happening before our eyes, and yet it is also a testament to just how far basic logic has been eroded.... Advanced social atomization and a radical absence of social change. Today, I might argue, at least in the U.S. (and likely much of Europe) there is a profound sense of repetitiveness to daily life. No matter one's occupation, and quite possibly no matter one's class. Certainly the repetitiveness of the high-net-worth one percent is of a different quality than that of an Uber driver. And yet, the experience of life is an experience of repetition.

A kind of flaccid grimness accompanies this sensibility. Humor is absent, and the only kind of laughter allowed is the mocking kind that hides a nihilistic spirit of resignation—a sense of inevitability that mocks the spirit of rebellion. Everything is solipsistic and even jokes are taken as revelations of one's personal life.

The other day I was going grocery shopping. My wife had written on the list: "heavy cream or whipping cream." Not knowing if there was a difference, I asked her which she preferred. "I prefer whipping," she said.

I replied, "But I don't have a whip nor do they sell them at the supermarket."

We both laughed, although I found it funnier than she. She slipped, and I found humor in that. Because it was an innocent slip of the tongue with no significance and she had done the slipping, there was also a slippage between our senses of humor.

But when I told this to a few people, they hesitated to laugh as if I might be revealing some sado-masochistic personal reality, and they didn't know whether to laugh or not.

It's harder to laugh at yourself because we get uptight and are afraid to say the "wrong" things. Many people come to the end of their lives hearing the tolling for their tongues that never spoke freely because of the pale cast of thought that has infected them. Not their own thoughts, but thoughts that have been placed into their minds by their controllers in the mass media.

Freud famously wrote about slips of the tongue and tried to pin them down. In this he was a bit similar to a lepidopterist who pins butterflies. We are left with the eponymous Freudian slips that sometimes do and sometimes don't signify some revelation that the speaker does not consciously intend to utter.

It seems to me that in order to understand anything about ourselves and our present historical condition—which no doubt seems very confusing to many people as propagandists and liars spew out disinformation daily—we need to develop a way to cut through the enervating miasma of fear that grips so many. A fear created by elites to cower regular people into submission, as another doctor named Anthony Fauci has instructed: "Now is the time to just do what you are told."

But obviously words do matter, but what they matter is open to interpretation and sometimes debate. To be told to shut up and do what you're told, to censor differences of opinion, to impose authoritarian restrictions on free speech as is happening now, speech that can involve slips of the tongue, is a slippery slope in an allegedly democratic society.

So how can we break out of this deeply imbedded impasse?

This is the hard part, for digital addiction has penetrated deep into our lives.

I believe we need to disrupt our routines, break free from our habits, in order to clearly see what is happening today.

We need to slip away for a while. Leave our cells. Let their doors clang shut behind us. Abandon television. Close the computer. Step out without any mask, not just the paper kind but the ones used to hide from others. Disburden our minds of their old rubbish. Become another as you go walking away. Find a park or some natural enclave where the hum and buzz quiets down and you can breathe. Recall that in Orwell's *Nineteen Eighty-Four* the only place Winston Smith can escape the prying eyes and spies of Big Brother, the only place he can grasp the truth, was not in analyzing Doublethink or Crimestop, but "in a natural clearing, a tiny grass knoll surrounded by tall saplings that shut it in completely" and bluebells bloomed and a thrush sang madly. Here he meets his lover, and they affirm their humanity and feel free and alive for a brief respite. Here in the green wood, the green chaos, new thoughts have a chance to grow. It is an old story and old remedy, transitory of course, but as vital as breathing. In his profound meditation on this phenomenon, *The Tree*, John Fowles, another Englishman, writes, "It is not necessarily too little knowledge that causes ignorance; possessing too much, or wanting to gain too much, can produce the same thing."

I am not proposing that such a retreat is a permanent answer to the propaganda that engulfs us. But without it we are lost. Without it, we cannot break free from received opinions and the constant mental noise the digital media have substituted for thought. Without it, we cannot distinguish our own thoughts from those slyly suggested to us to make us "available." Without it, we will always feel ourselves lost, "shipwrecked upon things," in the words of the Spanish philosopher Ortega Y Gasset. If we are to take a stand against the endless lies and a worldwide war waged against regular people by the world's elites, we must first take "a stand within the self, *ensimismamiento*" by slipping away into contemplation. Only then, once we have clarified what we really believe and don't believe, can we take meaningful action.

There's an old saying about falling or slipping between the cracks. It's meant to be a bad thing and to refer to a place where no one is taking care of you. The saying doesn't make sense. For if you end up between the cracks, you are on the same ground where habits hold you in learned helplessness. Better to slip into the cracks where, as Leonard Cohen sings, "the light gets in."

It may feel like you are slipping away, but you may be exploring your roots.

The Music of Forgetting

I remember when we first came to this small Mexican island in the Caribbean. The pace of life was very slow and time seemed to spiral, not chug straight ahead. It seemed as if local people far outnumbered visitors, most of whom came for the off-beat rhythm of life. The days floated by as did the people along the narrow streets, in and out of the little cafes and aqua water as if everyone were a sea bird soaring on the up notes and dancing down with the swaying palms. Celestial music filled the air.

Now that we have returned to the place where destiny conceived me and I sit on the sandy shore looking out to sea, cut off for a few days from the news of another war and the endless staged propaganda pouring from the Western media about Ukraine and Gaza—being out of touch, so to speak—I contemplate the sea's musical cadence as it breaks on the shore under the rising sun. The beach is deserted except for some singing birds and me. I am for the birds, heart and soul. They are beautiful spirits.

Then he appears from the rear out of the coconut palm trees and dense flowering gardens. A man armed with a drone and his Barbie Doll. He launches his mechanical bird over the water while his lady friend prances and poses for its camera. He shoots her again and again, as if once were not enough to still her mechanical gestures.

I need no entrails to read this early sign. Yet the Sphinx asks me its riddle anyway: What at first can't grasp its own image, then learns to see it, and finally can see nothing else?

I get up and walk away down the beach. When I look back, the drone man and his doll have disappeared. The rosy-fingered dawn, like a radiant remonstrance on the altar of the world, returns me to reality and I plunge into Aphrodite's warm waters. I float in her arms. I swim and forget. With each stroke of my pen the waters of forgetfulness grow stronger, and I turn on my back and spout winged words of joy and adoration.

Many people have heard of Friedrich Nietzsche, and even many more, whose numbers are growing, have not. Quite a few who have probably think he is a dead rapper and others, just some crazy artist like Van Gogh. His general reputation is that of a dark and depressing thinker who went mad. This negative reputation even holds for many somewhat familiar with his writing, the so-called educated classes, who readily believe the media's lies and erroneously associate him with supporting Nazis even as they embrace the Nazis in Ukraine and Tel Aviv.

I have little doubt that this rejection of Nietzsche, based on their groundless "knowledge," is because he told his truths that few want to hear, because he long ago grasped what people would become. And it's not a pretty picture, which all the self-images they take and worship reveal.

Nietzsche was obsessed with the theater and the theatrical nature of life. Not in its aesthetic sense or theater on a literal stage, but life itself. At the core of this was the actor, what was an actor, who was an actor, and what did it mean to act or to be "a genuine actor," if possible. This was because he saw acting as imitation at the core of epistemology, the fundamental issue of knowledge and reality.

In his own way, he was true to ancient Greek philosophy whose core theme was the relationship between Being and Seeming. "To stamp on Becoming the nature of Being" was his goal, which flipped the terms in a way that offers little solace to those who act as if their knowingness is not groundless and imitative, and their acting not a feigned relationship with reality. Unable to play the music of forgetting, he knew they would turn on their false selves with every weapon at their disposal.

Ah reality, here, with the sun risen, she comes down the beach with exposed buttocks quavering and cell phone and tripod in hand. She sets her camera up and smiles at the machine in pose after pose. She is so beautiful she tells herself and sees nothing else but her grotesque smiling image. And she comes every morning to this stage of sand to play her part for an audience of one.

Later, with the sun at its zenith, hordes of actors arrive with their image-making machines. They primp and pose on the sand and in the sea, holding their little mechanical gods high above the water as they walk out up to their necks in the water, grinning and clicking their visages. The sea bobs with hundreds of unreflective skulls, a watery cemetery for modern times.

They are students in what Eduardo Galeano calls "the looking-glass school" where ignorance is the rule:

> There are no admission exams, no registration fees, and courses are offered free to everyone everywhere on earth as well as in heaven. It's not for nothing that this school is the child of the first system in history to rule the world.
>
> In the looking-glass school, lead learns to float and cork to sink. Snakes learn to fly and clouds drag themselves along the ground.

This is the world of nihilists that Nietzsche knew would come to dominate, the self-regarding ones for whom the world does not exist beyond the masks they wear to face the faces that they face.

"Are you genuine?" he asked. "Or merely an actor? A representative? Or that which is represented? In the end, perhaps you are merely a copy of an actor?"

Yes, I think, copies of copies of copies without end. Nothing original, for that would suggest the groundless freedom of becoming when you forget yourself and move only to the music.

It is sardonically comical to observe these actors playing the part of Dionysian people—those who once in their forgetfulness could live out life's tragedy but who are now nearly extinct—parasitically imitating that which they cannot be or comprehend. They cannot forget or open their eyes to reality because they must remember how to act, to imitate all the images, and perform their lives in front of their mirrors. Do they think their machines can stop time for them, freeze their becoming, or "make memories" that prevent them from dying?

I remember coming here when it wasn't so, or at least when the performances were not so blatant. The cell phone has unlocked the largely unconscious secret of the masses: That feigning is all we can do, but since we are doing it blatantly, it is real. We are real fakes. They are imitating their oppressors.

The world has been turned inside out and upside down. Some know it, most don't, and then there are those who play the music of forgetting where each note, each word is forever new, a gift out of the blue.

As for me, my name is Diego Sandoval, but my name, it means nothing. I come from this island, at least my parents told me I was conceived here when they were traveling to Cuba from Mexico City. My father fought with Fidel, but Fidel knocked him out. They had met in Los Angeles when Fidel was in Hollywood to make his movie debut and my father, who was a psychiatrist, was hired by the production company to analyze the acting because the film took place in a mental hospital where even the staff was crazy. It was an unusual movie for its time. It wasn't a comedy, but my father laughed at one scene where Fidel, who was playing a young staff psychiatrist, flubbed his lines. I never knew what my father found so funny, but Fidel was incensed and punched my father. When my father woke up, he thought he was a patient in the hospital and Fidel was his doctor. So many role reversals. Fidel also woke up soon thereafter, abandoned Hollywood for a better role. He became a genuine actor in a different world.

Anyway, that's the story my father told me, but being a psychiatrist, he often made stuff up. He often wove tall tales to entertain me. He loved magic and considered himself quite an amateur magician. I guess my interest in acting started then.

Nietzsche? Maybe that began when I was fourteen years old in a bilingual school in Mexico City and first saw his photo in a book with his Emiliano Zapata mustache. I had found a discarded Spanish copy of his book, *Thus Spoke Zarathustra,* and read it, although I must say I didn't understand much, yet something in it struck a deep chord in me. I only had some wispy hairs then but by seventeen you should have seen me; I was ferocious looking. Still am, some say. When I became a poet and singer, I took the stage name Mr. Z to honor my heroes. Perhaps you've heard of me. Few who come to hear me perform know my name's origins and I never explain.

As my popularity grew and fame pursued me, I grew many disguises. I answered questions with questions and gave answers so enigmatic that no one understood me. I didn't understand myself much of the time since more and more I said whatever popped out of my mouth, but this delighted me. I laughed a lot and stopped taking myself seriously. I kept forgetting more and more and my poetry and music seemed to come from some unbidden place. I guess you could call it intuition. But I'd often forget the lyrics and have to improvise. That became so enjoyable that even when I remembered the lyrics I would change them just for fun. The audience hated this, but I didn't care. Forgetting became my musical forte and over time I realized that it must permeate my life and so I became a genius at active, conscious forgetting.

I even forget why I am writing this. Perhaps it is to remind myself to forget what I have seen on my return to the island. To write about it as a form of exorcism. It is all so utterly changed. To see all these poor players on the stage of self, so serious and self-absorbed makes me want to never return, to fly away. I ask myself how can I ever forget the images of all those shaking, flabby buttocks staring me in the face. Maybe if their cameras captured their asses, they would reconsider showing them. As for me, to paraphrase a wise man, if you gaze too long into an ass, the ass gazes also into you.

I should work on my music, so I can simply soar like a sea bird on the up notes and dance down with the swaying palms, and in the playing I will forget everything and be lost in the celestial music. Nietzsche said truly:

> I do not know of any more profound orientation of an artist than this, whether he looks at his work in progress (at himself) from the point of view of the witness, or whether he has forgotten the world, which is the

essential feature of all monological art: it is based on forgetting, it is the music of forgetting.

The Past Lives On: The Elite Strategy to Divide and Conquer

"They call my people the White Lower Middle Class these days. It is an ugly, ice-cold phrase, the result, I suppose, of the missionary zeal of those sociologists who still think you can place human beings on charts. It most certainly does not sound like a description of people on the edge of open, sustained and possibly violent revolt," wrote the marvelous New York journalist, Pete Hamill in "The Revolt of the White Lower Middle Class" in *New York* magazine. He added:

> The White Lower Middle Class? Say that magic phrase at a cocktail party on the Upper East Side of Manhattan and monstrous images arise from the American demonology. Here comes the murderous rabble: fat, well-fed, bigoted, ignorant, an army of beer-soaked Irishmen, violence-loving Italians, hate-filled Poles. Lithuanians and Hungarians.... Sometimes these brutes are referred to as "the ethnics" or "the blue-collar types." But the bureaucratic, sociological phrase is White Lower Middle Class. Nobody calls it the Working Class anymore.

He wrote that on April 14, 1969. Yesterday. Little changes.

Transferred from NYC to the middle of the country half a century later, these people are referred to as Trump's "deplorables." They come in baskets, as Hillary Clinton said. And even though they represent nearly half the voting public in the last two presidential elections—70+ million Americans—their complaints are dismissed as the rantings of ignorant, conservative racists.

Name calling substitutes for understanding. This is not an accident.

Like Hamill, I am a NYC born and bred Irish American—my working-class Bronx to Pete's Brooklyn. We both attended the same Jesuit high school in different years. Unlike Hamill, known for his gritty street reporting, I could falsely be categorized as a northeastern liberal intellectual oozing with disdain for those who voted for Trump because I have been a college sociology professor. This is false, because, like Hamill, I see it as my intellectual duty to understand what motivates these voters, just as I do with those who voted for Biden.

I didn't vote for Donald Trump, nor did I vote for Joseph Biden, or Hillary Clinton in 2016. I am not one of those sociologists Hamill refers to; I use the term Working Class and am acutely aware of the social class nature of life in the U.S.A., where the economic system of neoliberal capitalism is constructed to try to convince working Americans that the system cares for them, and if they grow disgusted with its lies and inequities and rage against the machine by voting for anyone who seems to be with them (even a super-rich reality TV real estate magnate named Trump, who is not with them), they are dumb-ass bigots whose concerns should be brushed off.

The truth is that both the Trump voters and the Biden voters have been taken for a ride. It is a game, a show, a movie, a spectacle. It hasn't changed much since 1969; the rich have gotten richer and the poor, working, and middle classes have gotten poorer and more desperate. Those who have profited have embraced the fraud.

The Institute for Policy Studies has just released a new analysis showing that since the start of the COVID-19 "pandemic" in mid-March and the subsequent transfer upwards of $5 trillion to the wealthy and largest corporations through the Cares Act, approved 96–0 in the U.S. Senate, 650 U.S. billionaires have gained over a trillion dollars in eight months as the American people have suffered an economic catastrophe. This shift upward of massive wealth under Trump is similar to Obama's massive 2009 bailout of the banks on the backs of American workers. Both were justified through feats of legerdemain by both political parties, accomplices in the fleecing of regular people, many of whom continue to support the politicians that screw them while telling them they care.

If the Democrats and the Republicans are at war as is often claimed, it is only over who gets the larger part of the spoils. Trump and Biden work for the same bosses, those I call the Umbrella People (those who own and run the country through their intelligence/military/media operatives), who produce and direct the movie that keeps so many Americans on the edge of their seats in the hope that their chosen good guy wins in the end. The Umbrella People's con job is to convince regular people that they protect them from the rain while soaking them for everything they can get.

I am well aware that most people disagree with my analysis. It does seem as if I am wrong and that because the Democrats and their accomplices have spent years attempting to oust Trump through Russia-gate, impeachment, etc. that what seems true is true and Trump is simply a crazy aberration who somehow slipped through the net of establishment control to rule for four years. To those 146+ million people who voted for Biden and Trump this seems self-evident. But if that is so, why, despite their superficial differences—and Obama's, Hillary Clinton's and George W. Bush's for that matter—have the super-rich gotten richer and richer over the decades and the war on terror continued as the military budget has increased each year and the armament industries and the Wall Street crooks continued to rake in the money at the expense of everyone else? These are a few facts that can't be disputed. There are many more. So what's changed under Trump? We are talking about nuances, small changes. A clown with a big mouth versus traditional, "dignified" con men.

Variety is necessary. You wouldn't want to repeat the film from 2008 when a well-spoken black man came into town out of nowhere to clean up the mess created by the poorly spoken white sheriff who loved war and then the black hero went on to wage war in seven countries while his fans sat contented in the audience loving the show and making believe they didn't see what was happening on the screen even though their hero jailed whistle blowers and greatly expanded the surveillance state right in front of their eyes.

No, as the years passed, those two guys turned out to be buddies, and their wives hit it off, and a famous photograph appeared of the good guy's wife hugging the bad guy, which was not a good thing for the script that has the Republicans warring against the Democrats.

A new story line was needed. How about an opéra bouffe, someone suggested, and the rest is history. Or pseudo-history. This is the real matrix. The most sophisticated mind control operation up to this point, with the coronavirus lockdown added to propel it to what the producers hope is a conclusion.

What more can I say?

Billy Joel said it: "JFK blown away."

The Towers pulverized. David Ray Griffin told us the truth in a number of books from various angles.

Minds of this generation destroyed, as Allen Ginsberg said in "Howl": "I saw the best minds of my generation destroyed by madness."

It's been many generations now. There has been a form of social madness growing over the decades and it is everywhere now. Look at people's faces, if you can see them behind the masks; everywhere the strained and stressed looks, the scared rabbit eyes that you see on the wards of mental hospitals. The look that says: what the fuck has happened as they stare into a blank screen in a tumbling void, to paraphrase Don DeLillo from his new book *Silence,* where people speak gibberish once their digital world is mysteriously taken down and they wander in the dark. We are in the dark now, even though the lights and screens are still shining for the time being.

Let those who think I am wrong about Trump and Biden being players in the same show consider this. If Trump is truly the opponent of the Deep State, the Swamp, the corrupt establishment, he will pardon Julian Assange, Chelsey Manning, and

Edward Snowden who have been persecuted by these forces. He has nothing left to lose as he exits stage right.

The journalist Julian Assange has done more than anyone to expose the sick underbelly of the gangster state, its intelligence and military secrets, its illegal and immoral killings. That is why he has been hounded and locked away for so long. It's a bipartisan persecution of an innocent man whose only "crime" has been to tell the truth that is allegedly the essence of a democratic society.

Chelsey Manning has also suffered tremendously for exposing the savagery of U.S. military operations.

And Edward Snowden has been forced into Russian exile for telling us about the vast global surveillance systems run by the NSA and CIA to spy on the American people.

Three innocent truth-tellers at war with the Deep-State forces that Donald Trump says he opposes.

If he is what his supporters claim, he will pardon these courageous three. It's all in his power. A simple, clear message as he goes out the door. If by the smallest chance he does pardon them, I will be very happy and publicly apologize. If he doesn't, as I expect, please don't say a word in his defense. My ears will be stuffed with wax. For he won't, because, like Biden, he is controlled by the very forces that these truth-tellers have exposed.

But back to the working class "deplorables" that voted for Trump. They aren't going anywhere. Their grievances remain. For decades, under Democratic and Republican administrations, their lives have been hollowed out, their livelihoods taken as corporate thieves have ravaged their towns and cities by closing down the factories where they worked and sending them overseas for greater profits. Small farmers have been "liquidated" for agribusiness.

As always, the coastal urbanites have considered rural people stupid, uncouth, and clownish, ignorant of the fact that the words clown, boor, and villain have all originally meant farmer or countryman or lower-class peasant. Such hidden etymological social class prejudices have a way of persisting over the years.

Towns and small businesses disappear, traditional values are ridiculed, drug addiction and suicide increase, the fabric of traditions crumble, etc. This list is long. The people who voted for Trump feel betrayed; they feel like victims. Of course, as Pete Hamill wrote of the NYC white working class in 1969, there are racists among them, and with all racists, they have their reasons, and these reasons are poison and despicable. But overall, these Trump voters are, in Hamill's words, "actually in revolt against taxes, joyless work, the double standards and short memories of professional politicians, hypocrisy and what he [they] considers the debasement of the American dream." Any politician, he added, who leaves these people out of the political equation, does so at a very large risk. That risk has been growing over the decades.

Yet desperate people do desperate things, and for many Americans these are desperate times. Everywhere you look, there are long lines at food pantries and soup kitchens. The unemployment numbers are staggering. Homelessness. Suicides. Drug and alcohol addictions rising. Clear signs of social disintegration. This is true not just in the United States but is happening around the world as neoliberal capitalist economic policies are exacerbated by the widespread lockdowns that have given rise to massive protests worldwide, protests that the corporate press has failed to publicize since doing so would give the lie to their promotions of the lockdowns.

In England, the *Mirror* newspaper just printed an article by the legendary Australian journalist John Pilger about his 1975 interviews with impoverished English families with this lead:

> John Pilger interviewed Irene Brunsden in Hackney, east London about only being able to feed her two-year-old a plate of cornflakes in 1975. Now he sees nervous women queueing at foodbanks with their children as it's revealed 600,000 more kids are in poverty now than in 2012.

Vast numbers of people are suffering.

Many Trump voters no doubt know that Trump was never going to save them. But he said the right things, and desperation and disgust will grasp onto the slightest will-o'-the-wisp when disbelief in the whole rotten system is widespread.

Let's not bullshit: everyone knows the game is rigged.

Trump is a liar.

Biden is a liar.

Great Britain's Boris Johnson is a liar.

Fill in the names of the political charlatans.

The system is built on lies to keep the illusions brightening the screen of the great picture show, what Neil Gabler has rightly called "life the movie."

Biden voters no doubt desperately hope that we can go back to some semblance of "normal," even while knowing this is a losing game. Many of them try hard to conceal their true feelings, that their hatred for Trump and their love of living in times when imperialism is concealed as democracy is what they want. They don't want to know. Concealment of the atrocious underbelly of normal is their hope and desire, even while they too are being fleeced and secretly know that the "new normal" will be far from their restorative dreams. There are exceptions, of course, true believers who think Biden will significantly change things, but I would say they are a very small minority. Many Biden voters say they have voted for the "lesser of two evils," an old, worn-out excuse that in a rigged system will perdure.

Little changes. The past lives on.

Next year's Academy Awards will be interesting. A wit I know suggested that perhaps Trump and Biden will be nominees for the Best Actor in a Leading Role and they will tie for the Oscar. That will be the second time that has ever happened. The first was in 1932 when Fredric March and Wallace Beery shared the award. March starred in *Dr. Jekyll and Mr. Hyde a*nd Beery in the boxing film, *The Champ.*

Both winners will be announced as starring in the same film, confusing the audience until it's named: *The American Nightmare.* Then raucous cheering will erupt from the jaded audience. Dr. Jekyll will embrace Mr. Hyde and the melded Champ will take a bow as he winks for the cameras.

The Houses of Dead and Crooked Souls

"A house constitutes a body of images that give mankind proofs or illusions of stability."
—GASTON BACHELARD, *The Poetics of Space*

There is a vast and growing gulf between the world's rich and poor. An obscene gulf. If we can read houses, they will confirm this. They offer a visible lesson in social class.

Houses stand before us like books on a shelf waiting to be read, and when the books are missing, as they are for a vast and growing multitude of homeless exiled wandering ones, their absence serves to indict the mansion-dwelling wealthy and to a lesser extent those whose homes serve to shield them from the truth of the ill-begotten gains of the wealthy elites who create the world's suffering through their avarice, lies, and war making.

Many regular people want to say with Edmund in Eugene O'Neill's play, *Long Day's Journey into Night*:

> The fog is where I wanted to be. Halfway down the path you can't see this house. You'd never know it was here. Or any of the other places down the avenue. I couldn't see but a few feet ahead. I didn't meet a soul. Everything looked and sounded unreal. Nothing was what it is. That's what I wanted—to be alone with myself in another world where truth is untrue and life can

> hide from itself.... Who wants to see life as it is, if they can help it?

Yet the rich don't hide or give a damn. They flaunt their houses. They know they are crooks and creators of illusions. Their nihilism is revealed in their conspicuous consumption and their predatory behavior; they want everyone else to see it too. So they rub it in our faces. Their wealth is built on the blood and suffering of millions around the world, but this is often hidden knowledge.

Many regular people prefer the fog to the harsh truth. It shields them from intense anger and the realization that the wealthy elites who run the world and control the media lie to them about everything and consider them beneath contempt. For that would demand a response commensurate with the outrage—rebellion. It would impose the moral demand to look squarely at the other kind of housing on offer, with its tiny cells in which the wealthy elites and their henchmen imprison and torture truthtellers like Julian Assange, an innocent man housed in a living hell; to make connections between wealth and power and the obscene flaunting of the rich elite's sybaritic lifestyles in houses where every spacious room testifies to their moral depravity.

The recent news of Barack Obama's vile selfie birthday celebration for his celebrity "friends" at his 29-acre estate and mansion (he has another eight-million-dollar mansion in Washington, D. C.) on Martha's Vineyard is an egregious recent case in point. If he thinks this nauseating display is proof of his stability and strength—which obviously he does—then he is a deluded fool. But those who carry water for the military-intelligence-media complex are amply rewarded and want to tell the world that this is so. It's essential for the Show. It must be conspicuous so the plebians learn their lesson.

Obama's Vineyard mansion stands as an outward sign of his inner disgrace, his soullessness.

Trump's golden towers and his never-ending self-promotion or the multiple million-dollar mansions of high-tech, sports, and Hollywood's superstars send the same message.

Take Bill Gates' sixty-three-million-dollar mansion, Xanadu, named after William Randolph Hearst's estate in *Citizen Kane*, that took seven years to build.

Take the house up the hill from where I live in an erstwhile working-class town that sold for one million plus and now is being expanded to double its size with a massive swimming pool that leaves no grass uncovered. Every week, three black window-tinted SUVs arrive with New Jersey plates to join two white expensive sedans to oversee the progress in this small western Massachusetts town where McMansions rise throughout the hills faster than summer's weeds.

Take the blue dolomite stone Searles Castle with its 60 acres, 40 rooms, and "dungeon" basement down the hill on Main St. that was recently bought by a NYC artist who also owns seven grand estates around the country that he showcases as examples of his fine artistic taste. "All these houses have endless things to do—it's just mind-boggling," he has said. The artist, Hunt Slonem, calls himself a "glamorizer," and his "exotica" paintings, inspired by Andy Warhol's repetition of soup cans and Marilyn Monroe, hang in galleries, museums, cruise ships, and the houses of film celebrities. Like his showcase houses, his exotica must have endless things to do.

What would Vincent van Gogh say? Perhaps what he wrote to his brother Theo: that the greatest people in painting and literature "have always worked *against the grain*" and in sympathy with the poor and oppressed. That might seem "mind-boggling" to Slonem.

Such ostentatious displays of wealth and power clearly reveal the delusions of the elites, as if there are no spiritual consequences for living so. Even if they read Tolstoy's cautionary tale about greed, *How Much Land Does A Man Need?*, it is doubtful that its truth would register. Like Tolstoy's protagonist Pahóm, they never have enough. But like Pahóm, the Devil has them in his grip, and like him, they will get their just rewards, a small space, a bit of land to imprison them forever.

"His servant picked up the spade and dug a grave long enough for Pahóm to lie in, and buried him in it. Six feet from his head to his heels was all he needed."

Where does the money for all these estates, not just Slonem's, come from? Who wants to ask?

Getting to the roots of wealth involves a little digging. Slonem's castle was originally commissioned in the late 1800s by Mark Hopkins for his wife. Hopkins was one of the founders of the Central Pacific Railroad, which was built by Irish and Chinese immigrants. Labor history is quite illuminating on the ways immigrants have always been treated, in this case "the dregs of Asia" and the Irish dogs. Interestingly enough, the great black scholar and radical, W. E. B. Du Bois, a town native, worked at the castle's construction site as a young man. No doubt it informed his future work against racism, capitalism, and economic exploitation.

Wealthy urbanites flooded this area after September 11, 2001, and now, in their terror of disease and death, they have bought every house they could find. Their cash-filled pockets overflow with blood-money and few ask why. To suggest that massive wealth is almost always ill-begotten is anathema. But innocence wears many masks, and the Show demands washed hands and no questions asked.

It is rare that one becomes super-wealthy in an honest and ethical way. The ways the rich get money almost without exception lead downward, to paraphrase Thoreau from his essay, "Life Without Principle."

Since the corona crisis began, investment firms such as the Blackstone Group have been gobbling up vast numbers of houses across the United States as their prices have gone through the roof. The lockdowns—an appropriate prison term—have set millions of regular people back on their heels as the wealthiest have gotten exponentially wealthier. Poverty and starvation have increased around the world. This is not an accident. Despair and depression are widespread.

There is a taboo in life in general and in journalism: Do not ask where people's money comes from. Thoreau was so advised long ago:

> Do not ask how your bread is buttered; it will make you sick....

But the super-wealthy do not get sick. They are sick. For they revel in their depravity and push it in the faces of regular people, many who envy them and wish to become super-rich and powerful themselves. Of course there are the blue bloods whose method is understatement, but it takes many decades to enter their theater of deception. In many ways, these people are worse, for their personae have been crafted over decades of play-acting and public relations so their images are laundered to smell fresh and benevolent. They often wear the mask of philanthropy, while the history of their wealth lies shrouded in an amnestic fog.

Yet soul murder includes suicide, and while the old and new moneyed ones smoothly justify their oppression of the vast majority, many regular people kill the best in themselves by envying the rich.

Years ago, I discovered some documents that showed that one of this country's most famous philosophers, known for his lofty moral pronouncements, owned a lot of stock in companies that were doing evil things—warmaking, poisoning and killings huge numbers with chemicals, etc. But his image was one of Mr. Clean, Mr. Good Guy. I suspect this is typical and that there are many such secrets in the basements and attics of the rich.

But let us also ask where the writers and presenters of the mainstream and alternative media get their money. Although "to follow the money" is a truism, few do. If we do, we will learn that money talks and those who take it toe the line, nor do they live in shacks by the side of the road or rent like so many others. They invest with Blackrock and their ilk and have money managers who can increase their wealth while shielding them from the ways that money is made on the backs of the poor and working people. And they lie about people like Assange, Daniel Hale, Reality Winner, Craig Murray, et al., all imprisoned for daring to reveal the depredations of the power elites, the violence at the heart of predatory capitalism.

Yes, houses speak. But few ever speak of where their money comes from. Those that are on the take—which has multiple meanings—always plead innocent. Yes, I can hear you say that I am being too harsh; that there are exceptions. That is obvious. So let's skip the exceptions and focus on the general principle. There is a Buddhist principle that right livelihood is a core ethic in earning money. Jesus had another way of putting it but was of course in agreement, as were so many others whom people hold in highest esteem.

The truth is that for most people, work, if they can find it, is drudgery and hard, a matter of survival. The late great Studs Terkel called it hell and rightly said that most jobs are not big enough for people because they crush the soul, they lack meaning. And behind all ledgers of great wealth lie crushed souls. This reality is so obvious and goes by many names, including class warfare, that further commentary would be redundant.

A few years ago, I visited Mark Twain's house in Hartford, Connecticut. It is advertised as "a house with a heart and a soul." It is not a house but a mansion, and it was an ostentatious display in Twain's time. Similar or worse than Obama's mansion on Martha's Vineyard today. It has no soul or heart. It was built with Twain's wife's family money. Her father was an oil and coal tycoon from upstate New York. Twain reveled in opulent respectability. He lived the life of a Gilded Age tycoon, an American magnate. It is not a pretty story, but the Twain myth says otherwise. Not that he catered to popular tastes to please the crowd and his domineering wife and that he lived in luxury, but that he was a radical critic of the establishment. This is false. For he withheld for the most part the publication of his withering take on American imperialism until after his death. He committed soul murder. But his mansion impressed his neighbors and his humor distracted from his luxurious lifestyle. His house still stands as a cautionary tale for those who will read it.

Baudelaire once said that in palaces "there is no place for intimacy." This is no doubt why in people's dreams small, simple houses with a light in the window loom large. Bachelard says, "When we are lost in darkness and see a distant glimmer of light, who does not dream of a thatched cottage or, to go more deeply still into legend, of a hermit's hut." For here man and God meet in solitude; here human intimacy is possible. "The hut can receive none of the riches 'of this world.' It possesses the felicity of intense poverty; indeed, it is one of the glories of poverty; as destitution increases, it gives access to absolute refuge."

He is not espousing actual poverty, but the oneiric depths of true desire, the dreams of hope, reconciliation, and simple living that run counter to the amassing of wealth to prove one's power and majesty. A humble house of truth, not a mansion of lies. This, to borrow the title of William Goyen's novel, is "the house of breath," where the spirit can live and pseudo-stability gives way to faith, for insecurity is the essence of life.

There is such a hermit's hut where the light shines. It is the tiny cell in Belmarsh Prison where Julian Assange hangs onto his life by a thread. His witness for truth sends an inspiring message to all those lost in the world's woods to look to his fate and not turn away. To follow to their sources the money that greases the palms of all the so-called journalists and politicians who want him dead or imprisoned for life, who tell their endless lies, not just about him, but about everything.

The house of propaganda is built on unanimity. When one person says no, the foundation starts to crumble. The houses of the rich dead and crooked souls, erected to project the stability of their bloody illusions, start to crumble into sand when people dissent one by one.

Soon the fog lifts and there is no hiding any more. At the end of the path, you can see the vultures circling overhead as their prey go running out of their mansions in terror.

Sing Hallelujah!

The Assassination and Resurrection of Martin Luther King, Jr.

"I don't believe in death without resurrection. If they kill me, I will rise again in the Salvadorian people...."
—ARCHBISHOP OSCAR ROMERO, martyred, 24 March 1980

Whether we are aware of it or not, we live by stories. We live by others' stories while we tell our lives by how we live. Our actions tell our stories. Then when we die, others tell our stories as they wish.

This is the spiritual thread that links the meanings of our lives. It is the way we pass over to other lives and return to our own. But without truth, we end up in the wrong place, living the wrong stories.

And don't the stories of certain special people inspire us to carry on their legacies because their spirits are far stronger than death? Their courage contagious? Their witness the triumph of life over death? Love over hate?

Don't they challenge us to imitate them, to kindle in ourselves the fire of their resurrected spirits?

For Christians, Holy Week is the time for deep reflection on the story of the death and resurrection of Jesus and what this means for us today. This year, the anniversary of the murder of the Christian prophet and martyr, Martin Luther King, Jr., falls on Easter Sunday, April 4, which gives rise to doubly deeper thoughts that cross religious boundaries where people of all faiths or none can unite in the spirit of nonviolent resistance to the forces of war, poverty, racism, and materialism—violence in all its forms. Everything that stands in the way of what King called "the Beloved Community."

That Jesus met violence with nonviolent love and voluntarily entered the darkness of death and abandonment is at the heart of the Christian faith. So, too, his Resurrection. If the Jewish radical Jesus had not been executed by the Roman state occupiers of Palestine, if all hope for his followers had not seemingly been lost, then the Resurrection that followed could not have given birth in turn to hope in his followers, spurring them to carry on his spirit of love for the poor, the downtrodden, and the outcasts—his resistance to violence.

Like Oscar Romero in El Salvador, gunned down by U.S. trained death squads at the altar while offering Mass and subsequently named a saint by the Roman Catholic Church, Martin Luther King, Jr.'s witness and the truth about his death should be a central meditative focus this year. For the convergence of King's death on April 4, 1968 with Easter this April 4th and the last day of Passover impels us to contemplate what is now demanded of all people who yearn for an end to hatred, violence, and injustice, and the creation of a beloved world community where love and kindness reign.

The spirit of all the prophets and martyrs is about now, not then; about us, not them; it confronts us with the challenge to interrogate our beliefs and deeds.

Shall we turn away from their witness? What truly animates our souls? Where do we stand? Do we support the state's power to kill and wage war, to deny people freedom, to discriminate, to oppress the poor?

It is always about now; the living truth is now.

To contemplate the lives of the prophets takes us very deep into the darkness where we encounter the murders of Jesus, King, Romero, and all those who have died trying to make peace and justice a reality. But only if we go into the darkest truths will we be able to see the light that leads us to resurrect the spirit of their resistance to evil.

Another prophet of our broken world, the Hindu Mohandas Gandhi, soul brother to King, echoed the words that many have heard, that "God chose what is weak in the world to shame the strong," when, in crossing over to the Christian tradition, he told us: *"We dare not think of birth without death on the cross. Living Christ means a Living Cross, without it life is a living death."*[1]

So what do we need to know about MLK, and why does it matter?

King's True Story

Very few Americans are aware of the truth behind the assassination of Dr. Martin Luther King, Jr., the United States' celebrated civil rights icon. Few books have been written about it, unlike other significant assassinations, especially JFK's. For more than fifty years there has been a media blackout supported by government disinformation to hide the truth. And few people, in the public's massive act of self-deception, have chosen to question the official explanation, choosing, rather, to embrace a mythic fabrication intended to sugarcoat the bitter fruit that has resulted from the murder of a man capable of leading a mass movement for transformative change in the United States. Today we are eating the fruit of our denial as ongoing racial discrimination, poverty, and police violence garner the headlines.

After more than a decade as America's best-known and most respected civil rights leader, by 1968 Reverend Martin Luther King, Jr. had increasingly focused on poverty issues and publicly declared his intense opposition to the U.S. war against Vietnam in a famous speech—"Beyond Vietnam: Time to Break

1 As quoted in James W. Douglass, *The Non-Violent Cross: A Theology of Revolution and Peace* (New York: MacMillan, 1968), p. 57.

the Silence"—at New York's Riverside Church on April 4, 1967, one year to the day before he was assassinated.[2]

On winning the Nobel Peace Prize in 1964, he emerged as an international figure, whose opinions on human and economic rights and peaceful coexistence became influential worldwide. Shortly before his assassination, he was organizing the Poor People's Campaign that would involve hundreds of thousands of Americans who would encamp in Washington, D.C to demand the end to economic inequality, racism, and war.

At the same time, Reverend King was hated by an array of racists throughout America, especially in the American South. Among his greatest declared enemies was FBI Director J. Edgar Hoover, who seemed convinced that King's backers were Communists out to damage America's interests. In the late 1960s, the FBI's COINTELPRO program created a network of informants and agent provocateurs to undermine the civil rights and anti-war movements with a special focus on King.[3]

After King's "I Have a Dream" speech in 1963, William Sullivan, the head of the FBI's domestic intelligence division, wrote in a post-speech memo:

---

2 See David T. Ratcliffe, "50 Years Ago: Riverside Church and MLK's Final Year of Experiments With Truth," rat haus reality press, April 4, 2017. A significant moment in Dr. King's odyssey occurred on January 14, 1967, when he first saw a photographic essay by William Pepper about the children of Vietnam. Initially, while he hadn't had a chance to read the text, it was the photographs that stopped him. Bernard Lee, who was present at the time, never forgot Martin King's shock as he looked at photographs of young napalm victims: "Martin had known about the [Vietnam] war before then, of course, and had spoken out against it. But it was then that he decided to commit himself to oppose it." The truth force in these photographs led directly to Dr. King's Riverside Church exhortation in April. See David T. Ratcliffe, "The Truth of The Children of Vietnam: A Way of Liberation—How Will We Challenge Militarism, Racism, and Extreme Materialism?," rat haus reality press, November 30, 2017.

3 Dr. Martin Luther King, Jr., Case Study, U.S. Senate Select Committee to Study Governmental Operations with Respect to Intelligence Activities ("Church Committee"), *Final Report—Book III: Supplementary Detailed Staff Reports on Intelligence Activities and the Rights of Americans,* April 23, 1976, pp. 79–184.

> Personally, I believe in the light of King's powerful, demagogic speech that he stands head and shoulders over all other Negro leaders put together when it comes to influencing great masses. We must mark him now, if we have not done so before, as the most dangerous Negro of the future in this Nation from the standpoint of communism, the Negro and national security.[4]

The FBI, after extensive eavesdropping on King, subsequently sent him an anonymous letter urging him to kill himself or else his extramarital sex life would be exposed. The FBI's and its Director J. Edgar Hoover's hatred for King was so great that nothing was too low for them.[5]

This history is common knowledge as reported in the *Washington Post,* the *New York Times*, etc.

During the Senate Church Committee hearings in the mid-1970s, a parallel group within the CIA, code-named CHAOS, was uncovered. Despite its charter disallowing it from operating inside the United States, the CIA similarly used illegal means to disrupt the civil rights and anti-war movements.

Because MLK, in his Riverside Church speech, spoke clearly to what he identified there as "the greatest purveyor of violence in the world today—my own government" and continued to relentlessly confront his own government on its criminal war against Vietnam, he was universally condemned by the mass media and the government that later—once he was long and safely dead and no longer a threat—praised him to the heavens. This has continued to the present day of historical amnesia.

Today Martin Luther King's birthday is celebrated with a national holiday, but his death day disappears down the memory hole. Across the country—in response to the King Holiday and Service Act passed by Congress and signed by President Bill Clinton in 1994—people are encouraged to make the day one of

---

4 Tony Capaccio, "MLK's speech attracted FBI's intense attention," *Washington Post,* August 27, 2013.

5 Beverly Gage, "What an Uncensored Letter to M.L.K. Reveals," *New York Times,* November 11, 2014.

service (from Latin, *servus* = slave). Etymological irony aside, such service does not include King's commitment to protesting a decadent system of racial and economic injustice or nonviolently resisting the warfare state that is the United States. Government sponsored service is cultural neoliberalism at its finest.

The word service is a loaded word; it has become a smiley face and vogue word over the past thirty-five years. Its use for MLK Day is clear: individuals are encouraged to volunteer for activities such as tutoring children, painting senior centers, delivering meals to the elderly, etc., activities that are good in themselves but far less good when used to conceal an American prophet's message. After all, Martin Luther King's work was not volunteering at the local food pantry with Oprah Winfrey cheering him on.

But service without truth is slavery. It is propaganda aimed at convincing decent people into thinking that they are observing the essence of MLK's message while they are following a message of misdirection.

Educating people about who killed King, and why, and why it matters today, is the greatest service we can render to his memory.

What exactly is the relationship between King's saying that "the greatest purveyor of violence in the world today—my own government" and his murder?

Let's look at the facts.

Martin Luther King, Jr. was assassinated on April 4, 1968, at 6:01 PM as he stood on the balcony of the Lorraine Motel in Memphis, Tennessee. He was shot in the lower right side of his face by one rifle bullet that shattered his jaw, damaged his upper spine, and came to rest below his left shoulder blade. The U.S. government claimed the assassin was a racist loner named James Earl Ray, who had escaped from the Missouri State Penitentiary on April 23, 1967. Ray was alleged to have fired the fatal shot from a second-floor bathroom window of a rooming house above the rear of Jim's Grill across the street. Running to his rented room, Ray allegedly gathered his belongings, including the rifle, in a bedspread-wrapped bundle, rushed out the front door onto the adjoining street, and in a panic dropped the bundle in the doorway of the Canipe Amusement Company a few doors down. He was then said to have jumped into his white Mustang and to have driven to Atlanta where he abandoned the car. From there he fled to Canada and then to England and then to Portugal and back to England where he was eventually arrested at Heathrow Airport on June 8, 1968, and extradited to the U.S. The state claims that the money Ray needed to purchase the car and for all his travel was secured through various robberies and a bank heist. Ray's alleged motive was racism and that he was a bitter and dangerous loner.

When Ray, under extraordinary pressure, coercion, and a payoff from his lawyer to take a plea, pleaded guilty (only a few days later to request a trial that was denied) and was sentenced to 99 years in prison, the case seemed to be closed, and was dismissed from public consciousness. Another hate-filled lone assassin, as the government also termed Lee Harvey Oswald and Sirhan Sirhan, had committed a despicable deed.

Ray had received erroneous advice from his attorney, Percy Foreman. Foreman had a long history representing government, corporate, intelligence, and mafia figures, including Jack Ruby, in cases where the government wanted to keep people silent. Ray was told that the government would go after Ray's father and brother, Jerry, and that he'd get the electric chair if he didn't plead guilty,

Ray initially acquiesced. He entered what is known as an Alford plea before Judge Preston Battle. In making his plea, Ray did not admit to any criminal act and asserted his innocence. The following day, he fired Percy Foreman, who, by offering money to induce a guilty plea, had committed a criminal offense. Foreman had also lied to Judge Battle about his contract with Ray. And, the transcript of Ray's testimony was doctored to help support the government's case. Ray was sentenced to life in prison. After three days, Ray tried to retract his plea and maintained his innocence for almost 30 years until his death.

The United States government's case against James Earl Ray was extremely weak from the start, and in the intervening years has grown so weak that it is no longer believable. A vast body of evidence has accumulated that renders it patently false.

But before examining such evidence, it is important to point out that MLK, Jr, his father, Rev. M. L. King, Sr, and his maternal grandfather, Rev. A.D. Williams, all pastors of Atlanta's Ebenezer Baptist Church, were spied on by Army Intelligence and the FBI since 1917.[6] All were considered dangerous because of their espousal of racial and economic equality. None of this had to do with war or foreign policy, but such spying was connected to their religious opposition to racist and economic policies that stretched back to slavery, realities that have been officially acknowledged today. But when MLK, Jr. forcefully denounced unjust and immoral warmaking as well, especially the Vietnam war, and announced his Poor People's Campaign and intent to lead a massive peaceful encampment of hundreds of thousands in Washington, D.C., he set off panic in the inner sanctums of the government. Seventy-five years of spying on black religious leaders here found its ultimate "justification."

The corporate mass media has for more than fifty years echoed the government's version of the King assassination. Here and there, however, mainly through the alternative media, and also through the monumental work and persistence of the King family's lawyer, William Pepper, the truth about the assassination has surfaced. Through decades of research, a TV trial, a jury trial, and three meticulously researched books, Pepper has documented the parts played in the assassination by F.B.I. Director J. Edgar Hoover, the F.B.I., Army Intelligence, Memphis Police, and southern Mafia figures. In his last two books, *An Act of State (2003)* and later *The Plot to Kill King* (2016), Pepper presents his comprehensive case.

William Pepper's decades-long investigation not only refutes the flimsy case against James Earl Ray, but definitively proves that King was killed by a government conspiracy led by J. Edgar Hoover and the FBI, Army Intelligence, and Memphis Police, assisted by southern Mafia figures. He is right to assert that *"we have probably acquired more detailed knowledge about this*

6 Stephen G. Tompkins, "Army feared King, secretly watched him, Spying on blacks started 75 years ago," *The Commercial Appeal,* March 21, 1993.

political assassination than we have ever had about any previous historical event." This makes the silence around this revelation even more shocking.

This shock is accentuated when one is reminded (or told for the first time) that in 1999 a Memphis jury, after a thirty-day trial with over seventy witnesses, found the U.S. government guilty in the killing of MLK.

In that 1999 Memphis civil trial (see complete transcript at ratical.org) brought by the King family, the jury found that King was murdered by a conspiracy that included governmental agencies.[7] The corporate media, when they reported it at all, dismissed the jury's verdict and those who accepted it, including the entire King family led by Coretta Scott King,[8] as delusional. *Time* magazine called the verdict a confirmation of the King family's "lurid fantasies." The *Washington Post* compared those who believed it with those who claimed that Hitler was unfairly accused of genocide. A smear campaign ensued that has continued to the present day and then the fact that this trial ever occurred disappeared down the memory hole so that today most people still assume MLK was killed by a crazy white racist, James Earl Ray, if they know even that.

The civil trial was the King family's last resort to get a public hearing to disclose the truth of the assassination. They and Pepper knew and proved that Ray was an innocent pawn, but Ray nonetheless died in prison in 1998 after trying for thirty years to get another trial to further prove his innocence. During all these years, Ray had maintained that he had been manipulated by a shadowy figure named Raul, who had supplied him with money and his white Mustang and coordinated all his complicated travels, including having him buy a rifle and come to Jim's Grill and the

---

7 For an overview of the trial with links back into the court transcript see Jim Douglass, "The Martin Luther King Conspiracy Exposed in Memphis," *Probe Magazine,* Spring 2000. Apart from the courtroom participants, Douglass was one of only two people who attended the entire thirty-day trial.

8 See Transcript of the King Family Press Conference on the Martin Luther King Assassination Conspiracy Trial Verdict, Atlanta, Georgia, December 9, 1999.

boarding house on the day of the assassination to give it to Raul. The government has always denied Raul existed. Pepper proved that that was a lie.

Slowly, however, glimmers of light have been shed on that trial and truth of the assassination.

On March 30, 2018, *The Washington Post*'s crime reporter, Tom Jackman, published a four-column front-page article, "Who killed Martin Luther King, Jr.? His family believes James Earl Ray was framed." While not close to an endorsement of the Memphis trial's conclusions, it is a far cry from past nasty dismissals of those who agreed with the jury's verdict as conspiracy nuts or Hitler supporters. After decades of clouding over the truth of MLK's assassination, some rays of truth have come peeping through, and on the front page of the *WP* at that.

Jackman makes it very clear that all the surviving King family members—Bernice, Dexter, and Martin III—are in full agreement that James Earl Ray, the accused assassin, did not kill their father, and that there was and continues to be a conspiracy to cover up the truth. He adds to that the words of the highly respected civil rights icon and now deceased U.S. Congressman from Georgia, Rep. John Lewis (D-Ga.), who said:

> I think there was a major conspiracy to remove Dr. King from the American scene,

and former U.N. ambassador and Atlanta mayor Andrew Young, who was with King at the Lorraine Motel when he was shot, who concurs:

> I would not accept the fact that James Earl Ray pulled the trigger, and that is all that matters.

Additionally, Jackman adds that Andrew Young emphasized that the assassination of King came after that of President Kennedy, Malcolm X, and a few months before that of Senator Robert Kennedy.

"We were living in a period of assassinations," he quotes Young as saying, a statement clearly intimating their linkages and coming from a widely respected and honorable man.

In the years leading up to Pepper's 1978 involvement in the MLK case, only a few lonely voices expressed doubts about the government's case, such as, Harold Weisberg's *Frame Up* in 1971 and Mark Lane and Dick Gregory's *Code Name "Zorro"* in 1977. While other lonely researchers dug deeper, most of the country put themselves and the case to sleep.

As with the assassinations of President Kennedy and his brother, Robert (two months after MLK), all evidence points to the construction of scapegoats to take the blame for government executions. The cases of Ray, Oswald, and Sirhan Sirhan all bear striking resemblances in the ways they were chosen and moved as pawns over long periods of time into positions where their only reactions could be stunned surprise when they were accused of the murders.

It took Pepper many years to piece together the essential truths, once he and Reverend Ralph Abernathy, Dr. King's associate, interviewed Ray in prison in 1978. The first giveaway that something was seriously amiss came with the 1976 House Select Committee on Assassinations' report on the King assassination. Led by Robert Blakey, suspect in his conduct of the other assassination inquiries, who had replaced Richard Sprague, who was deemed to be too independent, *"this multi-million-dollar investigation ignored or denied all evidence that raised the possibility that James Earl Ray was innocent,"* and that government forces might be involved. Pepper lists in his book over twenty such omissions that rival the absurdities of the magical thinking of the Warren Commission. The HSCA report became the template *"for all subsequent disinformation in print and visual examinations of this case"* for the past forty-two years.

Blocked at every turn by the authorities and unable to get Ray a trial, Pepper arranged an unscripted, mock TV trial that aired on April 4, 1993, the twenty-fifth anniversary of the assassination. Jurors were selected from a pool of U.S. citizens, a former U.S. Attorney and a federal judge served as prosecutor and judge, with Pepper serving as defense attorney. He presented extensive evidence clearly showing that authorities had withdrawn all security for King; that the state's chief witness was falling down drunk; that the alleged bathroom sniper's nest was empty right before the shot was fired; that three eyewitnesses, including the *New York Times*' Earl Caldwell, said that the shot came from the bushes behind the rooming house; and that two eyewitnesses saw Ray drive away in his white Mustang before the shooting, etc. The prosecution's feeble case was rejected by the jury that found Ray not guilty.

As with all Pepper's work on the case, the mainstream media responded with silence. And though this was only a TV trial, increasing evidence emerged that the owner of Jim's Grill, Loyd Jowers, was deeply involved in the assassination. Pepper dug deeper, and on December 16, 1993, Loyd Jowers appeared on ABC's *Primetime Live* that aired nationwide. Pepper writes:

> *Loyd Jowers cleared James Earl Ray, saying that he did not shoot MLK but that he, Jowers, had hired a shooter after he was approached by Memphis produce man Frank Liberto and paid $100,000 to facilitate the assassination. He also said that he had been visited by a man named Raul who delivered a rifle and asked him to hold it until arrangements were finalized. . . . The morning after the Primetime Live broadcast there was no coverage of the previous night's program, not even on ABC. . . . Here was a confession, on prime-time television, to involvement in one of the most heinous crimes in the history of the Republic, and virtually no American mass-media coverage.*

In the twenty-eight years since that confession, Pepper has worked tirelessly on the case and has uncovered a plethora of additional evidence that refutes the government's claims and indicts it and the media for a continuing cover-up. The evidence he has gathered, detailed and documented in *An Act of State* and *The Plot to Kill King*, proves that Martin Luther King was killed by a conspiracy masterminded by the U.S. government. The foundation of his case proving that was presented at the 1999 trial, while other supporting documentation was subsequently discovered.

Since the names and details involved make clear that, as with the murders of JFK and RFK, the conspiracy was very sophisticated with many moving parts organized at the highest level, I will just highlight a few of his findings in what follows.

- Pepper proves, through multiple witnesses, telephonic, and photographic evidence, that Raul existed, that his full name is Raul Coelho and that he was James Earl Ray's intelligence handler, who provided him with money and instructions from their first meeting in the Neptune Bar in Montreal, where Ray had fled in 1967 after his prison escape, until the day of the assassination. It was Raul who instructed Ray to return from Canada to the U.S. (an act that makes no sense for an escaped prisoner who had fled the country), gave him money for the white Mustang, helped him attain travel documents, and moved him around the country like a pawn on a chess board. The parallels to Lee Harvey Oswald are startling.

- He presents the case of Donald Wilson, a former FBI agent working out of the Atlanta office in 1968, who went with a senior colleague to check out an abandoned white Mustang with Alabama plates (Ray's car, to which Raul had a set of keys) and opened the passenger door to find that an envelope and some papers fell out onto the ground. Thinking he may have disturbed a crime scene, the nervous Wilson pocketed them. Later, when he read them, their explosive content intuitively told him that if he gave them to his superiors they would be destroyed. One piece was a torn-out page from a 1963 Dallas telephone directory with the name Raul written at the top, and the letter "J" with a Dallas telephone number for a club run by Jack Ruby, Oswald's killer. The page was for the letter H and had numerous phone numbers for H. L. Hunt, Dallas oil billionaire and a friend of FBI Director J. Edgar Hoover. Both men hated MLK. The second sheet contained Raul's name and a list of names and sums and dates for payment. On the third sheet was written the telephone number and extension for the Atlanta FBI office. (Read James W. Douglass's important interview with Donald Wilson in *The Assassinations*, pp. 479–91.)

- Pepper shows that the alias Ray was given and used from July 1967 until April 4, 1968—Eric Galt—was the name of a Toronto U.S. Army Intelligence operative, Eric St. Vincent Galt, who worked for Union Carbide with Top Secret clearance. The warehouse at the Canadian Union Carbide Plant in Toronto that Galt supervised "housed a top-secret munitions project funded jointly by the CIA, the U.S. Naval Surface Weapons Center, and the Army Electronics Research and Development Command. . . . In August 1967, Galt met with Major Robert M. Collins, a top aide to the head of the 902nd Military Intelligence Group (MIG), Colonel John Downie." Downie selected four members for an Alpha 184 Sniper Unit that was sent to Memphis to back up the primary assassin of MLK. Meanwhile, Ray, set up as the scapegoat, was able to move about freely since he was protected by the pseudonymous NSA clearance for Eric Galt.

- To refute the government's claim that Ray and his brother robbed the Alton, Illinois bank to finance his travels and car purchase (rather than Raul, whom the government claimed never existed), Pepper "called the sheriff in Alton and the president of the bank; they gave the same statement. The Ray brothers had nothing to do with the robbery. No one from the HSCA, the FBI, or *The New York Times* had sought their opinion." CNN later reiterated the bank robbery claim that became part of the official false story.

- Pepper shows that the fatal shot came from the bushes behind Jim's Grill and the rooming house, not from the bathroom window. He presents overwhelming evidence for this, showing that the government's claim, based on the testimony of a severely drunk Charlie Stephens, was absurd. His evidence includes the testimony of numerous eyewitnesses and that of

Loyd Jowers (a nine-and-a-half-hour deposition), the owner of Jim's Grill, who said he joined another person in the bushes, and after the shot was fired to kill King, he brought the rifle back into the Grill through the back door. Thus, Ray was not the assassin.

- He presents conclusive evidence that the bushes were cut down the morning after the assassination in an attempt to corrupt the crime scene. The order to do so came from Memphis Police Department Inspector Sam Evans to Maynard Stiles, a senior administrator of the Memphis Department of Public Works.

- He shows how King's room was moved from a safe interior room, 201, to balcony room, 306, on the upper floor; how King was conveniently positioned alone on the balcony by members of his own entourage for the easy mortal head shot from the bushes across the street. (Many people only remember the iconic photograph taken after-the-fact with Jesse Jackson, Andrew Young, et al., standing over the fallen King and pointing across the street.) He uncovers the role of black Memphis Police Department Domestic Intelligence and military intelligence agent Marrell McCollough, attached to the 111th MIG, within the entourage. McCollough can be seen kneeling over the fallen King, checking to see if he's dead. McCollough officially joined the CIA in 1974 (see Douglass Valentine's "Deconstructing Kowalski: The DOJ's Strange MLK Report."

- Pepper confirms that all of this, including that the assassin in the bushes was dutifully photographed by Army Intelligence agents situated on the nearby Fire House roof.

- He presents evidence that all security for Dr. King was withdrawn from the area by the Memphis Police Department, including a special security unit of black officers, and four tactical police units. A black detective at the nearby fire station, Ed Redditt was withdrawn from his post on the afternoon of April 4, allegedly because of a death threat against him.

And the only two black firemen at Fire Station No. 2 were transferred to another station.

- He confirms the presence of "Operation Detachment Alpha 184 team," a Special Forces sniper team in civilian disguise at locations high above the Lorraine Motel balcony, and he names one soldier, John D. Hill, as part of Alpha 184 and another military team, Selma Twentieth SFG, that was in Memphis.
- He explains the use of two white mustangs in the operation to frame Ray.
- He proves that Ray had driven off before the shooting; that Lloyd Jowers took the rifle from the shooter who was in the bushes; that the Memphis police were working in close collaboration with the FBI, Army Intelligence, and the "Dixie Mafia," particularly local produce dealer Frank Liberto and his New Orleans associate Carlos Marcello; and that every aspect of the government's case was filled with holes that any person familiar with the details and possessing elementary logical abilities could refute.
- So importantly, Pepper shows how the mainstream media and government flacks have spent years covering up the truth of MLK's murder through lies and disinformation, just as they have done with the Kennedy and Malcom X assassinations that are of a piece with this one.

There is such a mass of evidence through depositions, documents, interviews, photographs, etc. in Pepper's *An Act of State* and *The Plot to Kill King* that makes it abundantly clear that the official explanation that James Earl Ray killed Martin Luther King is false and that there was a conspiracy to assassinate him that involved the FBI and other government agencies. Only those inoculated against the truth can ignore such evidence and continue to believe the official version.

Martin Luther King was a transmitter of a radical non-violent spiritual and political energy so plenipotent that his very existence was a threat to an established order based on institutionalized violence, racism, and economic exploitation. He was a very dangerous man to the U.S. government and all the institutional and deep state forces armed against him.

Revolutionaries are, of course, anathema to the power elites who, with all their might, resist such rebels' efforts to transform society. If they can't buy them off, they knock them off. Fifty-three years after King's assassination, the causes he fought for—civil rights, the end to U.S. wars of aggression, and economic justice for all—remain not only unfulfilled, but have worsened in so many respects.

They will not be resolved until this nation decides to confront the truth of why and by whom he was killed.

It was the government that honors Dr. King with a national holiday that killed him. This is the suppressed truth behind the highly promoted MLK Day of service. It is what you are not supposed to know.

But it is what we need to know in order to resurrect his spirit in us, so we can carry on his mission and emulate his witness.

The time is now.

Mr. Blue and the CIA

"This is slavery, not to speak one's thoughts"
—EURIPIDES, *The Phoenician Women*

Some time ago on a Sunday evening when my wife and I had just sat down to dinner, our phone rang. Since I didn't recognize the phone number and it was dinnertime, I hesitated to answer it, but for some chance reason I did. The voice on the other end was agitated, intense, and asked for me.

Could he visit immediately because he had urgent news for me, he asked. He told me his name, one I was not familiar with, and said he was a big fan of my book, *Seeking Truth in a Country of Lies* —that he had read it numerous times. He wondered how I knew so much about the workings of what we might call the deep state, the power elite, the intelligence/moneyed class connections, the assassinations of JFK, RFK, et al. He had also read a newspaper Op Ed I had written about Robert F. Kennedy, Jr. and wished to talk to me about that as well. He said he had a very important story to tell me. The urgency in his voice was palpable.

Naturally I was wary, so I put him off for a few days. But New England is a relatively small area, the home to so many of the country's ultra-wealthy families and the traditional Blue Blood ruling power structure, and the little bit he had told me about himself intrigued me. So a few days later I travelled to meet him where he lived, not wanting to open my home to an unknown visitor. On the way I realized that his last name did ring a bell and it was one connected to important U.S. history of the 1960s. For reasons of privacy, I will not disclose his name.

Call him Mr. Blue. Like Dylan did. As I did:

> This is out of the blue,
> In the wink of an eye.
> No conspiracy that I know of,
> Though something on that order
> Is not impossible. Between me
> And you I would say it flows.
> No sense in telling them
> What we are up to, or why.
> We don't know ourselves, do we?
> Who cares, the knowing is overrated.
> What is this, school we are still in,
> Or haven't we graduated to the world
> Of living? Out of the blue,
> In the wink of an eye,
> Long before we know it,
> But not after, never after.

We arranged to meet in a café, but when we did, he asked to converse away from the cafe on a bench in the open air instead. The first thing he said to me was that he was not CIA. I took that in two ways: he was and he wasn't. But I said little and listened to his story, even while questioning myself for agreeing to meet a stranger after such a bizarre phone call. I was glad not to be sitting over cups of coffee.

He began by telling me about his Blue Blood family heritage, how his family was connected to all the prominent wealthy families whose names are very familiar to many people: the Forbes, Morgans, Choates, Rockefellers, et.al., an index of The Social Register of old money and high society well-connected to all the levers of political and economic power. Primarily based in the northeastern United States, their tentacles stretch around the world because of their power and influence. They attend Yale, Harvard, Princeton and the elite New England prep schools. They have long held important positions in the media, government, and Wall Street. In short, his family was part of what C. Wright Mills termed "the power elite," and as he made clear, he and the children of these families were brought up to assume they were born to make the major decisions for the country. To rule.

But Mr. Blue said he always felt like an outsider even while being an insider in this family nexus. He seemed burdened with guilt for something, and as he told a long story I became a bit impatient, waiting for the crux of the pressing news he wanted to convey to me. But I listened silently.

He told me about some of what he has done over the decades, which was good work trying to repair the damage caused by major corporations. It seemed to me he did this as a way of atoning for his family's sins. I would interrupt him from time to time to ask a point of clarification about some connection between the people he mentioned and their links to U.S. government agencies or the well-known media people connected to his family. He was very forthright in his answers. I grew to trust him the more he talked.

After about an hour, I asked him to please tell me the urgent news he had phoned about. It concerned the assassination of Robert F. Kennedy in 1968. He said he told RFK, Jr. decades ago that the CIA killed his father. This, he said, he learned two days after the assassination from a relative who was a CIA officer. This relative said to him in person, "We knew." When I asked him what that meant, he told me it meant that the CIA had killed Senator Kennedy. Then he traced this relative's connections through the military-intelligence-industrial-political-wealth complex and how it all wound through his family's history and the prominent families he was connected to. He named many names, including the CIA relative. I wasn't surprised by all the interconnections, for they confirmed what I already knew about the upper echelons of power and money. But this was the first time that an insider told me personally, and I kept marveling at their extent and how the names were connected to key events in U.S. history, particularly those involving the intelligence agencies.

We were sitting in a town deeply steeped in the famous names and historic mansions of the old money elites, and as he talked, I kept drawing on my knowledge of these people, which was not just academic but based on personal experience. We were sitting in the heart of the place where these traditional ruling elites congregated and socialized.

In another similar New England town years before, I had heard endless stories told to me by the famous theologian Reinhold Niebuhr's widow, Ursula Niebuhr, who was a big name dropper, and liked to point out all the Niebuhrs'elite connections. (Niebuhr was the most famous U.S. theologian of the 20th century; his photo appeared on the cover of Time magazine; he influenced politicians of many stripes; was quoted approvingly and often by Barack Obama and even John McCain; in short, he was the establishment's God-man during the Cold War and a theological underpinning for the neoliberal warfare state.) She would regularly note how so-and so, her friend and local resident (usually these people had their massive summer homes in addition to city residences)—e.g. Adolph Berle, an intelligence officer in WW I, a member of FDR's original Brain Trust, Ambassador, Columbia law professor, power broker involved in above and below board foreign intrigue, Cold Warrior—did this and that, etc. For some reason she shared with me much of her inside knowledge of her elite "friends" as if I shared her values, which I didn't. It must have been my theological background. And I guess playing dumb helped. But I listened—and learned in doing so—that people will tell you many things you may or may not want to hear if they think you are receptive. Her stories about some of the most famous people of the 20th century—Einstein, T.S. Eliot, her Princeton associates, et al., always referred to by their first names—told me much about the workings of the power elites. Sometimes the stories were weirdly funny if not revealing of something else.

At lunch with her son Christopher one day, she told me about her "friend" (all the famous people were "friends") the famous German-American psychoanalyst Erik Erikson. She said he encouraged her husband Reinhold to stop smoking cigarettes by turning to Danish cigarillos. She quoted him as saying: "Remember what Freud said, Reinhold: 'It's been a long time since I had something hot and wet between my lips.'" I was taken aback by this seventy-five year-old woman saying this, knowing as I did that Freud smoked cigars his whole life.

But it was typical of a type of double entendre that she often gave about her elite associates that opened my eyes to the inner workings of a social class I was not familiar with. I took note of all of it and drew connections between various organizations these elites were involved with, many of which at first blush one would not think were involved in their power operations, such as conservation and nature groups, organizations allegedly formed to fight corporate misdeeds, etc. For decades after, I have come to see more connections than seemed possible, and many in a small geographic area but all connected to the upper class elites and their control of land, resources, and media outlets.

Mr. Blue confirmed all this and more. He told me about the Cold War bomb shelters under the mansions of his and other wealthy families, the connections between the CIA and corporations, how those seen as the "good guys" were really working for the bad guys, that CIA and Mossad operatives would contact him under the assumption he was on their side, the seamless socializing between all the elite families with so many names and places connected to operations of "deep state" operators—the stuff I have been researching for years and the subject of much of my recent book. Mr. Blue corroborated for me the essence of what I had discovered through my own work. And as I told him, I did it by studying, researching, and listening, something anyone could do if so inclined.

Weeks after our first meeting, Mr. Blue agreed to meet again, this time together with me and a documentary filmmaker. He told all the same stories, elaborating on many of them and adding others. He was loose and easy and we talked for nearly five hours. At one point, when I asked him to repeat what he had told me weeks before about his CIA relative and what that relative meant by the phrase "We knew" about the RFK assassination, and Mr. Blue had then told me that he meant that the CIA had killed Kennedy, he jumped to say, "I never said that." This denial startled me. But he had said it. After our initial conversation, I had written his exact words in my notes before driving home. And he had also said that he told RFK, Jr. that the CIA killed his father. This was the only time during our long conversation that he grew very agitated.

This was obviously the one revelation that scared him among all the other stories he shared. I understand his fear. But time is relentless; we run out of it. There comes that day when it is too late to find your public tongue. It is why he remains Mr. Blue, an anonymous good man caught in a family history for which he has tried to atone. An outsider on the inside still, calling to be heard by another person, in the wink of an eye, out of the blue.

Perhaps someday he will tell the world. I am still waiting for him to change his mind.

Rise Up, Say the Birds to the Bread

It was early morning on St. Patrick's Day and I was sitting in the kitchen eating a few slices of delicious Irish Soda Bread. My wife had made it at 5 A.M. while I was still in bed half-asleep, but its smell wafting through the rooms induced me to get up. From outside the window came the sound of mourning doves cooing and crows playing their little raw saxophones.

It's not every day that such an invitation to awaken arrives through the air. Some people are never so invited and others refuse the call, but the bread is always rising, if only we knew it.

The bread is always rising.

The Irish soda bread's smell and taste with my coffee was extremely sensuous and brought me back to our time in Ireland long before the world was locked down by the machine people into a virtual world in front of screens because of coronavirus. The bread was real, not virtual. I felt as though for a few slow hours I would luxuriate in the silence and allow my mind to go on vacation and wander through the narrow lanes of reverie and memory.

My wife, Jeanne Lemlin, a James Beard Award–winning cookbook writer, had created the recipe after visiting the bakery department at Field's supermarket in Skibbereen, County Cork, where she observed Dennis McSweeney and his staff preparing their breads in the early morning.

I was returning to my Irish rebel roots, thinking of how my ancestors rose up against their oppressors, the British colonizers. How those Irish rebels became an inspiration for colonized people around the world. How the enslaved and oppressed need the bread of hope.

The bread is always rising. Can you hear its music?

By being lost in reverie, I was violating the terms the machine people have laid down for us to start and spend and end each day in fear and trembling.

They are the experts who, as the English essayist Adam Philips has said, "construct the terror, and then the terror makes them expert."

Contrarian that I am, I refuse to be terrorized, now or later. For twenty years, the U.S. government "experts" have lied about Muslim terrorists coming to get us as they have killed millions of innocent Muslims around the world.

Now it's an invisible virus that has arrived to slay us.

Of course, the Russians are always coming to get us, but they are very slow; they've been coming for at least eighty years and the lies about them continue. Here they come again!

It is just an odd happenstance that each of these three terrors has in its turn resulted in further losses of freedoms and increased "emergency" powers for the government. We all know why the caged bird sings.

Freedom is under assault.

Outside on a large tree I see nine black vultures looking my way. Behind them in the sky are another four or five soaring majestically. The birds have recently returned after wintering farther south. They roost in the tall pine streets on the other side of the house. They are beautifully ugly.

Love is a mystery.

Their return gives me hope, as did the red-tailed hawks we saw the other morning doing clasped talon barrel-rolls as a bald eagle sailed before them. So too the little multi-colored moth I saw on the outside glass of the door yesterday. And the two insects that came up the drain into the kitchen sink. These little ones had no fear, although their chances of surviving cold nights and water were slim. But they took the risk of death as the world slowly rises into new life. All creation conspires toward resurrection in the spring.

But the machine people, like the colonizers and oppressors, are intent on burying us for good. They want to destroy our spirits through fear and falsehoods. They planted their seeds long ago. If we buy their poisonous fruit, we will reap what we sow.

"What," wrote Thomas Hobbes in the seventeenth century, "is the heart but a spring, and the nerves so many strings, and the joints so many wheels, giving motion to the whole body."

Now they want to make us all into machines, obedient artificial intelligence cyborgs, conspiring in our own enslavement. The only birds the machine people like are drones, satellites, war planes, flying missiles and bullets. They have filled the earth with the blood of the innocent, the blood that doesn't stop running. They have contaminated the air. They have filled it with electronic noise, the unheard cacophony of billions of desperadoes talking from their cells, caged and clipped-winged birds talking of the unknown. Lost in cyberspace while thinking they are free and grateful for the little talking machines the rulers have deemed to give them. Their cells.

The machine people have set their traps to capture any wild birds left. They want to inject them with their poisonous vaccines, to brand and band them as fit for further torture and control within a totally digitized world. The medical bureaucrats and their controllers create categories to which they assign people so that they can grant them permission to do or not do various human activities that are their natural rights. As Ivan Illich tells us in his classic *Medical Nemesis,* the template for this was set down more than two-and-a-half centuries ago:

> On November 5, 1766, the Empress Maria Theresa issued an edict requesting the court physician to certify fitness to undergo torture so as to ensure healthy, i.e. "accurate," testimony; it was one of the first laws to establish mandatory medical certification.

But out of the blue, like a wayward thought, last night's dream came to me while I was just typing those words.

In my dream, I went down to the basement of the house I grew up in. It was dark but I could see a large bird sitting on the floor. It startled me by its still presence. Off to the side stood the poet Allen Ginsberg, and next to him was a coffin. In the coffin was a blue-eyed man in a blue shirt. The man was me. Ginsberg said the man needed my help with his contact lenses, for they were preventing him from seeing clearly. So I spit on my fingers and removed his contact lenses so he could see. In each of his eyes a cross appeared. I heard the bird rustle and turned to see it stand up. It opened its huge wings and its feathers revealed dazzling colors when it fluttered them open and closed. The man rose from the coffin and smiled. I woke up.

It's not believable of course, although it's true, even if you think I just made it up, which I didn't. Dream and reality—what are they? In memory I can vaguely hear T.S. Eliot's words:

> Go, said the bird, for the leaves were full of children,
> Hidden excitedly, containing laughter.
> Go, go, go, said the bird: human kind
> Cannot bear very much reality.

Loren Eiseley, the great naturalist/scientist and enchanting writer, wrote in his 1959 essay, "The Bird and the Machine," that "I learned there [on an isolated expedition to the western American desert to capture birds—which he never did—circa 1910] that time is a series of planes existing superficially in the same universe. The tempo is a human illusion, a subjective clock ticking in our own kind of protoplasm."

Which is to say that the night country we inhabit when asleep and our day hours cross over in the same consciousness to create the strange human creatures that we are. We generally prefer to dismiss the night like the birds that keep watch on us because we have learned to think of ourselves as Hobbesian machines who live by clocks under the watchful embrace of the rational experts who tell us we are indeed "the incredible human machine[s]."

They lie. We are flesh and blood and bones, like our friends, the birds. There are profound reasons why birds and bread have held such important places in people's spiritual lives and imaginations for thousands of years. They symbolize our human solidarity in the breaking of bread and our need for freedom in the winged beauty and song of birds in flight.

Despite their moribund philosophy, the machine people can never defeat these two human realities. At the still point of the turning world, where past and future are gathered up in the music of the dance, their mechanical philosophies will be defeated.

I am going out for a walk now, up by the lake above the town and the railroad tracks, but in the spirit of that Irish soda bread and the Irish rebel spirit, I suggest that you listen to the song that I listened to on the evening of March 17 when I toasted my friends the black vultures with a glass of Guinness as they soared high in the evening sky above the mountains here. It is Van Morrison's "The Beauty of the Days Gone By."

Opening the CIA's Can of Worms

"The CIA and the media are part of the same criminal conspiracy," wrote Douglas Valentine in his important book, *The CIA As Organized Crime.*

This is true. The corporate mainstream media are stenographers for the national security state's ongoing psychological operations aimed at the American people, the same as they have done for an international audience. We have long been subjected to this "information warfare," whose purpose is to win the hearts and minds of the American people and pacify them into being victims of their own complicity, just as it was practiced long ago by the CIA in Vietnam and by *The New York Times,* the *Washington Post, CBS,* etc. on the American people then and over the years as the American warfare state waged endless wars, coups, false flag operations, and assassinations at home and abroad.

Another way of putting this is to say that, for all practical purposes when it comes to matters that bear on important foreign and domestic matters, the roles that the CIA and the corporate mainstream media play cannot be distinguished from each other.

For those who read and study history, it has long been known that the CIA has placed their operatives throughout every agency of the U.S. government, as explained by Fletcher Prouty in *The Secret Team*; that CIA officers Cord Myer and Frank Wisner operated secret programs to get some of the most vocal exponents of intellectual freedom among intellectuals, journalists, and writers to be their voices for unfreedom and censorship, as explained by Frances Stonor Saunders in *The Cultural Cold War* and Joel Whitney in *Finks*, among others; that Cord Myer was especially focused on and successful in "courting the Compatible Left" since right wingers were already in the Agency's pocket. All this is documented and not disputed. It is shocking only to those who don't do their homework.

With the rise of alternate media and a wide array of dissenting voices on the Internet, the establishment felt threatened and went on the defensive. It therefore should come as no surprise that those same elite corporate media are now leading the charge for increased censorship and the denial of free speech to those they deem dangerous, whether that involves wars, rigged elections, foreign coups, COVID-19, vaccinations, or the lies of the corporate media themselves. Having already banned critics from writing in their pages and or talking on their screens, these media giants want to make the stilling of dissenting voices complete.

Just the other day *The New York Times* had this headline: "Robert Kennedy, Jr. is barred from Instagram over false virus claims." Notice the lack of the word alleged before "false virus claims." No evidence for their falsity is given. This is guilt by headline. It is a perfect piece of propaganda posing as reporting, since it accuses Kennedy of falsity and stupidity, thus justifying the Instagram's ban, and it is an inducement to further censorship of Mr. Kennedy by Facebook that owns Instagram. That ban should follow soon, as *Times*' reporter Jennifer Jett hopes, since she accusingly writes that RFK, Jr. "makes many of the same baseless claims to more than 300,000 followers" at Facebook. Jett made sure her report also went to msn.com and *The Boston Globe*.

This is one example of the censorship underway with much, much more to follow. What was once done under the cover of omission is now done openly and brazenly, cheered on by those who, in an act of bad faith, still claim to be upholders of the First Amendment and the importance of free debate in a democracy. We are quickly slipping into an unreal totalitarian social order.

Which brings me to the recent work of Glenn Greenwald and Matt Taibbi, both of whom have strongly and rightly decried this censorship. As I understand their arguments, they go like this.

First, the corporate media have today divided up the territory and speak only to their own audiences in echo chambers: liberal to liberals (read: the "allegedly" liberal Democratic Party), such as *The New York Times*, NBC, etc., and conservative to conservatives (read: the "allegedly" conservative Donald Trump), such as Fox News, Breitbart, etc. They have abandoned old school journalism that, despite its shortcomings, involved objectivity and the reporting of disparate facts and perspectives, but within limits. Since the digitization of news, their new business models are geared to these separate audiences since they are highly lucrative choices. It's business driven since electronic media have replaced paper as advertising revenues have shifted and people's ability to focus on complicated issues has diminished drastically. Old school journalism is suffering as a result and thus writers such as Greenwald and Taibbi and Chris Hedges (who interviewed Taibbi and concurs) have taken their work to the internet to escape such restrictive categories and the accompanying censorship.

Secondly, the great call for censorship is not something the Silicon Valley companies want because they want more people using their media since it means more money for them, but they are being pressured to do it by the traditional old school media, such as *The New York Times*, who now employ "tattletales and censors," people who are power hungry jerks, to sniff out dissenting voices that they can recommend should be banned. Greenwald says, "They do it in part for power: to ensure nobody but they can control the flow of information. They do it partly for ideology and out of hubris: the belief that their worldview is so indisputably right that all dissent is inherently dangerous 'disinformation.'" Thus, the old-school print and television media are not on the same page as Facebook, Twitter, etc., but have opposing agendas.

In short, these shifts and the censorship are about money and power within the media world as the business has been transformed by the digital revolution.

I think this is a half-truth that conceals a larger issue. The censorship is not being driven by power hungry reporters at the *Times* or *CNN* or any media outlet. All these media and their employees are but the outer layer of the onion, the means by which messages are sent and people controlled. These companies and their employees do what they are told, whether explicitly or implicitly, for they know it is in their financial interest to do so. If they do not play their part in this twisted and intricate propaganda game, they will suffer. They will be eliminated, as are pesky individuals who dare peel the onion to its core. For each media company is one part of a large, interconnected intelligence apparatus—a system, a complex—whose purpose is power, wealth, and domination for the very few at the expense of the many. The CIA and media are parts of the same criminal conspiracy.

To argue that the Silicon Valley companies do not want to censor but are being pressured by the legacy corporate media does not make sense. These companies are deeply connected to U.S. intelligence agencies, as are the *NY Times, CNN, NBC,* etc. They too are part of what was once called Operation Mockingbird, the CIA's program to control, use, and infiltrate the media. Only the most naïve would think that such a program does not exist today.

In *Surveillance Valley,* investigative reporter Yasha Levine documents how Silicon Valley tech companies like Facebook, Amazon, and Google are tied to the military-industrial-intelligence-media complex in surveillance and censorship; how the Internet was created by the Pentagon; and even how these shadowy players are deeply involved in the so-called privacy movement that developed after Edward Snowden's revelations. Like Valentine, and in very detailed ways, Levine shows how the military-industrial-intelligence-digital-media complex is part of the same criminal conspiracy as the traditional media with its CIA overlords. They are all in one club.

Many people, however, might find this hard to believe because it bursts so many bubbles, including the one that claims that these tech companies are pressured into censorship by the likes of T*he New York Times*, etc. The truth is the Internet was a military and intelligence tool from the very beginning, and it is not the traditional corporate media that gives it its marching orders.

That being so, it is not the owners of the corporate media or their employees who are the ultimate controllers behind the current vast crackdown on dissent, but the intelligence agencies who control the mainstream media and the Silicon Valley monopolies such as Facebook, Twitter, Google, etc. All these media companies are but the outer layer of the onion, the means by which messages are sent and people controlled.

But for whom do these intelligence agencies work? Not for themselves.

They work for their overlords, the super wealthy people, the banks, financial institutions, and corporations that own the United States and always have. In a simple twist of fate, or it "just so happens," as some like to say, such super wealthy naturally own the media corporations that are essential to their control of the majority of the world's wealth through the stories they tell. It is a symbiotic relationship. As FDR put it bluntly in 1933, this coterie of wealthy forces is the "financial element in the larger centers [that] has owned the Government ever since the days of Andrew Jackson." Their wealth and power have increased exponentially since then, and their connected tentacles have further spread to create what is an international deep state that involves such entities as the IMF, the World Bank, the World Economic Forum, those who meet yearly at Davos, etc. They are the international overlords who are pushing hard to move the world toward a global dictatorship.

As is well known, or should be, the CIA was the creation of Wall St. and serves the interests of its wealthy owners. Peter Dale Scott, in *The State, the Deep-State, and the Wall St. Overworld*, says of Allen Dulles, the nefarious longest running Director of the CIA and Wall St. lawyer for Sullivan and Cromwell, "There seems to be little difference in Allen Dulles's influence whether he was a Wall Street lawyer or a CIA director." It was Dulles, long connected to Rockefeller's Standard Oil, international corporations, and a friend of Nazi agents and scientists, who was tasked with drawing up proposals for the CIA. He was ably assisted by five Wall St. bankers or investors, including the aforementioned Frank Wisner who later, as a CIA officer, said his "Mighty Wurlitzer" was "capable of playing any propaganda tune he desired." This he did by recruiting intellectuals, writers, reporters, labor organizations, and the mainstream corporate media, etc. to propagate the CIA's messages.

Greenwald, Taibbi, and Hedges are correct up to a point, but they stop short. Their critique of old school journalism à la Edward Herman and Noam Chomsky's *Manufacturing of Consent* model, while true as far as it went, fails to pin the tail on the real donkey. Like old school journalists who knew implicitly how far they could go, these guys know it too, as if there is an invisible electronic gate that keeps them from wandering into dangerous territory.

The censorship of Robert Kennedy, Jr. is an exemplary case. His banishment from Instagram and the ridicule the mainstream media have heaped upon him for years is not simply because he raises deeply informed questions about vaccines, Bill Gates, the pharmaceutical companies, etc. His critiques suggest something far more dangerous is afoot: the demise of democracy and the rise of a totalitarian order that involves total surveillance, control, eugenics, etc. by the wealthy led by their intelligence propagandists.

To call him a super spreader of hoaxes and a conspiracy theorist is aimed not only at silencing him on specific medical issues, but to silence his powerful and articulate voice on many other issues. To give thoughtful consideration to his deeply informed scientific critique concerning vaccines, the World Health Organization, the Bill and Melinda Gates Foundation, etc., is to open a can of worms that the powerful want shut tight.

This is because RFK, Jr. is also a severe critic of the enormous power of the CIA and its propaganda that goes back so many decades and was used to cover up the national security state's assassinations of his father and uncle, JFK. This is why his wonderful recent book, *American Values: Lessons I Learned from My Family*, that contains not one word about vaccines, was shunned by mainstream book reviewers; the picture he paints fiercely indicts the CIA in multiple ways while also indicting the mass media that have been its mouthpieces. These worms must be kept in the can, just as must the power of the international overlords represented by the World Health Organization and the World Economic Forum with its Great Reset. Such understandings must be dismissed as crackpot conspiracy theories not worthy of debate or exposure.

With the key exception of his full support for Israel in their long-term killing and persecution of Palestinians, Robert Kennedy, Jr conjures up his father's ghost, the last politician who, because of his vast support across racial and class divides, could have united the country and tamed the power of the CIA to control the narrative that has allowed for the plundering of the world and the country for the wealthy overlords.

So they killed Senator Kennedy.

The question remains: Will RFK, Jr. continue to oppose CIA control or will he succumb, as he has done with his support for the Zionist cause in Israel, to the Agency's pressure?

There is a reason Noam Chomsky is an exemplar for Hedges, Greenwald, and Taibbi. He controls the can opener for so many. He has set the parameters for what are considered acceptable views in order to be considered a serious journalist or intellectual. The assassinations of the Kennedys, 9/11, or a questioning of the official COVID-19 story are not among them, and so they are eschewed.

To denounce censorship, as they have done, is admirable. But now Greenwald, Taibbi, and Hedges need go up to the forbidden gate with the sign that says—"This far and no further"—and jump over it. That's where the true stories lie. That's when they'll see the worms squirm.

The Invincible Green Stick of Happiness

After a night of haunting dreams that flowed as if they were written like running water, written on air, as the Roman poet Catullus once said, in the depth of a dark winter morning, I decided that I would take a walk in the afternoon, hoping that the sun would then appear, and it did, so I went walking toward the woods through deep white new-fallen snow all around me and entered a path into the woods across from my house that led toward a deep ravine below which were deep dark caves that once sheltered runaway slaves searching for the happiness of freedom, and I thought of them as I poked under the snow on the odd chance that I might find the green stick of happiness that Leo Tolstoy's beloved brother, ten-year-old Nikolai, had once told the five-year-old Leo was buried by a ravine on the edge of the forest, a stick upon which were written the secret words that would bring love, peace, and happiness to everyone, and would do away with death, for their mother had died three years earlier and their father would die four years later, but I saw nothing and continued deeper into the forest to try to shed a sad feeling from a lockdown that had brought my spirits low as I tried to understand why so many people I knew were so enslaved, their minds forged in manacles, and how sad and dispirited it made me knowing that they were locked away from me in some conventional reality sold to them by liars, but perhaps you like the word depressed and you can use it if you want, but all I know is that the spirit of happiness had escaped me as I trudged deeper into the forest between the high pine trees until the trail I walked was intersected by another and a man met me there, as if he knew I was coming, a man with a long white beard and piercing eyes and we nodded and then he continued beside me and asked me what I was looking for, which startled me, and I was speechless and he said he's been through here many times, especially by the ravine, and Leo told me he never could find the green stick of happiness his brother once told him was buried there but he was not giving up, he never would do that since he loved his brother who would never lie, he knew the stick existed and that's why he himself was buried there, and he told me to continue seeking, because the stick was real and yes, those slaves knew it and were in that ravine for a reason, so we walked on as a man approached us who said his name was Albert, and I said Camus, and he said yes, let's walk together guys, for these woods are dark and deep I know, but look up at the sky, the clouds have parted and the sparkling sky is speaking to us, right Leo, who said yes, I remember when Andrei in my book *War and Peace* lay wounded on the battlefield and looked at the sky, I wrote that he realized then that that lofty sky was infinite and that happiness was possible, that especially in the midst of battle you have to look up and realize that, that there are deeper reasons for things and petty concerns shield the spirit of truth and that even in the midst of war you can glimpse that reality, and it sounded good, I had heard their spiels before, or had read them to be accurate, they were great writers but this was my life and I couldn't live in their books, but I wasn't reading, I was walking, or was I dreaming, and then we came to the end of the path leading out of the woods and the sky opened out from the vast tree cover and they were gone and I was all alone again as usual, dispirited and heading back home on the road by the lake when I looked up at the sparkling blue sky and light that radiated off the snowy frozen lake and rose back to the sky in columns of undulating glory and felt the sun that had warmed the day and heard birds in the trees and was overwhelmed with a rush of happiness I can't describe but it was not a dream and I walked in joy for a few minutes, knowing I had found the stick and that in the depth of winter, as Albert said, I had finally learned that there was in me an invincible summer, but that it came and went like running water, like flowing air, but it was enough.

The Incantational Bewitchment of Propaganda

All propaganda succeeds because it satisfies needs that it has first created. If you follow the daily rat-a-tat mainstream news reports and react to them, you will be caught in a labyrinth that has been set to entrap you. You will keep finding that your mind will be like a bed that is already made up and your daylight hours filled with nightmares. What you assume are your real needs will be met, but you will swiftly tumble into the free-floating anxiety that the media has created to keep you on edge and confused. They will provide you with objects—COVID-19, the U.S. "withdrawal" from Afghanistan, the Russian and Chinese "threats," the need to crack down on domestic dissidents, 9/11, etc. (an endless panoply of lies)—that you can attach your anxiety to, but they will be no help. They are not meant to; their purpose is to befuddle; to make you more anxious by wondering if currently there is any contrast between the real world and the apparent one. The corporate mainstream media serve phantasmagoria on a 24/7 basis, all shifting like quicksand. For anyone with a modicum of common sense, this should be obvious. But then again, as Thoreau put it:

> The commonest sense is the sense of men asleep, which they express by snoring.

Perhaps some health expert will soon recommend that 24 hours of sleep a day is optimal, but maybe I am dreaming or being redundant.

For many decades, the corporate mainstream media and the CIA/NSA have been synonymous. They were married down in hell and now daily do the devil's work up above. Now that news is conveyed primarily through digital media via the internet, their power to induce electronic trances has increased exponentially. Linguistic and visual mind control is their raison d'être. Fear is their favorite tactic. And since the fear and anxiety of death is the archetypal source of all anxiety, death becomes a core element in their fearmongering.

In a recent powerful article, Canadian independent journalist Eva Bartlett, a brave and free war correspondent who has reported from inside Syria, Gaza, and Russia, has shown how the ongoing COVID-19 "fear porn" spewed out by the media has dramatically increased people's anxiety levels and thrown so many into a perpetual state of near panic. This, of course, is not an accident.

Fear immobilizes people and drives them into a cataleptic state where clear thinking is impossible. They become hypnotized in a "private" space that is actually social, an instantaneous identification with the media news reports that are addressed to millions but feel personal and greatly exacerbate the great loneliness that lies at the core of high-tech society.

As I have written before, the new digital order is the world of teleconferencing and the online life, existence shorn of physical space and time and people. A world where shaking hands is a dissident act. A haunted world of masked specters, distorted words and images that can appear and disappear in a nanosecond. A magic show. A place where, in the words of Charles Manson, you can "get the fear," where fear is king. A locus where, as you stare at the screens, you are no longer there since you are spellbound.

In a high-tech society, loneliness is far more prevalent than in the past. The technology has imprisoned people behind their screens and now the controlling forces are intent on closing this mechanistic circle if they can. They call it The Great Reset.

They have spent decades using technology to invade and pare down people's inner private space where freedom to think and decide resides.

They have repeated ad nauseam the materialistic mantra that freedom is an illusion and that we are amazing machines determined by our genes and social forces.

They have reiterated that God and the spiritual and transcendent realms are illusions.

And they have pushed their transhuman agenda to assert more and more power and control.

This is the essence of the corona crisis and the push to vaccinate everyone.

Drip by drip, year by year, they have cultivated the necessary preconditions and predispositions for this technological fascism with its nihilistic underpinnings to succeed.

When the inner dimension of existence is lost, there is no way to critique the outer world, its politics, and social structure. Dissent becomes a useless passion when people instantly identify with the social. Human nature doesn't change but social structures and technology do, and they can be used to try to destroy people's humanity. Herbert Marcuse put it clearly long before the latest digital technology:

> This immediate, automatic identification (which may have been characteristic of primitive forms of association) reappears in high industrial civilization; its new "immediacy," however, is the product of a sophisticated, scientific management and organization. In this process, the "inner" dimension of the mind in which opposition to the status quo can take root is whittled down. The loss of this dimension, in which the power of negative thinking—the critical power of Reason—is at home, is the ideological counterpart to the very material process in which advanced industrial society silences and reconciles the opposition.

Once upon a time, people sat together and talked. They even touched and shared their thoughts and feelings. They conspired in a most natural way apart from the prying eyes and ears of the electronic spies. Now so many sit and check their cell phones.

They "connect," thinking they are with it while not knowing they have been lured into another dimension where frenetic passivity reigns and trance states are the rule.

Propaganda provides a doorway to pseudo-community, a place to lose oneself in the group, to satisfy the need to believe and obey in mass technological society where emotional emptiness and lack of meaning are widespread and the need to fill up the empty self is dutifully met by propaganda, which is a drug by any other name, indeed the primary drug. The empty self craves fulfillment, anything to consume to fill the void that a consumer culture dangles everywhere. Think alike, buy alike, dress alike—and you will be one big happy community. It is all abstract of course, even as its rational character is irrational, but that doesn't matter a whit since the fear of "not going along" and appearing dissident plagues people.

Now we have endless digital propaganda that is the "remedy" for loneliness. Ah, all the lonely people, keeping their masks in a jar by the side of the door together with Eleanor Rigby. They think they know what their masks are for but don't know why they are lonely or that they have been played with. Masks upon masks are donned to ward off the fear that is pumped out through the electronic airwaves. It is doubtful that many ever heard of William Casey or can imagine the breadth and depth of the propaganda that he and his current protégés in the intelligence agencies and corporate media dispense daily.

A grim submissiveness has settled over the lives of millions of hypnotized people in so many countries. Grim, grim, grim, as Charles Dickens wrote of his 1842 visit to the puritanical Shaker religious sect in western Massachusetts. He said:

> I so abhor, and from my soul detest, that bad spirit, no matter by what class or sect it may be entertained, which would strip life of its healthful graces, rob youth of its innocent pleasures, pluck from maturity and age their pleasant ornaments, and make existence but a narrow path to the grave....

And yet, the fundamental things still do apply as time goes by. Love, glory, loneliness, beauty, fear, faith, and courage. Lovers and true artists, fighters both, resist this machine tyranny and its endless lies because they smell a rat intent on destroying their passionate love of the daring adventure that is life. They feel life is an agon, an arena for struggle, "a fight for love and glory," a case of do-and-die. They have bull-shit detectors and see through the elites' propaganda that is used to literally kill millions around the world and to kill the spirit of rebellion in so many others. And they know that it is in the inner sanctuary of every individual soul where resistance to evil is born and fear is defeated. They know too that the art and love must be shared and this is how social solidarity movements are created.

The Last Temptation of Things at the Lost and Found

"I cling like a miser to the freedom that disappears as soon as there is an excess of things."
—ALBERT CAMUS, *Lyrical and Critical Essays*

Let me tell you a story about a haunted house and all the thoughts it evoked in me.

Do we believe we can save ourselves by saving things?

Or do our saved possessions come to possess their saviors?

Do those who save many things or hoard believe that there are pockets in shrouds? Or do they collect things as a magical protection against the shroud?

These are questions that have preoccupied me for weeks as my wife and I have spent long and exhausting days cleaning out a friend's house. Many huge truckloads of possessions have been carted off to the dump. Thousands of documents have been shredded and thousands more taken to our house for further sorting. Other things have been donated to charity. This is what happens to people's things; they disappear, never to be seen again, just as we do, eventually.

Tolstoy wrote a story—"How Much Land Does A Man Need"—that ends with the answer: a piece six feet long, enough for your grave. As in this story, the devil always has the last laugh when your covetousness gets the best of you. Yet so many people continue to collect in the vain hope that they are exceptions. Ask almost anyone and they will reluctantly admit that they hoard to some degree.

In capitalist consumer societies, getting and spending and hoarding not only lay waste our powers, but it is done on the backs of the poor and destitute around the world. It is a system built to inflame the worst human tendencies of acquisitiveness and indifference since it teaches that one never has enough of everything. It denies the primal sympathy of human care for all humans as it teaches that if you surround yourself with enough things—have ten pair of shoes, twenty shirts, an attic filled with things in reserve—you will be safe from the fate of the majority of the world's poor who have next to nothing. It is an insidious form of soul murder wherein one pulls the shades on the prison-house, counts one's possessions, and shakes hands with the Devil. And it is sadly common.

From attic to cellar to garage, every little cubbyhole, closet, and drawer in this relative's house was filled with "saved" items. Nothing was ever thrown away. If you walked in the front door, you would never know that the occupants were compulsive keepers. While there were plenty of knick-knacks in evidence like so many houses where the fear of emptiness rules (the emptiness that is the source of freedom and creativity), once you opened a drawer or closet, a secreted lunacy spilled out seriatim like circus clowns from a small car. Like all clown shows, it was funny but far more frightening, as though all the saved objects were tinged with the fear of death and dissolution, were futile efforts to stop the flow of time and life by sticking a finger in a dike. All this stuff serving as an anchor to prevent them getting somehow "lost." But those who are never lost are forever lost.

Samuel Beckett's words come to mind: "Nothing is more real than nothing."

Let me begin with the bags. Hidden in every corner and closet, there were bags stuffed in bags. Big bags and little bags, hundreds if not thousands, used and unused, plastic, paper, cloth bags with price tags still on them. The same was true for boxes, especially empty jewelry boxes. Cardboard boxes that once held a little something, wooden boxes, cigar boxes, large cartons, boxes from every device ever purchased—all seemingly being saved for some future use that would never come. But the bags and boxes filled each other so that no emptiness could survive, although desolation seemed to cry out from within: "You can't suffocate me."

Tens of thousands of photographs and slides were squirreled into cabinets, closets, and their own file cabinets, each neatly marked with the date and place of their taking. Time in a "bottle" from which one would never drink again—possessing the past in a vain attempt to stop time. These photos were kept in places where their taker would never see them again but could find a weird comfort in the fact that they were saved somewhere in this vast collection. Cold comfort by embalming time.

It so happens that while emptying the house, I was rereading the wonderful novel, *Zorba The Greek*, by Nikos Kazantzakis. There is a passage in it where a woman has died, and while her corpse lies in her house, the villagers descend on her possessions like shrieking vultures on a carcass.

> Old women, men, children went rushing through the doors, jumped through the open windows, over the fences and off the balcony, each carrying whatever he had been able to snatch—sauce pans, frying pans, mattresses, rabbits. . . . Some of them had taken doors or windows off their hinges and had put them on their backs. Mimiko had seized the two court shoes, tied on a piece of string and hung them round his neck—it looked as though Dame Hortense were going off astraddle on his shoulders and only her shoes were visible. . . .

This avidity for things drives many people mad, to get and to keep stuff, to build walls around life so as to protect themselves from death. To consume so as not to be consumed. Kazantzakis brilliantly makes this clear in the book. Zorba, the Greek physical laborer and wild man, is different, for he knows that salvation lies in dispossession. One day he encounters five little children begging in a village. Their father has just been murdered. "I don't know why, divine inspiration I suppose, but I went up to them."

He gives the children his basket of food and all his money. He tells his interlocutor, a writer whom he calls "Boss," a man whom Zorba accuses of not being able to cut the string that ties him to a life of living-death, that that was how he was rescued.

> Rescued from my country, from priests, and from money. I began sifting things, sifting more and more things out. I lighten my burden that way. I—how shall I put it?—I find my own deliverance, I become a man.

In the jam-packed attic where there is little room to move with boxes and objects piled on top of each other, I found a large metal four-drawer file cabinet packed with files. In one file folder there was a small purse filled with the following: four very old unmarked keys, six paper clips, two old unworkable watches, a bobby pin, a circular case that contained what looked like a piece of a human bone, a few old medallions, tweezers, four buttons, an eye screw, a safety pin, a nail, a screw, two ancient tiny photos, and a lock of human hair. Similar objects were stored throughout the house in various containers, bags, boxes, the pockets of clothes, in old ancient furniture in the basement, on shelves, in cigar boxes, in desks, etc. Old receipts for purchases made forty years ago, airline baggage tags, ticket stubs, school papers, jewelry hidden everywhere, old foreign and domestic coins, perhaps twenty-five old unworkable watches, clocks, radios, clothes and more clothes, more than anyone could ever have wear, scores of old pens and pencils, hand-written notes with no dates or any semblance of order or meaning, chaos and obsessive account-keeping hiding everywhere in contradictory forms shared by two people: one the neat freak and the other disorganized. One dead and the other forced by fate to let her stuff go, to stand naked in the wind.

How does it help a person to record that they bought a toaster for $6.98 in 1957 or a bracelet for $20 in 1970 or that they called so-and-so some undated time in the past? What good does it do to save vast correspondences documenting your complaints, bitterness, and quarrels? Or boxes upon boxes of Christmas cards received thirty years ago? Or brochures and receipts from a trip taken long ago? Old sports medals? Scrapbooks? Photos of long dead relatives no one wants? Fashion designer shoes and coats and handbags hidden in a dusty attic where you don't even know they are there. An immigrant mother's ancient sewing machine weighing seventy-five pounds and gathering dust in the cellar?

Nothing I could tell you can come close to picturing what we saw in this house. It was overwhelming, horrifying, and weirdly fascinating. And aside from the useful things that were donated to charity and some that were taken to the woman's next dwelling, ninety percent was dumped in a landfill, soon to be buried.

In his brilliant novel *Underworld*, Don DeLillo writes about a guy named Brian who goes to visit a collector of old baseball paraphernalia—bats, balls, an old scoreboard, tapes of games, etc.—in a house where "a mood of mausoleum gloom" fills the air. The man tells Brian that "There's men in the coming years they'll pay fortunes for these objects. Because this is desperation speaking.... Men come here to see my collection.... They come and they don't want to leave. The phone rings, it's the family—where is he? This is the fraternity of missing men."

Men and women hoarders, collectors, and keepers are lost children, trying desperately to secure themselves from death while losing themselves in the process. In my friend's house I found huge amounts of string and rope waiting to tie something up neatly someday. That day never came.

> Zorba tells the Boss, who insists he's free, the following: No, you're not free. The string you're tied to is perhaps no longer than other people's. That's all. You're on a long piece of string, boss; you come and go and think you're free, but you never cut the string in two. And when people don't cut that string....
>
> It's difficult, boss, very difficult. You need a touch of folly to do that; folly, d'you see? You have to risk everything! But you've got such a strong head, it'll always get the better of you. A man's head is like a grocer; it keeps accounts. I've paid so much and earned so much and that means a profit of this much or a loss of that

> much! The head's a careful little shopkeeper; it never risks all it has, always keeps something in reserve. It never breaks the string. Ah, no! It hangs on tight to it, the bastard! If the string slips out of its grasp, the head, poor devil, is lost, finished! But if a man doesn't break the string, tell me what flavor is left in life? The flavor of chamomile, weak chamomile tea! Nothing like rum—that makes you see life inside out.

On the way out the door on our final day cleaning the house, I found a beautiful boxed fountain pen on a windowsill. I love pens since I am a writer. This one shone brightly and seemed to speak to me: think of what you could write with me, it said so seductively. I was sorely tempted, but knowing that I didn't need another pen, I left it there, thinking that perhaps the next occupants of this house would write a different story and embrace Camus' advice about an excess of things.

Perhaps, but very unlikely.

JFK vs. Allen Dulles by Greg Poulgrain

– A REVIEW –

Before I digress slightly, let me state from the outset that this book by Greg Poulgrain that I am about to review is extraordinary by any measure. The story he tells is one you will read nowhere else, especially in the way he links the assassination of President Kennedy to former CIA Director Allen Dulles and the engineering by the latter of one of the 20th century's most terrible mass murders. It will make your hair stand on end and should be read by anyone who cares about historical truth.

About thirteen years ago I taught a graduate school course to Massachusetts State Troopers and police officers from various cities and towns. As part of the course material, I had created a segment on the history of the United States' foreign policy, with particular emphasis on Indonesia.

No one in this class knew anything about Indonesia, not even where it was. These were intelligent, ambitious adults, eager to learn, all with college degrees. This was in the midst of the "war on terror"—i.e. war on Muslim countries—and the first year of Barack Obama's presidency. Almost all the class had voted for Obama and were aware they he had spent some part of his youth in this unknown country somewhere far away.

I mention this as a preface to this review of *JFK vs. Dulles*, because its subtitle is *Battleground Indonesia,* and my suspicion is that those students' lack of knowledge about the intertwined history of Indonesia and the U.S. is as scanty today among the general public as it was for my students a dozen years ago.

This makes Greg Poulgrain's remarkable book—*JFK vs, Allen Dulles: Battleground Indonesia*—even more important since it is a powerful antidote to such ignorance, and a reminder for those who have fallen, purposefully or not, into a state of historical amnesia that has erased the fact that the U.S. has committed systematic crimes that have resulted in the deaths of more than a million Indonesians and many more millions throughout the world over innumerable decades.

Such crimes against humanity have been hidden behind what the English playwright Harold Pinter in his 2005 Nobel Prize address called "a tapestry of lies." Of such massive crimes, he said:

> But you wouldn't know it. It never happened. Nothing ever happened. Even while it was happening it wasn't happening. It didn't matter. It was of no interest. The crimes of the United States have been systematic, constant, vicious, remorseless, but very few people have actually talked about them.

And when one examines the true history of such atrocities, again and again one comes up against familiar names of the guilty who have never been prosecuted. Criminals in high places whose crimes around the world from Vietnam to Chile to Cuba to Nicaragua to Argentina to Iraq to Libya to Syria, etc. have been—and continue to be—integral to American foreign policy as it serves the interests of its wealthy owners and their media mouthpieces.

In his new book on U.S./Indonesian history, Dr. Greg Poulgrain unweaves this tapestry of lies and sheds new light on the liars' sordid deeds. He is an Australian expert on Indonesia whose work stretches back forty years, is a professor at University of the Sunshine Coast in Brisbane and has written four highly-researched books about Indonesia.

In *JFK vs. Dulles,* he exposes the intrigue behind the ruthless regime-change strategy in Indonesia of the longest-serving CIA director, Allen Dulles, and how it clashed with the policy of President John F. Kennedy, leading to JFK's assassination, Indonesian regime change, and massive slaughter.

Poulgrain begins with this question:

> Would Allen Dulles have resorted to assassinating the President of the United States to ensure that his "Indonesian strategy" rather than Kennedy's was achieved?

To which he answers: Yes.

But let me not get ahead of myself, for the long, intricate tale he tells is one a reviewer can only summarize, so filled is it with voluminous details. So I will touch on a few salient points and encourage people to buy and read this important book.

Indonesia's Strategic Importance

The strategic and economic importance of Indonesia cannot be exaggerated. It is the world's 4th most populous country (275+ million), is located in a vital shipping lane adjacent to the South China Sea, has the world's largest Muslim population, has vast mineral and oil deposits, and is home in West Papua to Grasberg, the world's largest gold mine and the second largest copper mine, primarily owned by Freeport McMoRan of Phoenix, Arizona, whose past board members have included Henry Kissinger, John Hay Whitney, and Godfrey Rockefeller.

Long a battleground in the Cold War, Indonesia remains vitally important in the New Cold War and the pivot to Asia launched by the Obama administration against China and Russia, the same antagonists Allen Dulles strove to defeat through guile and violence while he engineered coups at home and abroad. It is fundamentally important to the Pentagon's Indo-Pacific strategy for what it euphemistically calls a "free and open Indo-Pacific." While not front-page news in the U.S., these facts make Indonesia of great importance today and add to the gravity of Poulgrain's historical account.

JFK

Two days before President John Kennedy was publicly executed by the U.S. national security state led by the CIA on November 22, 1963, he had accepted an invitation from Indonesian President Sukarno to visit that country the following spring. The aim of the visit was to end the conflict (*Konfrontasi*) between Indonesia and Malaysia and to continue Kennedy's efforts to support post-colonial Indonesia with economic and developmental, not military, aid. It was part of his larger strategy for ending conflict throughout Southeast Asia and assisting the growth of democracy in newly liberated post-colonial countries worldwide.

He had forecast his position in a dramatic speech in 1957 when, as a Massachusetts Senator, he told the Senate that he supported the Algerian liberation movement and opposed colonial imperialism worldwide. The speech caused an international uproar, and Kennedy was harshly attacked by Eisenhower, Nixon, John Foster Dulles, and even liberals such as Adlai Stevenson. But he was praised throughout the third world.

Poulgrain writes:

> Kennedy was aiming for a seismic shift of Cold War alignment in Southeast Asia by bringing Indonesia "on side." As Bradley Simpson stated (in 2008), "One would never know from reading the voluminous recent literature on the Kennedy and Johnson administrations and Southeast Asia, for example, that until the mid-1960s most officials [in the U.S.] still considered Indonesia of far greater importance than Vietnam or Laos."

Of course, JFK never went to Indonesia in 1964, and his peaceful strategy to bring Indonesia to America's side and to ease tensions in the Cold War was never realized, thanks to Allen Dulles. And Kennedy's proposed withdrawal from Vietnam, which was premised on success in Indonesia, was quickly reversed by Lyndon Johnson after JFK's murder on November 22, 1963. Soon both countries would experience mass slaughter engineered by Kennedy's opponents in the CIA and Pentagon. Millions would die.

While the Indonesian mass slaughter of mainly poor rice farmers (members of the Communist Party—PKI) instigated by Allen Dulles began in October 1965, ten years later, starting in December 1975, the American-installed Indonesian dictator Suharto, after meeting with Henry Kissinger and President Ford and receiving their approval, would slaughter hundreds of thousands of East-Timorese with American-supplied weapons in a repeat of the slaughter of more than a million Indonesians in 1965 when the CIA engineered the coup d'état that toppled President Sukarno. The American-installed dictator Suharto would rule for thirty years of terror. The CIA considers this operation one of its finest accomplishments. It became known as "the Jakarta Method," a model for future violent coups throughout Latin America and the world.

And in-between these U.S. engineered mass atrocities, came the bloody coup in Chile on September 11, 1973 and the ongoing colossal U.S. war crimes in Vietnam, Laos, and Cambodia.

Dulles's Secret

What JFK didn't know was that his plans for a peaceful resolution of the Indonesia situation and an easing of the Cold War were threatening a covert long-standing conspiracy engineered by Allen Dulles to effect regime change in Indonesia through bloody means and to exacerbate the Cold War by concealing from Kennedy the truth that there was a Sino-Soviet split. Another primary goal behind this plan was to gain unimpeded access to the vast load of natural resources that Dulles had kept secret from Kennedy, who thought Indonesia was lacking in natural resources. But Dulles knew that if Kennedy, who was very popular in Indonesia, visited Sukarno, it would deal a death blow to his plan to oust Sukarno, install a CIA replacement (Suharto), exterminate alleged communists, and secure the archipelago for Rockefeller controlled oil and mining interests, for whom he had fronted since the 1920s.

Reading Poulgrain's masterful analysis, one can clearly see how much of modern history is a struggle for control of the underworld wherein lie the fuel that runs the megamachine—oil, minerals, gold, copper, etc. Manifest ideological conflicts, while garnering headlines, often bury the secret of this subterranean Devil's game.

The Discovery of Gold

His murder mystery/detective story begins with a discovery that is then kept secret for many decades. He writes:

> In the alpine region of Netherlands New Guinea (so named under Dutch colonial rule—today, West Papua) in 1936, three Dutchmen discovered a mountainous outcrop of ore with high copper content and very high concentrations of gold. When later analyzed in the Netherlands, the gold (in gram/ton) proved to be twice that of Witwatersrand in South Africa, then the world's richest gold mine, but this information was not made public.

The geologist among the trio, Jean Jacques Dozy, worked for the Netherlands New Guinea Petroleum Company (NNGPM), ostensibly a Dutch-controlled company based in The Hague, but whose controlling interest actually lay in the hands of the Rockefeller family, as did the mining company, Freeport Sulphur (now Freeport McMoRan, one of whose Directors from 1988–95 was Henry Kissinger, Dulles' and the Rockefeller's close associate) that began mining operations there in 1966.

It was Allen Dulles, Paris-based lawyer in the employ of Rockefeller's Standard Oil, who in 1935 arranged the controlling interest in NNGPN for the Rockefellers. And it was Dulles, among a select few others, who, because of various intervening events, including WW II, that made its exploitation impossible, kept the secret of the gold mine for almost three decades, even from President Kennedy, who had worked to return the island to Indonesian control. JFK "remained uninformed of the El Dorado, and once the remaining political hurdles were overcome, Freeport would have unimpeded access." Those "political hurdles"—i.e. regime change—would take a while to effect.

The Need to Assassinate President Kennedy

But first JFK would have to be eliminated, for he had brokered Indonesian sovereignty over West Papua/West Irian for Sukarno from the Dutch who had ties to Freeport Sulphur. Freeport was aghast at the potential loss of "El Dorado," especially since they had recently had their world's most advanced nickel refinery expropriated by Fidel Castro, who had named Che Guevara its new manager. Freeport's losses in Cuba made access to Indonesia even more important. Cuba and Indonesia thus were joined in the deadly game of chess between Dulles and Kennedy, and someone would have to lose.

While much has been written about Cuba, Kennedy, and Dulles, the Indonesian side of the story has been slighted. Poulgrain remedies this with an exhaustive and deeply researched exploration of these matters. He details the deviousness of the covert operations Dulles ran in Indonesia during the 1950s and 1960s. He makes it clear that Kennedy was shocked by Dulles's actions, yet never fully grasped the treacherous genius of it all, for Dulles was always "working two or three stages ahead of the present." Having armed and promoted a rebellion against Sukarno's central government in 1958, Dulles made sure it would fail (shades of the Bay of Pigs to come) since a perceived failure served his long-term strategy. To this very day, this faux 1958 Rebellion is depicted as a CIA failure by the media. Yet from Dulles's standpoint, it was a successful failure that served his long-term goals.

"This holds true," Poulgrain has previously written, "only if the stated goal of the CIA was the same as the actual goal. Even more than five decades later, media analysis of the goal of The

Outer Island rebels is still portrayed as a secession, as covert U.S. support for 'rebels in the Outer Islands that wished to secede from the central government in Jakarta.' The actual goal of Allen Dulles had more to do with achieving a centralized army command in such a way as to appear that the CIA backing for the rebels failed."

Dulles the Devil

Dulles betrayed the rebels he armed and encouraged, just as he betrayed friend and foe alike during his long career. The rebellion that he instigated and planned to fail was the first stage of a larger intelligence strategy that would come to fruition in 1965–66 with the ouster of Sukarno (after multiple unsuccessful assassination attempts) and the institution of a reign of terror that followed. It was also in 1966 that Freeport McMoRan began their massive mining in West Papua at Grasberg at an elevation of 14,000 feet in the Alpine region. Dulles was nothing if not patient; he had been at this game since WW I. Even after Kennedy fired him following the Bay of Pigs, his plans were executed, just as were those who got in his way. Poulgrain makes a powerful case that Dulles was the mastermind of the murders of JFK, U.N. Secretary General Dag Hammarskjold (working with Kennedy for a peaceful solution in Indonesia and other places), and Congolese President Patrice Lumumba, the first president of a newly liberated Congo.

His focus is on *why* they needed to be assassinated (similar in this regard to James Douglass's *JFK and the Unspeakable*), though with the exception of Kennedy (since the *how* is well-known and obvious), he also presents compelling evidence as to the *how*. Hammarskjold, in many ways Kennedy's spiritual brother, was a particularly powerful obstacle to Dulles's plans for Indonesia and colonial countries throughout the Third World. Like JFK, he was committed to independence for indigenous and colonial peoples everywhere and was trying to implement his Swedish-style "third way," proposing a form of "muscular pacifism."

Poulgrain argues correctly that if the UN Secretary General succeeded in bringing even half these colonial countries to independence, he would have transformed the UN into a significant world power and created a body of nations so large as to be a counterweight to those embroiled in the Cold War.

He draws on documents from the South African Truth and Reconciliation Commission (TRC) and Chairman Archbishop Desmond Tutu to show the connection between South Africa's "Operation Celeste" and Dulles's involvement in Hammarskjold's murder in September 1961. While it was reported at the time as an accidental plane crash, he quotes former President Harry Truman saying, "Dag Hammarskjold was on the point of getting something done when they killed him. Notice that I said, 'When they killed him.'" Hammarskjold, like Kennedy, was intent on returning colonized countries to their indigenous inhabitants and making sure Papua was for Papuans, not Freeport McMoRan and imperial forces.

And Dulles sold his overt Indonesian strategy as being necessary to thwart a communist takeover in Indonesia. Cold War rhetoric, like "the war on terrorism" today, served as his cover. In this he had the Joint Chiefs of Staff on his side; they considered Kennedy soft on communism in Indonesia and Cuba and everywhere else. Dulles's covert agenda was to serve the interests of his power elite patrons.

While contextually different from David Talbot's portrayal of Dulles in *The Devil's Chessboard,* Poulgrain's portrait of Dulles within the frame of Indonesian history is equally condemnatory and nightmarish. Both describe an evil genius ready to do anything to advance his agenda.

Dulles and George de Mohrenschildt

Poulgrain adds significantly to our understanding of JFK's assassination and its aftermath by presenting new information about George de Mohrenschildt, Lee Harvey Oswald's handler in Dallas. Dulles had a long association with the de Mohrenschildt family, going back to 1920–21 when in Constantinople he negotiated with Baron Sergius Alexander von Mohrenschildt on behalf of Rockefeller's Standard Oil. The Baron's brother and business partner was George's father. Dulles's law firm, Sullivan

& Cromwell, was Standard Oil's primary law firm. These negotiations on behalf of elite capitalist interests, in the shadow of the Russian Revolution, became the template for Dulles's career: economic exploitation was inseparable from military concerns, the former concealed behind the anti-communist rhetoric of the latter. An anti-red thread ran through Dulles's career, except when the red was the blood of all those whom he considered expendable. And the numbers are legion. Their blood didn't matter.

Standard Oil is the link that joins Dulles [who controlled the Warren Commission investigating the assassination of JFK] and de Mohrenschildt. This connection was kept from the Warren Commission despite Dulles' prominent role and the importance of the testimony of de Mohrenschildt. Poulgrain argues convincingly that de Mohrenschildt worked in "oil intelligence" before his CIA involvement, and that oil intelligence was not only Dulles's work when he first met George's father, Sergius, in Baku, but also that that "oil intelligence" is a redundancy. The CIA, after all, is a creation of Wall Street and their interests have always been joined. The Agency was not formed to provide intelligence to U.S. presidents; that was a convenient myth used to cover its real purpose which was to serve the interests of investment bankers and the power elite, or those I call The Umbrella People who control the U.S.

While working in 1941 for Humble Oil (Prescott Bush was a major shareholder, Dulles was his lawyer, and Standard Oil had secretly bought Humble Oil sixteen years before), de Mohrenschildt was caught up in a scandal that involved Vichy (pro-Nazi) French intelligence selling oil to Germany. This was similar to the Dulles's brothers and Standard Oil's notorious business dealings with Germany.

It was an intricate web of the high cabal with Allen Dulles at the center.

In the midst of the scandal, de Mohrenschildt, suspected of being a Vichy French intelligence agent, "disappeared" for a while. He later told the Warren Commission that he decided to take up oil drilling, without mentioning the name of Humble Oil that employed him again, this time as a roustabout.

"Just when George needed to 'disappear,' Humble Oil was providing an oil exploration team to be subcontracted to NNGPM—the company Allen Dulles had set up five years earlier to work in Netherlands New Guinea." Poulgrain makes a powerful circumstantial evidence case (certain documents are still unavailable) that de Mohrenschildt, in order to avoid appearing in court, went incommunicado in Netherlands New Guinea in mid-1941 where he made a record oil discovery and received a $10,000 bonus from Humble Oil.

"Avoiding adverse publicity about his role in selling oil to Vichy France was the main priority; for George, a brief drilling adventure in remote Netherlands New Guinea would have been a timely and strategic exit." And who best to help him in this escape than Allen Dulles—indirectly, of course; for Dulles's modus operandi was to maintain his "distance" from his contacts, often over many decades.

In other words, Dulles and de Mohrenschildt were intimately involved for a long time prior to JFK's assassination. Poulgrain rightly claims that "the entire focus of the Kennedy investigation would have shifted had the [Warren] Commission become aware of the 40-year link between Allen Dulles and de Mohrenschildt." Their relationship involved oil, spying, Indonesia, Nazi Germany, the Rockefellers, Cuba, Haiti, etc. It was an international web of intrigue that involved a cast of characters stranger than fiction, a high cabal of the usual and unusual operatives.

Two unusual ones are worth mentioning: Michael Fomenko and Michael Rockefeller. The eccentric Fomenko—aka "Tarzan"—is the Russian-Australian nephew of de Mohrenschildt's wife, Jean Fomenko. His arrest and deportation from Netherlands New Guinea in 1959, where he had travelled from Australia in a canoe, and his subsequent life, are fascinating and sad. It's the stuff of a bizarre film. It seems he was one of those victims who had to be silenced because he knew a secret about George's 1941 oil discovery that was not his to share. "In April 1964, at the same time George de Mohrenschildt was facing the Warren Commission—a time when any publicity regarding Sele 40 [George's record oil discovery] could have changed history—it was decided that electro-convulsive therapy would be used on Michael Fomenko." He was then imprisoned at the Ipswich Special Mental Hospital.

Equally interesting is the media myth surrounding the disappearance of Michael Rockefeller, Nelson's son and heir to the Standard Oil fortune, who was allegedly eaten by cannibals in New Guinea in 1961. His tale became front-page news, "a media event closed off to any other explanation and the political implications of his disappearance became an ongoing tragedy for the Papuan people." To this very day, the West Papuan people, whose land was described by Standard Oil official Richard Archbold in 1938 as "Shangri-la," are fighting for their independence.

The Sino-Soviet Split

While the gold in West Papua was very important to Allen Dulles, his larger goal was to keep the Cold War blazing by concealing the dispute between China and the Soviet Union from Kennedy while instigating the mass slaughter of "communists" that would lead to regime change in Indonesia, with Major-General Suharto, his ally, replacing President Sukarno. In this he was successful. Poulgrain writes:

> Not only did Dulles fail to brief Kennedy on the Sino-Soviet dispute early in the presidency, but he also remained silent about the rivalry between Moscow and Beijing to wield influence over the PKI or win its support. In geographical terms, Beijing regarded Indonesia as its own backyard, and winning the support of the PKI would give Beijing an advantage in the Sino-Soviet dispute. The numerical growth of the PKI was seen by Moscow and Beijing for its obvious political potential. Dulles was also focused on the PKI, but his peculiar skill in political intelligence turned what seemed inevitable on its head. The size of the party [the Indonesian Communist Party was the largest outside the Sino-Soviet bloc] became a factor he used to his advantage when formulating his wedge strategy—the greater the

> rivalry between Moscow and Beijing over the PKI, the more intense would be the recrimination once the PKI was eliminated.

The slaughter of more than a million poor farmers was a trifle to Dulles.

The September 30, 1965 Movement

In the early hours of October 1, 1965, a fake coup d'état was staged by the CIA's man, Major-General Suharto. It was announced that seven generals had been arrested and would be taken to President Sukarno "to explain the rumor that they were planning a military coup on October 5." Suharto declared himself the head of the army. Someone was said to have killed the generals. In the afternoon, a radio announcement was made calling for the Sukarno government to be dismissed. This became Suharto's basis for blaming the fake coup on the communists and the so-called September 30 Movement, and he gave the order to kill the PKI leaders. This started the massive bloodshed that would follow.

With one hand, Suharto crushed the Movement, accusing the PKI of being the ultimate instigator of an attempt to oust Sukarno, and with the other hand he feigned to protect the "father of the Indonesian revolution," while actually stripping Sukarno of every vestige of political support.

When the generals' bodies were recovered a few days after Oct 1, Suharto falsely claimed the PKI women had tortured and sexually mutilated them as part of some primitive sexual orgy. This heinous perversion of power was the start of the Suharto era. In total control of the media, he manipulated popular wrath to call for revenge.

If this confuses you, it should, because the twisted nature of this fabricated coup was actually part of a real coup in slow motion aimed at ousting Sukarno and replacing him with the CIA's man Suharto. This occurred in early 1967 after the mass slaughter of communists. It was a regime change cheered on by the American mass media as a triumph over communist aggression.

New Evidence of U.S. Direct Involvement in the Slaughter

Poulgrain has spent forty years interviewing participants and researching this horrendous history. His detailed research is quite amazing. And it does take concentration to follow it all, as with the machinations of Dulles, Suharto, et al.

Some things, however, are straightforward. For example, he documents how, during the height of the slaughter, two Americans—one man and one woman—were in Klaten (PKI headquarters in central Java) supervising the Indonesian army as they killed the PKI. These two would travel back and forth by helicopter from a ship of the U.S. 7th Fleet that was off the coast of Java. The plan was that the more communists killed, the greater would be the dispute between Moscow and Beijing, since they would accuse each other of the tragedy, which is exactly what they did. This was the wedge that was mentioned in the Rockefeller Brothers Panel Report from the late 1950s in which Dulles and Henry Kissinger both participated.

The hatred drummed up against these poor members of the Communist Party was extraordinary in its depravity. In addition to Suharto's lies about communist women mutilating the generals' bodies, a massive campaign of hatred was directed against these landless peasants who made up the bulk of the PKI. False Cold War radio broadcasts from Singapore stirred up hostility toward them, declaring them atheists, etc. Wealthy Muslim landowners—the 1 per cent—made outrageous charges to assist the army's slaughter. Poulgrain tells us:

> Muhammadiyah preachers were broadcasting from mosques that all who joined the communist party must be killed, saying they are the "lowest order of infidel, the shedding of whose blood is comparable to killing a chicken."

For those Americans especially, who think this history of long ago and far away does not touch them, its compelling analysis of how and why Allen Dulles and his military allies would want

JFK dead since he was a threat to national security as they defined in it their paranoid anti-communist ideology might be an added impetus to read this very important book. Indonesia may be far away geographically, but it's a small world. Dulles and Kennedy had irreconcilable differences, and when Dulles was once asked in a radio interview what he would do to someone who threatened national security, he matter-of-factually said, "I'd kill him." The Joint Chiefs of Staff agreed.

I would be remiss if I didn't say that the introduction to *JFK vs. Dulles* by Oliver Stone and the afterward by James DiEugenio are outstanding. They add excellent context and clarity to a really great and important book

Why Is Everything Broken?

"Begin then with a fracture, a cesura, a rent; opening a crack in this fallen world, a shaft of light."
—NORMAN O. BROWN, *LOVE'S BODY*

Being sick for the past few weeks has had its advantages. It has forced me to take a break from writing since I could not concentrate enough to do so. It has gifted me with a deeper sympathy for the vast numbers of the seriously ill around the world, those suffering souls without succor except for desperate prayers for relief. And it has allowed thoughts to think me as I relinquished all efforts at control for a few miserable weeks of "doing nothing" except napping, reading short paragraphs in books, watching some sports and a documentary, and being receptive to the light coming through the cracks in my consciousness.

I suppose you could say that my temporary illness forced me, as José Ortega Y Gasset described it, virtually and provisionally to withdraw myself from the world and take a stand inside myself—"or, to use a magnificent word which exists only in Spanish, that man can *ensimismarse* ('be inside himself')."

But as I learned, being "inside myself" doesn't mean the outside world doesn't come visiting, both in its present and past manifestations. When you are sick, you feel most vulnerable; this sense of frailty breaks you open to strange and familiar thoughts, feelings, dreams and memories that you must catch on the fly, pin with words if you are quick enough. I've pinned some over these weeks as they came to me through the cracks.

"Broken flesh, broken mind, broken speech," wrote Norman Brown when he argued for aphoristic truth as opposed to methods or systematic form. These days the feeling that everything is broken is the norm, that madness reigns, that truth is being strangled and all we have are lies and more lies. Carefully constructed arguments fall on deaf ears as dissociation of the personality, post-modern attention-disorder, gender confusion, and corporate/intelligence mass media propaganda techniques are used daily to sow confusion. In simple colloquial language, people are badly fucked up.

Much of the world is suffering from megrims. Bob Dylan puts it simply:

> Broken lines, broken strings
> Broken threads, broken springs
> Broken idols, broken heads
> People sleeping in broken beds
> Ain't no use jiving
> Ain't no use joking
> Everything is broken.

Who can disagree? Everyone's mind seems to be at the end of its tether.

Why? There are obvious answers, and while so many are true, they are insufficient, for they usually scratch the surface of a worldwide crisis that has been developing for at least a century and a half. That crisis is spiritual. Many can feel it rumbling beneath the surface of world events. It's a rumbling in the bowels. It's unspoken. It's something very dark, sinister, and satanic. It seems to be a form of systemic evil almost with a will of its own that is sweeping the world.

For many decades I have studied, written, and taught in an effort to grasp the essence of what has been happening in our world. My tools have been philosophy, theology, literature, art, and sociology—all the disciplines really, including a careful study of popular culture. It was always a personal quest, for my "career" has been my vocation.

Being trained in the classics from high school through college, and then the scientific method and textual analysis, I adhered for the most part to logical analyses in the classical style. Such an approach, while possessed of a certain elegance and balance, has serious limitations since it suggests the world follows a neat Aristotelian logic and that there is a method to the world's madness that is easy to capture in logical argumentation. Romanticism and existentialism, to name two reactions to such thinking, arose in opposition. Each offered a needed corrective to the reductive, materialist nature of a scientific method that became deified while dismissing God, freedom, and the spiritual as leftover superstitions from olden times.

But I have no sustained argument to offer here, just some scraps I gathered while enduring weeks in the doldrums. I sense these bits of seemingly digressive little flashes in the dark were telling me something about what I have been trying to understand for many years: the grasp the demonic has on our world today.

It is easy to dismiss the use of such a word, for it sounds hyperbolic, and it easily plays into the ridiculous themes of popular Hollywood and tabloid entertainment, which have also become staples of the formerly "serious" media as well. It's all entertainment now, life the movie, the unreality of endless propaganda, sick, sordid, and what can only be termed "The Weirdness," a term my friend the writer and playwright Joe Green has suggested to me. I think it would be a serious mistake to dismiss the demonic nature of the forces at work in our world today.

- Like Rip Van Winkle, I awoke one recent day, a few weeks after I wrote my last article before I got sick, to see that the corporate media/intelligence narrative on the war in Ukraine had taken an abrupt turn. I had written on May 13, 2022 that certain leftists were parroting the official U.S. propaganda that Russia was losing its battle with the Ukrainian forces. Noam Chomsky had claimed the U.S. media were doing a good job reporting Russian war crimes in Ukraine and Chris Hedges had said that Russia had suffered "nine weeks of humiliating military failures." Now Th*e New York Times*, the *Washington*

Post, etc.—*mirabile dictu*—have suddenly changed their tune and the Russians are winning after all. Who was asleep? Or was it sleep that prompted such obviously false reporting? For the Russians were clearly winning from the start. Yet we can be assured the authoritative voices will continue to flip the switch and play mind games, for shock and confusion are keys to effective propaganda, and American exceptionalism with its divine mission, its manifest destiny, is to demonically try to destroy Russia.

- The slogan that I learned when I was a Marine before becoming a conscientious objector came to me when I was feverish. "My rifle is my life." I never thought so, but I did recall how when I was ten years old my cousin killed his brother with a rifle, and how I heard the news on the radio while talking with my father. *The New York Times* reported: "A 9-year-old boy was fatally wounded last night by his brother, 7, while the two were playing with a rifle in a neighbor's apartment in the northeast Bronx.... [the rifle] 'was secreted in a bedroom' [under the bed] and was loaded."

- Watched the new documentary about George Carlin—*George Carlin's American Dream.* What struck me in this interesting documentary was George's facile dismissal of God—"the God bullshit," as he put it. Funny, of course, and correct in certain ways, it was also jejune in significant ways and threw God out with the bathwater. It was something I had not previously noticed about his routine, but this time around it hit me as unworthy of his scathing critiques of American life. It got laughs at the expense of deeper and important truths and probably has had deleterious effects on generations who have been beguiled and besotted by how George's God critique consonantly fits with the shallow arguments of the new atheists.

- When I was young and teaching at another school and involved in anti-war activities, a fellow teacher stopped me on a staircase on a late Friday afternoon when no one was around and tried to get me to join Army Intelligence. "You are exactly the type we could use," he said with a smile, "since you are so outspoken in your anti-war positions." I will spare you my reply, which involved words you once could never say on TV. But the encounter taught me an early lesson about distinguishing friend from foe; how treachery is real, and evil often wears a smiley face. The man who approached me was the head of social studies curricula for the Roman Catholic Brooklyn Diocese of New York.

- Al Capone, while speaking to Cornelius Vanderbilt, Jr. in 1931: "People respect nothing nowadays.... It is undermining the country. Virtue, honor, truth, and the law have all vanished from our life."
- I also read this from *Literature and the Gods* by Roberto Calasso: "... all the mythologies now pass a largely indolent life in a no-man's-land haunted by gods and vagrant simulacra, by ghosts and Gypsy caravans in constant movement. They learn only to tell their stories again.... Yet it is precisely this ability that is so obviously lacking in the world around us. Behind the trembling curtains of what passes for 'reality,' the voices throng. If no one listens, they steal the costume of the first person they can grab and burst onto the stage in ways that can be devastating. Violence is the expedient of what has been refused an audience."
- Lying in bed after a feverish night early on in my sickness, I looked up at the ceiling where a fly was buzzing. I remembered how years ago, when my father was in the hospital after a terrible car accident in which he smashed his head, he told me he was seeing monkeys all over the ceiling of the hospital room. Later, when I was out of bed, I heard the news reports about monkeypox and thought I was also hallucinating. I started laughing, a sardonic laughter brought to a feverish pitch after more than two years of COVID propaganda. These are the same people who hope to create a transhuman future—mechanical monkeys.

- A trilogy of books—*Sinister Forces*—by Peter Levenda shocks by the amount of documented history they contain, history so bizarre and disturbing that reading them is not advisable before bedtime. Sinister forces that run through American history, indeed, but Levenda presents his material in a most reasonable and fair-minded way:

> The historical model I am proposing in these volumes should be obvious by now. By tracing the darker elements of the American experience from the earliest days of the Adena and Hopewell cultures through the discovery by Columbus, the English settlers in Massachusetts and the Salem witchcraft episode, the rise of Joseph Smith, Jr. and the Mormons via ceremonial magic and Freemasonry, up to the twentieth century and the support of Nazism by American financiers and politicians before, during, and after World War II, and the UFO phenomenon coming on the heels of that war, we can see the outline of a political ectoplasm taking shape in this historical séance: politics as a continuation of religion by other means. The ancillary events of the Charles Manson murders, the serial killer phenomenon, Jonestown, and the assassinations of Jack Kennedy, Bobby Kennedy, Martin Luther King, and Marilyn Monroe are all the result of the demonic possession of the American psyche, like the obscenities spat out by little Regan [*The Exorcist*], tied to her bed and shrieking at the exorcists. It is said that demonic possession is a way of testing us, and making us aware of the real conflict taking place within us every day. . . .
>
> The more I looked, however, the more I found men with bizarre beliefs and involved in questionable, occult practices at the highest levels of the American government, and buried deep within government agencies. I also discovered that occultism was embraced by the American military and intelligence establishments as a weapon to be used in the Cold War; and as they did so,

> they unleashed forces upon the American populace that cannot be called back....
>
> One inevitably was forced back to the CIA and the mind-control experiments that began in the late 1940s and extended nearly to the present day [no, to the present day]. Coincidence piled upon coincidence, indicating the existence of a powerful, subliminal force working at the level of chaos—at the quantum level—and struggling to manifest itself in our reality, our consciousness, our political agenda.

If that all sounds too bizarre for words, unbelievable really, I suggest that one read these books, for if only a minority of Levenda's claims are true, we are in the grip of evil forces so depraved that fiction writers couldn't imagine such reality.

As I finish these notes, I am sitting outside on a small porch, watching the rain subside. The sun has just emerged. It is 5:30 P.M. and across the driveway and a lawn of grass, eight foxes have come through the bushes. The parents watch as the six kits jump and scamper around the ground level porch of a cottage that is unoccupied. The foxes have a den under the porch, and every day for a few months we have been privileged to watch them perform their antics in the mornings and evenings. Cute would be an appropriate word for the kits, especially when they were smaller. But they are growing fast and suddenly one sees and seizes a squirrel and worries it to death by shaking it in its mouth. Soon they are ripping it to pieces. Cute has turned deadly. But as the aforementioned Ortega Y Gasset says, while people can be inside themselves, "The animal is pure *alteración.* It cannot be within itself." This is because it has no self, "no *chez soi*, where it can withdraw and rest." Foxes always live in pure exteriority, unlike me, sitting here with a small glass of wine and thinking about them and the various thoughts that have come to me over these past few weeks.

Before I came outside, I read this from a powerful new article by Naomi Wolf—"Dear Friends: Sorry to Announce a Genocide." "It is a time of demons sauntering around in human spaces, though they look human enough themselves, smug in their Italian suits on panels at the World Economic Forum."

In this piece she writes about what is in the 55,000 Internal Pfizer Documents which the FDA had asked a court to keep under wraps for 75 years, but which a court has released as a result of outside pressure. These documents reveal evil so depraved that words would fail her if not for her moral conscience and her growing awareness—that I share—that we are dealing with a phenomenon that demands an analysis that is theological, not sociological. She writes:

> Knowing as I now do, that Pfizer and the FDA knew that babies were dying and mothers' milk discoloring by just looking at their own internal records; knowing as I do that they did not alert anyone let alone stop what they were doing, and that to this day Pfizer, the FDA and other demonic "public health" entities are pushing to MRNA-vaccinate more and more pregnant women; now that they are about to force this on women in Africa and other lower income nations who are not seeking the MRNA vaccines, per Pfizer CEO Bourla this past week at the WEF, and knowing that Pfizer is pushing and may even receive a US EUA for babies to five year olds—I must conclude that we are looking into an abyss of evil not seen since 1945.
>
> So I don't know about you, but I must switch gears with this kind of unspeakable knowledge to another kind of discourse.

That discourse is religious, for Naomi Wolf has realized that our world is in satanic hands, and that only a recognition of that fact offers a way out. That those who wield weapons both medical and military can only be defeated by those who realize that a key part of the killers' propaganda has been a long campaign to convince people, not only that God does not exist, but that Satan doesn't either. This, while they assume the mantle of the evil one.

She says:

> This time could really be the last time; these monsters in the labs, on the transnational panels, are so very skillful; and so powerful; and their dark work is so extensive.
>
> If God is there—again—after all the times that we have tried his patience—and who indeed knows?—will we reach out a hand to him in return, will we take hold in the last moment out of this abyss, and simply find a way somehow to walk alongside him?

We will, but only if we also recognize the deeper forces informing our hidden history and haunting our present days. Sometimes an illness can crack you open to being receptive to shafts of light that can lead the way. Yet to do so we must go deep into very dark places. And since everyone and everything seems broken now—let's say everyone is just sick in some way—maybe courage is what we need, the simple courage to open ourselves to the voices of the hungry ghosts that haunt this country. Norman O. Brown referred to them and our stage set this way:

> Ancestral voices prophesying war; ancestral spirits in the *danse macabre* or war dance; Valhalla, ghostly warriors who kill each other and are reborn to fight again. All warfare is ghostly, every army an *exercitus feralis* (army of ghosts), every soldier a living corpse.

The U.S.A. and its allies are waging war on many fronts. It is a form of total war—cold, hot, medical, military, mind-control, spiritual, etc.—that demands a total response from us. None of us is completely innocent; we are all part of the deep evil that is happening all around us. But if we listen carefully, we might hear God asking for our help. For we need each other.

I watch in horror as the cute foxes kill their prey. I must remind myself that that is their nature. As for my fellow humans, I know that it isn't nature that drives them to kill, maim, hurt, lie, etc.

Everything is truly broken, and I'm not joking.
But someone is laughing.
And it's not God.

Inside the Iron Cage

"No one knows who will live in this [iron] cage in the future. . . ."

—MAX WEBER, *The Protestant Ethic and the Spirit of Capitalism*

This is one of those stories hard to believe. When I first heard it, I thought it was a joke, some sort of parable, and my friend who was telling it to me had had too much to drink or was just pulling my leg. I'm not sure. Like so much in today's world, the difference between fiction and fact has become very blurry.

Let me call him Sean, since these days holding a strong dissenting opinion can cost you your job. He is a professor who, like the character David in John Fowles' story, "The Ebony Tower," teaches art history. And like Fowles' character he is a very frustrated academic. In Sean's case, he has had to contend with the transformation of his college from a place of learning to a place where "Woke" ideology stifles dissent. Perhaps more importantly, he has suffered from extreme writer's block. He had just been telling me how, after years of writing copiously in his private journals, he had grown nauseated by it because it seemed so self-involved, concerning self and family stuff he was sick of. He wanted to write articles and books, yet when he tried, he couldn't. All his energy had been going into his futile daily journals where he felt trapped by family matters. Until one recent day at the bar where we regularly meet, he heard this strange story. It jolted him.

Here is what he told me over beer at the tavern. I am paraphrasing, but because his tale was so startling, I know I have the essentials right. He said:

"It was late in the afternoon last Wednesday when I came in here for a beer. I was feeling very tired that day, though depressed would be more accurate. The teaching routine seemed absurd to me. I wasn't writing. I felt at a dead end. I guess I was. Anyway, you know that guy Tom whom we've talked to here before? Well, he was here and we got talking. The place was empty. It turns out his last name is Finn—Tom Finn. His father was Russell Finn, the famous painter, you know, the one the mainstream media gush over. A realistic sentimentalist is the way I've heard him described, although I would say he was a sick fabulist trying to repaint history for Hallmark Cards. Anyway, so this Tom Finn had had a few beers, and as he got talking, both of us had a few more. It became obvious that he was obsessed with his father. He didn't say that exactly, but I could guess it from the snide remarks about him then he'd laugh out of the side of his mouth. I asked him about a big traveling exhibit of his father's paintings which I had recently read about in the newspapers; had he seen it? 'No,' he said, 'I don't go to that kind of crap. That's his bag of marbles.' Things like that.

"It turns out the son is also a painter, but he said nothing about his own work, just that he painted. He talked all about his father's work, how his father stole ideas, wasn't very good, etc. I told him I agreed that his father's work was overhyped and mediocre, but that my experience studying art taught me that was true for every era. I was trying to be nice, something I tend to overdo. I got the impression he turned to painting by default, it being some kind of knee-jerk reaction to his father, some kind of Oedipal contest.

"It turns out his real obsession is toys, no shit, and he got very animated as he talked about them. He wanted me to come over to his house to see his vast toy collection. The invitation was so weird, and with the beer's effects, I couldn't refuse. It was nearly dinner time, so I called Sara and told her I'd be late. I was actually interested in what made him tick. I mean, why would a grown man—I'd say he is in his mid-forties—collect fucking toys? And weirder still, he said his specialty was tiny plastic figures of all sorts. Of these he had more than 25,000—for some reason he emphasized that number—that he'd periodically put on display at local libraries.

"So I followed him over to his house which is on that street adjoining the university where a number of art history professors live. Oak Terrace, I think it is. I couldn't help laughing when I saw all those abstract sculptures decorating their lawns. It was getting dark and they were spotlighted. What a juxtaposition—so perfect—so-called realism and cerebral abstraction side-by-side. And both utter bullshit. I was reminded of a description of Russell Finn's paintings that I once read: Cute wallpaper for readers of *Reader's Digest.*

"Actually, Finn's house is quite cute itself. When we were going in, I had to restrain myself from saying to him, 'Life's cute, isn't it?' I don't think he would have appreciated that, although it's very possible that he wouldn't have known what the hell I was getting at. He's a toy collector after all and what's cuter than that.

"I'll tell you this. I wasn't prepared for what he showed me. He took me down to his finished basement, which he called 'the laboratory.' When he switched on the lights the room was empty except for the walls. They were covered with shelves about six inches apart that ran from wall to wall and ceiling to floor. It gave the large room this incredibly bizarre look as though it were a prison cell. There were even spotlights that illuminated the shelves, upon which, right along the outer edges looking out, he had lined up his collection of little figures. As we stood in the middle of the room, it was as though thousands of little people were staring at us, the giants. I felt as though I was hallucinating. Finn just chuckled when I said, 'Pretty fucking amazing!' Then he said, 'I like the perspective, don't you?' I knew he didn't expect an answer and I could only chuckle in response, even as I felt a chill on the back of my neck. It was so eerie that I had to contain a shudder. For a brief moment I had the feeling that the door we had entered was going to shut and be bolted and that something terrifying was about to unfold.

"But at that moment he gestured to me to follow him to another door, over which a sign read, 'The Family Fun Room.' 'This is my favorite,' he said with a smile.

"In the middle of this pink painted room there was a cage that extended from floor to ceiling, and in the cage, sitting on stools, were two life-sized and very realistic figures of a man and a woman. They were both dressed in those black and white stripped prison uniforms you've seen in old movies. The woman was facing away from the man. I couldn't tell who the woman was, but I immediately recognized the man. It was Finn's father, down to the most realistic detail. He was holding a small toy figurine and was looking into its face. The door to the cell was padlocked shut. 'That's to make sure they can't escape,' Finn said with a straight face. 'Now that I got them where I want them, I can't take any chances. They're dangerous and can cause me a lot of grief.'

"He then closed the door and we went upstairs. Neither of us said a word. He offered me a beer, but I declined. I felt spooked, some dreadful feeling in my gut. I told him I had to be leaving, which I did. On the way out I noticed a framed photograph in the foyer. It was a picture of Finn at about the age of nine or ten with his parents and sister. They are sitting together on a couch, the two kids caught between the parents. No one is smiling. Behind them on the wall is the father's famous painting of a family of four sitting on a couch. In that one, everyone is smiling and the father in the painting is Finn's father. As you probably know, that was one of his father's favorite techniques—to put himself in his paintings. Such a cute double-message: I did it, of course, but how could I have done it when I'm in it. You're left wondering: who really did it? Who executed the painting of these happy people. But since it's all supposed to be so amusing, you're left to chuckle, to think, how cute, how tricky. You're supposed to smile. But no one was smiling in the picture on the wall. It seemed like a house of smoke and mirrors and I was damn glad to leave.

"As I drove home, I sure as hell wasn't smiling. There was something terribly disturbing about it all. I felt nauseated, disgusted, really disturbed. Maybe it seems obvious, but I felt there was a connection between this weird experience and myself. A double connection, actually. I won't go into all the details now, and you know about my writer's block, but this bizarre experience has left me with a new sense of freedom, some kind of opening to a new way to write that at the time I couldn't put my finger on. I've come to think of it as writing beyond a cage of categories.

"I thought about all the stuff we talk about, the political propaganda about everything, the loss of a sense of reality, the illusions and delusions with the digital technology, the warmongering by the U.S against Russia, the COVID bullshit, all of it, all the stuff we share over beers. Especially the disconnect between the private and the public and the two-faced nature of a way of living that is so fucking phony. I realized why I had been hiding in my notebooks, how they had become my cage.

"To top it all off, when I got home and told Sara about my experiences with Tom Finn, the cage and all, she didn't believe me. She accused me of having drunk too much, which I had to admit I did. She said I was scaring her with such a ridiculous tale and that I was sounding like a deluded conspiracy nut.

"Anyway, I've told no one else about Finn. I'm afraid they wouldn't believe me either. You're a sociologist and know all about Max Weber's prediction of a coming disenchanted world with its iron cage. Shit, I feel like I had a small glimpse of it. Do you think anyone would believe me if I told this story?

"Do you?"

Masked, Homeless, and Desolate

Walk the streets in the United States and many countries these days and you will see streaming crowds of people possessed by demons, masked and anonymous, whose eyes look like vacuums, staring into space or out of empty sockets like the dead, afraid of their own ghosts. Fear and obedience oozes from them. Death walks the streets with people on leashes in lockstep.

That they have been the victims of a long-planned propaganda campaign to use an invisible virus to cower them into submission and shut down the world's economy for the global elites is beyond their ken. This is so even when the facts are there to prove otherwise. It is not a conspiracy theory but a blatant factual plan spelled out in the 2010 Rockefeller Report, the October 18, 2019 Event 201, and Agenda 21, among other places.

Who can wake up the sleepwalkers in this cowardly new world where culture and politics collude to create and exploit ignorance?

On July 20, 1965, Bob Dylan released his song, "Like a Rolling Stone." It arrived like a rocking jolt into the placid pop musical culture of the day. It was not about wanting to hold someone's hand or cry in the chapel. It wasn't mumbo-jumbo like "Wooly Bully," the number one hit. It wasn't like the pop pap that dominates today's music scene. It wasn't Woody Guthrie in slow time.

It beat you up. It attacked. It confronted you. Maybe, if you were alive then, you thought Dylan was kidding you. You thought wrong. Bitching about his going electric was a dodge. He was addressing all of us, including himself.

Still is. But who wants to hear his recent "Murder Most Foul" and read Dylan's scathing lyrics about the assassination of JFK, the killing that started the slow decay that has resulted in such masked madness. "And please, Don't Let Me Be Misunderstood," he tells us in capital letters for emphasis. Exactly what all the mainstream media have done, of course, and not by accident.

There are no alibis. "How does it feel/To be on your own/with no direction home/A complete unknown/Like a rolling stone?"

It was in the mid-1960s when confidence in knowing where home was and how to get there disappeared into thin air. If you left mommy and daddy, could you ever get back from where you were going? Who had the directions? Absolutes were melting and relativity was widespread. Life was wild and the CIA was planning to make it wilder and more confusing with the introduction of LSD on a vast scale. The CIA's MKUltra was expanding its scope. Operation Mockingbird was singing so many tunes that heads were spinning, as planned. The national security state killers were in the saddle, having already murdered President Kennedy and Malcolm X as they sharpened their knives for many more to come. The peace candidate, Lyndon Baines Johnson, had been elected nine months earlier with 61.1% of the popular vote and went immediately to work secretly expanding the war against Vietnam. War as an invisible virus. Who knew? Who, but a small anti-war contingent, wanted to know? War takes different forms, and the will to ignorance and historical amnesia endure. War is a disease.

Disease is weaponized for war. In 1968 Richard Nixon was elected on a "secret plan" to end the Vietnam War and then ramped it up to monstrous proportions, only to be reelected in 1972 by carrying 49 out of 50 states.

Who wants to know now? The historian Howard Zinn once said correctly that this country's greatest problem wasn't disobedience but obedience.

What's behind the masks? The lockstep?

On the same day that Dylan released "Like a Rolling Stone," Secretary of Defense Robert McNamara, just back from a "fact-finding" trip to Vietnam, recommended to LBJ that U.S. troop levels in Vietnam be increased to 175,000 and that the U.S. should increase its bombing of North Vietnam dramatically. This was the same McNamara who, in October 1963, had agreed with JFK when he signed NSAM 263 calling for the withdrawal of 1,000 military personnel from Vietnam by the end of 1963 and the remainder by the end of 1965. One of the moves that got Kennedy's head blown open.

Poor McNamara, the fog of war must have clouded his conscience, confused the poor boy, just as with Secretary of State Colin Powell holding up that vial of "anthrax" at the United Nations on February 5, 2003 and lying to the world about weapons of mass destruction in Iraq.

Powell recently said, "I knew I didn't have any choice. He's the President." How "painful," to use his word, it must have been for the poor guy, lying so that so many Iraqis could be slaughtered. Of course, he had no choice. These war criminals all wear masks. And have no choice.

Masks, or demonic possession, or both.

Also in that fateful year 1965, far out of sight and out of mind for most Americans, the CIA planned and assisted in the slaughter of more than a million Indonesians, led by their man, General Suharto. This led to the coup against President Sukarno, who two years earlier had been on good terms with JFK as they worked to solve the interrelated issues of Indonesia and Vietnam. Their meeting planned for early 1964 was cancelled in Dallas on November 22, 1963.

And the politicians and media luminaries came out in their masks and told the public that communists everywhere were out to get them.

It's tough being on your own. It hurts to think too much. Or think for yourself, at least. To obey an authority higher than your bosses. "I was tricked" is some sort of mantra, is it not?

"Oh, you never turned around to see the frowns on the jugglers and the clowns/When they all did tricks for you."

Dylan was lost and disgusted when he wrote the song. His own music sickened him, which, for an artist, means he sickened himself. He had just returned from a tour of England and was sick of people telling him how much they loved his music when he didn't. He needed to change.

What else is the point of art but change? If you're dead, or afraid of getting dead, you aren't going to change. You're stuck. Stuck is dead. Why wear a mask if you know who you are?

Knowledge, or more accurately, pseudo-knowledge or mainstream media lies, is a tomb "the mystery tramp" sold to us, a place to hide to avoid pain and guilt.

I have read more books than anyone I know. It sickens me.

I know too much. That sickens me.

I sicken myself. All the news sickens me.

I know so much no one believes me.

As Frank Serpico once told me: "It's all lies."

Of course. Dylan and Serpico are blood brothers.

Only art tells the truth. Real art.

Not bullshit pop art. Some say "Like a Rolling Stone" is about Edie Sedgwick, "the girl of the year" in 1965 and one of Andy Warhol's superstars. Perhaps to a degree it is, but it's far more than that. It's about us.

Poor Edie was poisoned by her wealthy family at a young age and barely had a chance. She was an extreme example of a rather common American story. People poisoned in the cradle. Thinking of her got me thinking of Andy Warhol, the death obsessed hoarder, the guy who called his studio "The Factory" in a conscious or unconscious revelation of his art and persona, his wigs and masks and the hold he has had on American culture all these years. Isn't he the ultimate celebrity?

Warhol once took my photo on a deserted street. His and my secret but this is the truth. West 47th Street in New York City on an early Sunday morning, 1980. I guess he thought he was doing art or collecting images for his museum of dead heads. When I asked him why, he said I had an interesting face. I told him he did too, rather transparent and creepy, but I didn't want to capture him. He was a ghost with a camera, a face like a death mask, trying to capture a bit of life. I told him I didn't give him permission to shoot me, but he turned and walked away into the morning mist. The shooters always just walk away in pseudo-innocence.

I then went down the street to the Gotham Book Mart that was my destination and asked James Joyce why he had written

"The Dead," and Joyce, secretive as ever, quoted himself, "Ed," he said, "Think you're escaping and run into yourself. Longest way round is the shortest way home." Now that was direction.

Only those who know how to play and be guided by intuition are able to escape the living tomb of so-called knowledge; what Dylan called, lifelessness. But that was from "Desolation Row," released as the closing track of *Highway 61 Revisited* on August 30, 1965. The only acoustic song on the album. Slow it down to make the point another way. "Like a Rolling Stone" was the opening track.

Do you feel all alone or part of a masked gang roaming the streets incognito? Ms. and Mr. Lonely, does that mask help? How do you feel?

Desolation means very lonely. From Latin, *de*, completely, *solare*, lonely.

Does that mask help? Do you feel alone together now, one of the crowd?

Do you really want to know about desolation row? It's here. It was here in 1965, too. Only the truly lonely know how it feels to really be all alone.

The Umbrella People, those who some call the deep state or secret government under whose protection all the politicians work, say they want to protect us all from death and disease. They are lying bastards who've gotten so many to imitate their masked ways. They can only sing a mockingbird's song.

Listen to real singers. Dylan has arched the years, as true artists do. Who has paid close attention to what he said this year about the assassination of President Kennedy in his song, "Murder Most Foul"? Or were many caught up in the propaganda surrounding corona virus, and rather than contemplating his indictment of the U.S. government and its media accomplices, were they contemplating their navels to see if a virus had secreted itself in there? Viruses lurk everywhere, they say, and the corporate media made certain to circulate a vaccine about the truth in Dylan's song. This is normal operating procedure.

We are on still on Desolation Row.

To Rebel Against Necessity and More

Autumn is the dying season. This morning when I came home from a walk, a bluejay was lying by the house on his back. He was dead.

Yet an autumn day like today in the mountains is so beautiful that everything vibrates with life. The air chimes. The clouds tango across the blue dance floor above. The leaves sway to some celestial tune. And the lake laps in synchronicity to singing hearts.

My heart was singing before I found him. His blueness and his beauty startled me. I touched him in the hope that he would move, but he stayed still, on his back with his eyes open. A still life. A life stilled. Only one of millions of fallen birds, yet I felt an immense sadness at the sight of him, as if he were waiting there to tell me something. I wanted so badly to resurrect him, for he seemed so alive in death. I felt myself returning to the blues I felt before my walk.

> Vincent Van Gogh wrote to his brother Theo these words: I feel more and more that we must not judge God on the basis of this world; it's a study that didn't come off. What can you do, in a study that has gone wrong, if you are fond of the artist? You do not find much to criticize; you hold your tongue. But you have a right to ask for something better. It is only a master who can make such a muddle, and perhaps that is the best consolation we

> have out of it, since then we have a right to hope that we'll see the same creative hand get even with itself.

This bluejay was a small creature, and many people hate his kind. He's a bully bird, they say. In the celebrated novel, *To Kill a Mockingbird*, the hero, Atticus Finch says one shouldn't kill a mockingbird but kill all the bluejays you can hit.

I am wondering who or what killed this beautiful bluejay at my feet, but I will never know.

I do know that "Operation Mockingbird" killed many minds and hearts, and resulted in untold numbers of deaths worldwide. This CIA media propaganda program in which all the major media were doing the bidding of the CIA was allegedly dismantled after its discovery in the 1970s, but it no doubt operates today under a different name. Perhaps its code name is Operation Bluejay, since the bluebird was already used for "Project Bluebird," a predecessor to MKULtra, the CIA's other massive mind control program.

The bird names migrate, but they seem to return under different nomenclature for people who are in the business of killing singers of songs of freedom.

They are the killers of Ernesto "Che" Guevara, the Argentinian revolutionary.

For before my walk, I had started to read an article, with declassified CIA and U.S. government documents from the National Security Archives, about his death on October 9, 1967. He was Fidel Castro's right-hand man in the Cuban Revolution, was executed by the CIA-led Bolivian military after having been captured in a firefight in the Bolivian mountains. Fascists killed the courageous Che as he fought to inspire the oppressed to rise up against U.S. imperialism. They executed him in cold blood, consciously and proudly. They posed with his dead body, like macho hunters pose while holding a bird they have just shot.

Writing in *The Nation* magazine three year ago, Peter Kornbluh, the director of the National Security Archives' Chile and Cuba Documentation Projects, described how he had met in Miami with Gustavo Villoldo, who had been the top Cuban-American CIA operative assigned to assist in tracking down and capturing Guevara, the iconic revolutionary, in Bolivia. Villoldo told Kornbluh how he cut off the dead Che's hands and pieces of his hair and beard before secretly burying his body, which was discovered and dug up in 1997, minus his hand bones. Kornbluh writes:

> At one point during the conversation, Villoldo opened the binder and pulled out a white envelope. Inside was a clump of brown hair. As the ultimate souvenir of this Cold War victory, Villoldo proudly stated, he had cut off strands of Che's hair before disposing of his body. "I basically took it because the symbol of the revolution was this bearded, long-haired guy coming down the mountain," Villoldo later explained. "To me, I was cutting off the very symbol of the Cuban revolution."

Maybe a hawk killed the bluejay, but if so, it didn't gloat over its body. It would have been operating under the laws of necessity, where as far as we know, compassion has no place. Not true for Che's killers. They posed for the camera, guns still aimed at the dead man, as if he still posed a great danger to them. They were right, at least in the long term.

Ernesto Che Guevara is also lying on his back, eyes open. Seeing the bluejay in a similar pose an hour after seeing this photograph, which I had studied for many minutes, gave me a jolt. The bird's blueness entered my soul. Blue blue blue—I felt I was sinking into a deep hole of sorrow and despair. My sorrow for the bird was nothing compared to the deep rage and anguish I felt when once again I viewed the photo of Che surrounded by cowards, and I thought of all the victims from Bolivia to the Congo and all around the world who have suffered and died—and continue to do so—at the hands of all the ruthless forces like those he opposed. I wanted so badly to resurrect him, for he seemed so alive in death. And his CIA killers so dead by comparison.

Here was a man of immense courage who gave his life for his beliefs, who was the embodiment of the Cuban Revolution, who cared deeply to liberate the world's oppressed from U.S.-led imperialism. I kept thinking of another revolutionary on the run from fascist forces, Pietro Spina in Ignazio Silone's great novel, *Bread and Wine*, who, disguised as a priest in Mussolini's Italy, tells a frightened girl who is worried what will ensue if the government captures the rebel leader, who is actually the "priest" she is talking to. "And if they catch him and kill him?" the girl asked.

> Killing a man who says "No!" is a risky business, the priest replied, because even a corpse can go on whispering "No! No! No!" with a persistence and obstinacy that only certain corpses are capable of. And how can you silence a corpse?

We know Che's voice has not been silenced where victims of imperialism continue to suffer and be killed around the world. But here in the United States, the image-makers have fashioned him into a celebrity whose message is lost, another casualty of mind control and the propagandists who control the corporate media. The people he fought against.

Everyone has seen Che's image somewhere. Posters of his visage adorn college dormitory rooms. You know, the man with the tousled hair and the beard. The cool charismatic guy! The handsome man who road a motorcycle, was articulate, and could write and speak eloquently. The Che on coffee mugs and tee-shirts everywhere. All derived from one photographtaken by Cuban photographer Alberto Korda for the revolutionary newspaper *Revolución* in Havana in 1960. A photograph that never earned Korda a cent, but has been exploited by countless money vultures, including the artist Andy Warhol. Che wrote in *Socialism and Man in Cuba*:

> A school of artistic inquiry is invented, which is said to be the definition of freedom; but this "inquiry" has its limits, imperceptible until there is a clash, that is, until the real problems of man and his alienation arise. Meaningless anguish or vulgar amusement thus become convenient safety valves for human anxiety. The idea

of using art as a weapon of protest is combated. Those who play by the rules of the game are showered with honours—such honours as a monkey might get for performing pirouettes. The condition is that one does not try to escape from the invisible cage.

Then as now, escaping from that invisible cage is our task, a cage that teaches us not to rebel against what is called "necessity," but to exploit others every way we can. To profit from their suffering, which is the nature of imperialism. To close our eyes and make believe it is possible to live in an imperialistic country abroad and have a democracy at home. Sooner or later, this pipe dream will come crashing down. Perhaps that is happening now.

> *"Compassion has no place in the natural order of the world, which operates on the basis of necessity. The laws of necessity are as unexceptional as the laws of gravitation. The human faculty of compassion opposes this order and is therefore best thought of as being in some way supernatural."*
>
> —JOHN BERGER, "A Man with Tousled Hair," from *The Shape of a Pocket*

Acting As If It Weren't Really So

"Laughing on the bus/Playing Games with the faces/
She said the man in the gabardine suit was a spy/
I said, 'Be careful his bowtie is really a camera.'"
—PAUL SIMON, "*America*"

Only people who listen to the chorus of reliable alternative media voices warning of the quickly growing threat of nuclear war have any sense of the nightmare that is approaching in 2024–25. Even for them, however, and surely for most others, unreality reigns. Reality has a tough time countering illusions. For we are cataleptically slow-walking to WW III. If it is very hard or impossible to imagine our own deaths, how much harder is it to imagine the deaths of hundreds of millions or more of others.

In 1915, amid the insane slaughter of tens of millions during WW I that was a shock to the meliorist fantasy of the long-standing public consciousness that had prevailed for a century—as Paul Fussell put it in *The Great War and Modern Memory*—"It reversed the idea of progress," Freud wrote:

> It is indeed impossible to imagine our own death, and whenever we attempt to do so, we can perceive that we are in fact still present as spectators. Hence the psychoanalytic school could venture on the assertion that, at bottom, no one believes in his own death, or to put the same thing another way, that, in the unconscious, every one of us is convinced of his own immortality.

The growing lunacy of the Biden administration's provocations against Russia via Ukraine seem lost on so many. The long-running and deep-seated demonization of Russia and its president, Vladimir Putin, by U.S. propagandists has sunk so deep into the Western mind that facts can't penetrate that depth to counteract it. It is one of the greatest triumphs of U.S. government propaganda.

A friend, a retired history professor at an elite university, recently told me that he can't think of such matters as the growing threat of nuclear war if he wants to sleep at night, but anyway, he's more concerned with the consequences of global warming. Readers at publications where my numerous articles about the nuclear war risk have appeared—the worst since the Cuban Missile Crisis of October 1962—have made many comments such as "nuclear weapons don't exist," that it's all a hoax, that Putin is in cahoots with Biden in a game of fear mongering to promote their secret agendas, etc. How can one respond to such denials of reality?

The other day I met another friend who likes to talk about politics. He is an intelligent and a caring man. He was sporting a tee-shirt with a quote from George Washington and quickly started talking about his obsessive fear of Donald Trump and the possibility that he could be elected again. I told him that I despised Trump but that Biden was a far greater threat right now. He spoke highly of Biden, and when I responded that Biden has been a warmonger throughout his political career and of course in Ukraine was instigating the use of nuclear weapons, and was in full support of Israel's genocide of Palestinians, he looked at me as if I were saying something he had never heard before. When I spoke of the 2014 U.S. engineered coup d'état in Ukraine, he, a man in his sixties at least, said he was unaware of it, but in any case Biden supported our military as he did and that was good. When I said Biden is mentally out of it and physically tottering, he emphatically denied it; said Biden was very sharp and fully engaged. He said Trump was fat and a great danger and George Washington would agree. I was at a loss for words. The conversation ended.

A third friend, just back from living overseas for a year, flew back east from California to visit old friends and relatives. He told me this sad tale:

> There were experiences that troubled me very deeply during my visit that had nothing to do with all the death and final goodbyes I was immersed in. My family I would say is pretty typical working class Democrat. Liberal/progressive in social outlook. Most are devout Catholics. All are kind, generous very loving people. What was troubling was that it was pretty much impossible to carry on a rational reasonably sane political conversation with all but a couple of them, as the "Trump Derangement Syndrome" symptoms were absolutely off the charts. It was quite stunning actually. It is almost as if Dementia-Joe isn't even in office as they had no interest in discussing his many failings, because their entire focus was the orange haired clown. If I had ten bucks for every time someone told me any one of the following NPR/PBS talking points I'd buy a nice meal for myself—(Trump will be a dictator if elected—Trump will prosecute his enemies if elected—Trump will destroy our democracy if he gets in—etc.) Any and all attempts to question these narratives and talking points by bringing the behavior of the current administration into the conversation were met with befuddlement—as if people couldn't believe that "I" wasn't as terrified as they were by the "Trump-Monster" lurking in the shadows.
>
> So I guess I'm sharing these thoughts with you Ed because it feels like I'm dealing with several different kinds of loss right now. The more obvious "loss" associated with the physical death of loved ones—but I'm also mourning the intellectual and psychological death of living loved ones who have somehow become completely untethered from the "material realities" I observe on planet earth. They can repeat "talking

> points" but can't explain the evidence or reason that needs to be attached to those talking points for them to be anything but propaganda. Physical death is a natural thing—something we will all face—but this intellectual and spiritual death I am witness to is perhaps even more painful and disconcerting for me. How do we find our way forward when reason, rational debate, evidence, and real-world events are replaced with fear—and rather irrational fears at that?

This intellectual and spiritual death that he describes is a widespread phenomenon. It is not new, but COVID-19 with its lockdowns, lies, and dangerous "vaccines" dramatically intensified it. It created vast gaps in interpersonal communication that were earlier exploited in the lead-up to the 2016 election and Trump's surprising victory. Families and friends stopped talking to each other. The longstanding official propaganda apparatus went into overdrive. Then in 2020 the normal human fear of death and chaos was fully digitized during the lockdowns. Putin, Trump, the Chinese, sexual predators, viruses, space aliens, your next door neighbor, etc.—you name it—were all tossed into the mix that created an amorphous fear and panic to replace the growing realization that the terror initiated by George W. Bush's war on terror in 2001 was losing its power. New terrors have since been created, censorship reinforced, and here we are in 2024 in a country supporting Israeli genocide in Gaza and with a population blind to the growing threat of WW III and the use of nuclear weapons.

The communication gap—what my friend aptly describes as "this intellectual and spiritual death"—is two-sided. On one hand there is simple ignorance of what is really going on in the world, greatly aided by vast government/media propaganda. On the other, there is chosen ignorance or the wish to be deceived, to maintain illusions.

We are thinking reeds as Pascal called us, vulnerable feeling creatures afraid of death; we only care enough to want to be deceived as to the impacts of our support for wars that make so much blood inside other people get to the outside for the earth to drink, since it is not our blood and we survive.

I could, of course, quote liberally from truth tellers down through history who have said the same thing about self-deception with all its shades and nuances. Those quotations are endless. Why bother? At some very deep level in the recesses of their hearts, people know it's true. I could make a pretty essay here, be erudite and eloquent, and weave a web of wisdom from all those the world says were the great thinkers because they are now dead and the hypocrisy they detected was in the past.

For the desire to be deceived and hypocrisy (Greek *hypokrites*, stage actor, a pretender) are kissing cousins. Grasping the theatrical nature of social life, the need to pretend, to act, to feel oneself part of a "meaningful" play explains a lot. To stand outside consensus reality, outside the stage door, so to speak, is not very popular. Despite the mass idiocy of the media's daily barrage of lies and stupidities that pass for news on the front pages and newscasts of the corporate media, people want to believe them to feel they belong.

Yet D. H. Lawrence's point a century ago still applies: "The essential American soul is isolate, stoic, and a killer. It has never yet melted."

But this killer soul must be hidden behind a wall of deceptions as the U.S. warfare state ceaselessly wages wars all around the world. It must be hidden behind feel good news stories about how Americans really care about others, but only others that they are officially allowed to care about. Not Syrians, Yemenis, Russian speakers of the Donbass, Palestinians, et al. The terrorist nature of decades upon decades of U.S. savagery and the indifference of so many Americans go hand-in-hand but escape notice by the corporate media propagandists. The major theme of these media is that the United States government is the great defender of freedom, peace, and democracy. Every once in a while, a scapegoat, one rotten apple in the barrel, is offered up in admission that all is not perfect in paradise. Here or there a decent article appears to reinforce the illusion that the corporate media tell the truth. This is essential for good propaganda.

Here's an anecdote about a very strange encounter, one I couldn't make up. A communication of some sort that also has a make-believe quality to it. I'm not sure what the message is.

I was recently meeting with a writer and researcher who has interviewed scores of people about the famous 1960s assassinations and other sensitive matters. I only knew this person through internet communication, but he was passing my way and suggested that we meet, which we did at a local out-of-the-way cafe. We were the only customers and we took our drinks out the back to a small table and chairs under a tree in the café's large garden that bordered open land down to a river. About 10 yards away a woman sat at a table writing in a notebook that I took to be journaling of some sort.

The researcher and I talked very openly for more than two hours about our mutual work and what he had learned from many of his interviewees about the assassinations. Neither of us paid any attention to the woman at the table—naively?—and our conversation naturally revolved around the parts played by intelligence agencies, the CIA, etc. in the assassinations of the Kennedys and MLK, Jr. The woman sat and wrote.

Near the end of our two plus hours, my friend went inside the café, which had closed to new customers, to use the men's room. The woman called to me and said I hope you don't mind but I overheard some of your conversation and my father worked for U.S. intelligence. She then told us much more about him, where he went to college, etc. or at least what she said she knew because when growing up he didn't tell her mother, her, or siblings any details about his decades of spying. But when she attended his memorial service in Washington D.C., the place was filled with intelligence operatives and she learned more about her father's secretive life.

Then, out of the blue, it burst out of her how he was obsessed with the high school he attended, one she assured us we probably never heard of (we were in Massachusetts)—Regis High School, a Jesuit scholarship prep school for boys in NYC. To say I was startled is an understatement, since I went to Regis myself (as did Anthony Fauci and many other establishment media and political types), and the anomalous "coincidence" of this encounter in the back garden of an empty café spooked my friend as well.

Who had set up whom?

I wondered who wore the bowtie and if what just happened entailed more than it seemed.

Sick, and Sick of It All

Sometimes it takes our bodies to return us to our souls. And our little pains to remind us of the indescribable pain of the savage killing and dismemberment of innocent children and adults in Gaza and many other places by U.S. weapons produced in clean factories by people just doing their jobs and collecting their pay at "defense" contractors Raytheon, Lockheed Martin, Pfizer, etc. Abstraction is the name of the game as human bodies are torn to pieces "over there" and the obscene profits are transferred at the computer terminals day and night.

Living in a technological world of the internet divorces us from real life as it passes into inert, abstract, and dead screen existence. It should not be surprising that people grow sick and tired of the steady streams of "news" that fills their days and nights. So much of the news is grotesque; propaganda abounds. Stories twisted right and left to tie minds into knots. After a while, as Macbeth tells us, life seems like "a walking shadow, a poor player, that struts and frets its hour upon the stage, and then is heard no more. It is a tale told by an idiot, full of sound and fury, signifying nothing."

Being sick and out of it for a while allows one a different perspective on the world. This is especially true for those of us who often write about politics and propaganda. A recent illness has forced me to step away from my usual routine of following political events closely. Fleeting headlines have been all I've noted for the past two weeks. While lying around waiting for the illness to leave, I would drift in and out of reveries and memories that would float to semi-consciousness. Feeling miserable prevented any focus or logical thinking, but not, I emphasize, thinking in a deeper, physical sense. But it also gave me a reprieve from noting the repetitive and atomizing nature of internet postings, as if one needs to be hammered over the head again and again to understand the world whose realities are much simpler than the endless scribblers and politicians are willing to admit.

Jonathan Crary, in a scathing critique of the digital world in *Scorched Earth*, puts it thus:

> For the elites, the priority remains: keep people enclosed within the augmented unrealities of the internet complex, where experience is fragmented into a kaleidoscope of fleeting claims of importance, of never-ending admonitions on how to conduct our lives, manage our bodies, what to buy and who to admire or to fear.

I completely agree with Crary. During my sickness, I did manage to read a few brief pieces, an essay, a short story, and a poem. Serendipitously, each confirmed the trend of my thinking over recent years as well as what my bodily discomfit was teaching me.

The first was an essay by the art critic John Berger about the abstract expressionist, avant-garde painter Jackson Pollock, titled "A Kind of Sharing." It struck me as very true. Pollock came to prominence in the late 1940s and early 1950s. He was described as an "action" painter who poured paint on large canvases to create abstract designs that were lauded by the New York art world. Some have sold for hundreds of millions of dollars. The description of Pollock as an untalented pourer, Berger says, is false, for Pollock was a very precise master of his art who was aware of how he was putting paint to canvas and of the effects of his abstractions. His work made no references to the outside world since such painting at that time was considered illustrative. Berger says that Pollock's paintings were violent in that "The body, the flesh, had been rejected and they were the consequence of this rejection." He argues that Pollock, who died in a drunken car crash in Easthampton, Long Island on August 11, 1956, was committing art suicide with his abstract paintings because he had rejected the ancient assumption of painting that the visible contained hidden secrets, that behind appearances there were presences. For Pollock, there was nothing beyond the surfaces of his canvases. This was because he was painting the nothingness he felt and wished to convey. A nihilism that was both personal and abroad in the society.

Pollock's story is a sad one, for he was praised and used by forces far more powerful than he. Nelson Rockefeller, who was president of the Museum of Modern Art (MOMA) that his mother had cofounded, called Pollock's work "free enterprise paintings," and the CIA, through its Congress for Cultural Freedom, secretly promoted it as a Cold War weapon against the Soviet Union's socialist realism art, even as right-wing congressmen ripped Pollock as a perverse artist. So in the name of openness, the CIA secretly promoted Pollock's avant-gardism as real America art in a campaign of propaganda, while the right-wing bashed him as a perverted leftist. This sick double game became a template for future mind-control operations that are widespread today.

As was his habit, Berger brilliantly places Pollock's work within social and political history, a description of *a time very similar to today* when the word "freedom" was bandied about. Then it was the freedom of the Voice of America extolling the Cold War tale of the freedom of the "Free World"; freedom for artists to be free of rhetoric, history, the past, and to jettison the tyranny of the object; freedom of the market amidst a strident yet incoherent sense of loss. He writes:

> At this moment, what was happening in the outside world? For a cultural climate is never separate from events. The United States had emerged from the war as the most powerful nation in the world. The first atom bomb had been dropped. The apocalypse of the Cold War had been placed on the agenda. McCarthy was inventing his traitors. The mood in the country that had suffered least from the war was defiant, violent, haunted. The play most apt to the period would have been Macbeth, and the ghosts were from Hiroshima.

Today there are still ghosts from Hiroshima and Macbeth is still apposite, and the ghosts of all the many millions killed since then would haunt us now if we could see them. Although their bodies have disappeared out the back door of the years—and continue to do so daily—true art is to realize their presence, to hear their cries and conjure their images. While the word freedom is still bandied about in this new Cold War era where the sense of social lostness is even more intense than in Pollock's time, it often comes from a nihilistic despondency similar to Pollock's and those who used atomic weapons, a belief that appearances and surfaces are all and behind them there is nothing. Nada, nada, nada. A society that Roberto Calasso calls "an agnostic theocracy based on nihilism." Berger concludes:

> Jackson Pollock was driven by a despair which was partly his and partly that of the times that nourished him, to refuse this act of faith [that painting reveals a presence behind an appearance]: to insist, with all his brilliance as a painter, that there was nothing behind, that there was only *that which was done to the canvas on the side facing us.* This simple, terrible reversal, born of an individualism that was frenetic, constituted the suicide.

This short essay by Berger about Pollock's denial of the human body struck me as my own body was temporarily failing me. It seemed to contain lessons for the augmented realities of the internet and the new Cold War being waged for the control of our minds and hearts today. Inducements to get lost in abstractions.

Then one day I picked up another book from the shelf to try to distract myself from my physical misery. It was a collection of stories by John Fowles. I read the opening novella—*The Ebony Tower*—haltingly over days. It was brilliant and eerily led me to a place similar to that of Berger's thoughts about Pollock. Fowles explores art and the body against a dreamy background of a manor house in the French countryside. As I read it lying on a couch, I fell in and out of oneiric reveries and sleep, induced by my body's revolt against my mind. Trying to distract myself from my aches and pains, I again found myself ambushed by writing about corporality. Both Berger and Fowles sensed the same thing: that modernity was conspiring to deny the body's reality in favor of visual abstractions. That in doing so our essential humanity was being lost and the slaughters of innocent people were becoming abstractions. Then the Internet came along, at first to offer hope only to become an illusion of freedom increasingly controlled by media in the service of deep-state forces. Soon the only way to write and distribute the truth will be retro—on paper and exchanged hand to hand. This no doubt sounds outlandish to those who have swallowed the digital mind games, but they will be surprised once they fully wake up.

Fowles's story is about David, an art historian who goes to visit a famous, cranky old painter named Henry Breasely. The younger man is writing about the older and thinks it would be interesting to meet him, even though he thinks it isn't necessary in order to write the article he has already composed in his mind. The art historian, like many of his ilk, lives in his mind, in academic abstractions. He is in a sense "pure mind," in many ways a replica of T.S. Eliot's neurotic J. Alfred Prufrock. The old painter lives in the physical world, where sex and the body and nature enclose his world, where paint is used to illuminate the physical reality of life, its sensuousness, not abstractions, where physical life and death infuse his work, including political realities. Obviously not new to William Butler Yeats' discovery as expressed in the conclusion to his poem "The Circus Animals' Desertion":

> Those masterful images because complete
> Grew in pure mind but out of what began?
> A mound of refuse or the sweepings of a street,
> Old kettles, old bottles, and a broken can,
> Old iron, old bones, old rags, that raving slut
> Who keeps the till. Now that my ladder's gone
> I must lie down where all the ladders start
> In the foul rag and bone shop of the heart.

The old man fiercely defends the "foul rag and bone shop of the heart" against all abstractions and academic bullshit, which are the young man's métier. He accuses the young critic of being afraid of the human body. When the critic responds, "Perhaps more interested in the mind than the genitals," the caustic and funny painter says, "God help your bloody wife then." He accuses the younger man of being in the game of destruction and castration, of supporting abstractions at the expense of flesh and blood life. "There are worse destroyers around than nonrepresentational art," the critic says in his defense. To which the painter roars, "You'd better tell that to Hiroshima. Or to someone who's been napalmed."

Back and forth they go, as a nubile art student, who is there to help the elderly artist, acts as a sort of an interlocutor. Her presence adds a sexual frisson throughout the story, a temptation to the milk-toast critic's life of sad complacency. The wild old man's rants—he calls Jackson Pollock Jackson Bollock—are continually paraphrased by the girl. She says, "Art is a form of speech. Speech must be based on human needs, not abstract theories of grammar. Or anything but the spoken word. The real word. . . . Ideas are inherently dangerous because they deny human facts. The only answer to fascism is the human fact."

The old painter's uncensored tongue brought tears of laughter to my eyes and a bit of relief to my aches and pains. I was primarily taken aback by the weirdness of haphazardly reading a second piece that coincided with my deepest thoughts that had been intensified by my body's revolt. The narrator's words struck me as especially true to our current situation:

> What the old man still had was an umbilical cord to the past; a step back, he stood by Pisanello's side. In spirit, anyway. While David was encapsulated in book knowledge, art as social institution, science, subject, matter for grants and committee discussion. That was the real kernel of his wildness. David and his generation, and all those to come, could only look back, through bars, like caged animals, born in captivity, at the old green

freedom. That described exactly the experience of those
last two days: the laboratory monkey allowed a glimpse
of his lost true self.

The Internet life has made caged monkeys of us all. We seem to think we are seeing the real world through its connectivity bars, but these cells that enclose us are controlled by our zoo keepers and they are not our friends. Their control of our cages keeps increasing; we just fail to see the multiplying bars. They have created a world of illusions and abstractions serving the interests of global capitalism. Insurgent voices still come through, but less and less as the elites expand their control. As internet access has expanded, the world's suffering has increased and economic inequality heightened. That is an unacknowledged fact, and facts count.

Toward the end of my two-week stay in the land of sickness, I read this poem by the Palestinian poet Refaat Alareer, who was killed in Gaza by an IDF airstrike on December 6, 2023 along with his brother, nephew, sister, and three of her children. My sickness turned to rage.

IF I MUST DIE

If I must die,
you must live
to tell my story
to sell my things
to buy a piece of cloth
and some strings,
(make it white with a long tail)
so that a child, somewhere in Gaza
while looking heaven in the eye
awaiting his dad who left in a blaze —
and bid no one farewell
not even to his flesh
not even to himself —
sees the kite, my kite you made, flying up above,

and thinks for a moment an angel is there
bringing back love.
If I must die
let it bring hope,
let it be a story.

The Cell Phone Is a Pair of Red High Heels

It is comical how easily one can be ignored for pointing out that new technology is dangerous and fetishistic. So-called "smart" cell phones are a prime example. For years I have been pointing out their dangers on many levels. To say most people are devoted to them is an understatement. Maybe it is an exaggeration to say they revere them, but if asked, they will say they couldn't live without them. It's sort of like saying I don't revere my partner but couldn't live without her or him. Ah love!

But what's love got to do with it? Love and romance are out of date. Sex is a just a quick fill-in when there's a break in the technological action. Creative and erotic energy is pissed away on trivia. Being lost and confused and having no time is in. But only the latter can be admitted.

Busy busy busy! Beep beep beep as the eyes go down to the screens. Thumbs athumbing or voices talking to the gadgets, while the busy beavers forget who is under whose thumbs.

Eros is replaced by Chaos while Aphrodite weeps in the woods, but no one hears.

Pass the remote. The silence stings.

We are children of Greece but we forget its truths in our time of digital dementia, if we ever knew them. Beauty is banished for ugliness and technology is worshipped as a god. Art has become meaningless unless it's falsely connected to celebrities and entertainment culture. There are no limits; everything is permitted. Hubris reigns. Even the thought that Digital IDs, Central Bank

Digital Currencies, and vaccination passports are on the agenda does not dissuade the lovers. It's a game of control abetted by radical stupidity, and it is not a mistake.

Floating in a void of gibberish and double-talk, heads barely above the water, alienated from reality while fixated on the Spectacle, while sometimes when panicky looking for a life preserver but never to the right source, this is where technology and capitalism have taken us. On any issue—the bombing of the Nord Stream pipelines, the facts about the U. S. proxy-war against Russia in Ukraine, the Israeli genocide of Palestinians, COVID-19, electoral politics, the economy, etc.—the mainstream media daily pumps out contradictory stories to confuse the public whose attention span has been reduced to a scrolling few seconds. Sustained attention and the ability to dissect the endless propaganda is a thing of the past and receding faster than the computer jargon of milliseconds and nanoseconds. Planned chaos is the proper name for the daily news reports.

Fetishism, in all its forms, rules.

What else is the cell phone but a pair of red high heels?

What else are all those phone photos millions are constantly taking as they antique reality to store in their mausoleums of loss?

What about the constant messaging, the being in touch that never touches?

Despite the fact that everything digital is extremely ephemeral, the "smart" phone itself seems god-like, a way to transcend reality while entering it. "My phone is my rock, and my fortress, and my deliverer; my God, my strength, in whom I will trust; my buckler, and the horn of my salvation, and my high tower."

A toehold on "reality." A machine in hand that saves nine—million abstractions. And prevents boredom from overwhelming minds intent on floating, because, as Walter Benjamin wrote in "The Storyteller," "Boredom is the dream bird that hatches the egg of experience. A rustling in the leaves drives him away." Vibrating and dinging phones will suffice to disturb that dream bird of creative silence that is the antidote to floating in the void of noise.

But fetishes come in many forms because the need for false gods is so attractive. To think you have a way to control reality is addictive.

I recently saw an article about an auction sale at Sotheby's in New York of the movie stars Paul Newman's and Joanne Woodward's personal effects. These include Woodward's (who is still alive and suffering from Alzheimer's disease) wedding ring and dress, the shackles Newman wore in the film *Cool Hand Luke,* a suit from his auto racing days, etc.—over three hundred items in all. According to a Sotheby spokesperson, the Newman-Woodward family, who will receive the proceeds, are doing this to "continue telling the stories of their parents." Don't laugh. The article mentions that one of Paul's watches sold at auction a few years ago for $17.8 million dollars and another for $5.4.

So I ask: what are the wealthy purchasers of these objects really buying? And the answer is quite obvious. They are buying fetishes or transference objects that they think will grant them a piece of the immortal stars' magic. They are buying idols, Oscars, illusions to worship and to touch in place of reality. Ways to enter the cultural hero system.

Ernest Becker put it this way in *The Denial of Death*: "The fetish object represents the magical means for transforming animality into something transcendent and thereby assuring a liberation of the personality from the standard bland and earthbound flesh." If one can possess a piece of the demi-god's power - a signature, a watch, a ring - one will somehow live forever. It's not about "trusting the science" but about believing in the magic.

Newman's daughters who have pushed this sale, as well as a new documentary, *The Last Movie Stars*, and the memoir *Paul Newman: The Extraordinary Life of an Ordinary Man*—compiled from their father's transcripts of conversations with his friend, Stewart Stern, over thirty years ago—have done something supremely ironic. On one hand, they are selling their father's and mother's memorabilia, allegedly to tell their stories, through things that are fetishes for those desperate for holy secular relics (or for storing value in unique objects when the currency seems shaky), while at the same time publishing a book in which Paul honestly knocks himself off the pedestal and says he was always an insecure guy, numbed by his childhood and the false face Hollywood created for him. In other words, an ordinary man with talent who was very successful in Hollywood's dream factory, where illusions are the norm.

"I was my mother's Pinocchio, the one that went wrong," he tells us right away, leading us to the revelations of his human, all-too-human reality. His was a life of facades and dead emotions, false faces, and his struggles to become who he really was. He tells us he wasn't his film roles, not Hud or Brick or Fast Eddie or Cool Hand Luke, but he wasn't really the guy playing them either. He was a double enigma, an actor playing an actor. He says:

> I've always had a sense of being an observer of my own life. . . . I have a sense of watching something, but not of living something. It's like looking at a photograph that's out of focus . . . . It's spacey; I guess I always feel spaced out.

His courageous honesty reminds me of Friedrich Nietzsche's final work, *Ecce Home* (Behold the Man), not because Paul waxes philosophical but because he's brutally honest. If a movie star's truths strike you as not comparable to those of a great philosopher, I would suggest considering that Nietzsche's key concern was the theater and how we are all actors, a few genuine and most false. In *The Twilight of the Idols* he asked, "Are you genuine? Or merely an actor? A representative? Or that which is represented? In the end, perhaps you are merely a copy of an actor."

Paul Newman lived for 17 years after speaking to his friend Stewart Stern. I like to think those conversations helped him break through to becoming who he really was. From what I know of the man, he was generous to a fault and did much to ease others' pains, especially to bring joy to children with cancer. I think he changed. While his things that are on the auction block now serve as illusionary fetishes for those looking for crutches, I believe he finally threw away the mental crutches he used when playing

Brick in *Cat on A Hot Tin Roof.* Perhaps the wooden ones will be in the auction and some desperado will bid on them.

There is something very chilling in the way the reality of flesh and blood humans living in a natural world has been replaced by all types of fetishes—drugs, objects, celebrities, machines, etc. While all are connected, the cell phone is key because of its growing centrality to the elites' push for a digitized world. No matter how many articles and news reports about Artificial Intelligence (AI) that appear, it is all just a gloss on a long-developing problem that goes back many years—machine worship.

"Smart" cell phones are the current apotheotic control mechanism promoted as liberation. They are a form of slavery promoted by the World Economic Forum, their bosses, and their minions. As Alastair Crooke, a former British diplomat, puts it, "It is that a majority of the people are so numbed and passive—and so in lockstep—as the state inches them through a series of repeating emergencies towards a new kind of authoritarianism, that they don't fuss greatly, or even notice much." Freedom is slavery.

Here is Ernest Becker again:

> Boss [Medard Boss, Swiss psychanalyst and psychiatrist] says that the terrible guilt feelings of the depressed person are existential, that is, they represent failure to live one's own life, to fulfill one's own potential because of the twisting and turning to be "good" in the eyes of the other. The other calls the tune to one's eligibility for immortality, and so the other takes up one's unlived life. . . . In short, even if one is a very guilty hero he is at least a hero in the same hero-system [personal and cultural]. The depressed person uses guilt to hold onto his objects and to keep his situation unchanged. Otherwise he would have to analyze it or be able to move out of it and transcend it. . . . Better guilt and self-punishment when you cannot punish the other—when you cannot even dare to accuse him [the social system], as he represents the immortality ideology with which you have identified. If your god is discredited, you yourself die;

the evil must be in yourself and not in your god, so that
you may live.

I wonder if I should bid on the shackles Paul Newman wore as the prisoner in *Cool Hand Luke*. They are probably the cheapest item on the auction menu. I think they will remind me that the Captain of the chain gang was wrong when he said to Luke, "What we've got here is failure to communicate."

"Where are you calling from," she asked. "My cell," he said.

"Of course," she answered.

Is a Happy New Year Possible?

"The struggle itself toward the heights is enough to fill a man's heart. One must imagine Sisyphus happy."
—ALBERT CAMUS, T*he Myth of Sisyphus*

Really? Or was he joking?

Whenever January rolls around and a new year begins with its implied ending, I think of my father and Albert Camus, both born in 1913. Camus died on January 4, 1960 in a strange car crash, which might have been an assassination according to Italian author Giovanni Catelli, while my father, who almost died in a car crash, was born on January 9. They did not know each other personally, although they were kindred souls in the way that seeming opposites attract.

One a Nobel Prize winning author who wrote *The Fall*, the confession of a lawyer, Jean-Baptiste Clamence, whose monologue from a seedy bar reveals his guilt for living a phony, cowardly, and inauthentic life—"When one has no character one *has* to apply a method," he says; the other (my father) a lawyer with character, an eloquent and witty writer who always, unlike Clamence, downplayed and did not parade his good deeds because he did them out of a pure heart.

Camus said he did not believe in God, yet I think a part of him did as filtered through his secular saint Tarrou in *The Plague* and his dialogue with Dominican Friars, among other writing, although he kept it publicly well hidden. My father, baptized a Catholic like Camus, was a life-long believer, never letting any doubts directly show, except for his love for Graham Green's book, *Monsignor Quixote*. Both were reserved men in the best sense of the word.

For faith and doubt always play their shadow show in all souls.

In a review of *Bread and Wine* by Ignazio Silone, Camus wrote, "For the grandeur of a faith can be measured by the doubts it inspires." In this case he was referring to secular faith, but he was lavishing praise on a novel that explores the interplay between secular and sacred faith, the former having its deepest roots in the later.

It is the story of Pietro Spina, the anti-fascist Italian revolutionary during Mussolini's time, who is in hiding disguised as a priest, and his former teacher, the priest Don Benedetto. Hunted and surveilled by Italy's fascist government, they secretly meet and talk of the need to resist the forces of state and church collaborating in violence and suppression. Don Benedetto tells Pietro, "But it is enough for one little man to say 'No!' murmur 'No!' in his neighbor's ear, or write 'No!' on the wall at night, and public order is endangered."

And Pietro says, "Liberty is something you have to take for yourself. It's no use begging it from others."

The two characters represent one truth, that the spirit of rebellion is sacred and profane. This Camus knew from the start, despite his reputation for being an unbeliever. When Pietro and Don Benedetto meet and talk about the need to resist the fascist government—two priests, so to speak, one disguised and one actual—we come to fully realize that they are one genuine person separated at birth for story-telling purposes. The younger tells the older that "it was a religious impulse that led me into the revolutionary movement," but that he had lost his faith in God many years before.

To which the elderly priest replies, "It does not matter. In these times of conspiratorial and secret struggle the Lord is obliged to hide Himself and assume pseudonyms. Besides, and you know it, He does not attach much importance to His name. . . ."

Silone writes: "The idea of God Almighty being forced to go about under a false passport amused the younger man greatly.

He looked at his old schoolmaster in astonishment, and suddenly saw him in a very different light from the image of him that he had preserved during the long years since they had last met."

If one carefully reads Camus' oeuvre, it becomes apparent that his sense of the sacred was profound even while saying that he didn't believe in God; so too was his commitment to resist evil and to see the sense of the absurd as a starting point and not a destination. "But does nothing have a meaning? I have never believed that we could remain at this point," he said. "Even as I was writing *The Myth of Sisyphus* I was thinking about the essay on revolt (*The Rebel*) that I would write later on. . . ."

Not to wallow in the absurd but to rebel against human suffering and oppression and to also serve beauty were always his twin goals. He saw his vocation as an artist as a call to give voice to the sorrows and joys of everyone, not as a solitary elitist, but as a writer engaged in the world.

In an illuminating essay, "Thomas Merton's Affinity with Albert Camus," Jim Forest wrote the following, which I would second:

> In fact what Camus rejected was not the person of Christ but a pseudo-Christianity that had become a mechanism for blessing the established order, a religion of accommodation that provides chaplains to witness executions without raising a word of protest, a religion committed to the status quo rather than the kingdom of God. What Camus was missing in the world were Christians who reminded him of Christ.

Which sounds like Silone's Pietro Spina and Don Benedetto in dialogue.

But then there is Sisyphus and this happiness issue, which is my central concern. Camus always fought against injustice and was well aware that he was living in a world where soulless and ruthless force was the context for all he wrote. The specifics have changed today, but the general principal prevails with social convulsions, violence, and endless wars in many guises. The old Cold War is now the new.

For Camus, the Greek myth of Sisyphus, the never-ending need to roll our rocks to the hilltop only to watch them come tumbling back down, these rolling stones of effort upon effort to resist the world's predators with their death-loving violence and the feeling of the uselessness of these uphill battles with our stones falling back at our feet as we try and try again to say "no"—this, and the indifferent silence of the natural world that devours people as appetizers—he called the absurd, the unbridgeable chasm between our desires for happiness and the world's indifference, including the hateful indifference of the world's elites and their evil efforts to control and murder regular people.

And lest I forget one tiny insignificant detail, and one that was at the heart of Camus' writing, the fact that we all die and that the day-to-day grind of struggling "to make a living" and be normal social beings can collapse in an instant on any street corner when one asks "why," and the absurd enters as "the stage sets collapse."

For Camus, Sisyphus and the feeling of the absurd were entwined, but why *must* we then imagine Sisyphus happy? The endless struggle against violence, lies, and injustice is exhausting and one must fight against falling into the pit of despair. So I ask again: Was Camus joking? He was not known for his humor.

Happy is a funny word; its etymology tells us so: it derives from the Old Norse *happ,* meaning chance, good luck, fortune. And I think for anyone who contemplates it, happiness, however one defines it, is not a constant state. It comes and goes if one is lucky. There are so many suffering people throughout the world for whom the word is a foreign language, since they are so victimized by violence and poverty that just to survive is their kind of luck.

Happiness cannot be sought, although there are countless books and happiness gurus who will take your money to tell you it can and they have the method. It's interesting to note that over the past twenty-five years or so the happiness industry has grown in equal measure to the overwhelming deterioration of the world situation. The more depressed, deprived, and distracted more people have become as the world's elites have waged war in all its forms everywhere, the more the clamor to "just be happy" has been heard. If it weren't so "absurd," I'd think someone would have claimed to have invented happiness pills.

After reading Edmund Gosse's 1907 memoir about his Victorian childhood and his relationship with his very religious father, *Father and Son*, my father wrote to me saying that it reminded him of the two of us, a father who remained conventionally religious while the son rejected conventional Christianity for a dissident's path. But then he added, commenting on the seeming difference, "Quién sabe? (Who knows?).

Contradictions abound, which he knew, and such contradictions cut through the human heart. So I wonder, what can cut through the contradictions?

For we are all full of contradictions in our different ways, but the question remains how we might be happy in the midst of life's struggles. How to live with our contradictions, how to reconcile them. How not to be so single-minded that we can't say, "Happy New Year" and mean it simply in all its complexity.

Although I think Camus was slightly wrong to say "we *must*" imagine Sisyphus happy, I think we may. Albert himself famously said that "In the midst of winter, I finally learned that there was in me an invincible summer." This "invincible summer" is the love of life despite all the struggles we go through. Camus was no stranger to them—the delights and the struggles—nor my father nor I nor anyone. Life is an *agon*—a conflict, struggle. contest—as the Greeks would put it. But it is also, if we are lucky, filled with love, beauty, and passionate delights, that, although they may not manifest themselves constantly, slumber within like cats on a hearth in our hearts, as Albert wrote of the writer's task, to be true to and awaken "those two or three great and simple images in whose presence his [our] heart[s] first opened."

So I must conclude by saying Camus wasn't joking, but humor was not his forte. It was my father's, his seeming opposite. With humor we might summon the dozing genie. I think it true what Lewis Hyde writes in *Trickster Makes This World:* "A touch of humor or levity, then, is one mark by which we know that a creative spirit working in the force field of contradictions has kept his promise, has not fallen from his tree, and so might actually move beyond the enclosing oppositions."

And since tomorrow is my father's birthday, I will recount a little story he wrote to me in his eloquent and inimitable style. It differs slightly from Attorney Jean-Batiste Clamence's confession from the "Mexico City" bar in Amsterdam, with the exception of the booze. It goes like this:

> On ecclesiastical matters I have a funny true story for you. Dennis Casey, one of the attorneys I used to work with, told it. He had an uncle who was a Bishop of some county in Ireland and, like a few citizens of the Ould Sod, could put away a drop or two of the creature. When Cardinal Cooke was alive in the late '70s, the Bishop attended some ceremony at St. Patrick's Cathedral where he was to give the homily. Dennis Casey was with him and said the good Bishop fortified himself with quite a few shots or smiles, as Uncle Tim used to call the creature, before ascending the pulpit. He then went on and on ad infinitum, saying in his thick Irish brogue, "if he had the cathedral filled with gold, I'd give it to the poor; if I had it filled with food, I'd give it the hungry," etc., etc., etc. Finally they gave him the hook after a few nods from the Cardinal. After the Mass the hierarchy retired to the Chancery for a reception. The place was filled with Bishops, Monsignors, and prelates of all shapes and sizes and everyone partook of liquid refreshments, including our friend, the Bishop. All went well until someone started a singalong when they coaxed Cardinal Cook for a solo. He tried to beg off, saying, "I'm not much of a singer," but the majority prevailed and he started a few notes of Danny Boy or some such song. After a couple of lines and false notes, the Bishop's stentorian brogue burst through the hall, shouting, "You are right. You can't sing a Fucking

> note." I think he was whisked back to Erin forthwith and now he sings with the heavenly choir or in the devil's band—having departed for his just reward.

Happy New Year, Albert and Edward. Let's raise our laughing glasses high to the beauty of the days gone by and those to come, even as we rebel. Hope for the future lies in resistance and contemplation.

The Assassination and Mrs. Paine

– A REVIEW ESSAY OF *MAX GOOD'S DOCUMENTARY FILM* –

Human duplicity is a marvel to contemplate. This riveting documentary is an excellent example of such cunning in action, not on the part of the filmmaker who is eminently fair, perhaps overly so, but on the part of some of those who appear in the film. It demands that viewers use every skill in their possession to determine who is lying and who is telling the truth about the involvement of a woman named Ruth Paine (and her husband Michael) in the assassination of President Kennedy. In many ways, it is akin to sitting in a jury box, listening to trial testimony from witnesses for the defense and prosecution and from a few whose slippery words seem meant to create uncertainty and never-ending debate about Paine's innocence or guilt in the president's murder.

The film will be an eye-opener for anyone unfamiliar with Mrs. Ruth Paine's fundamental role at the heart of the president's murder; and for those knowledgeable about her, it will be greeted as an important contribution to the case. I believe it is not just a must watch for those interested in JFK's assassination, which is the key to all subsequent American history, but for anyone trying to unravel today's tapestry of lies and propaganda spewing out from the mainstream media (MSM) that go by different names—CBS, ABC, the Washington Post, etc.—but all of whom speak for the Central Intelligence Agency (CIA). The basic equation is: CIA = MSM.

Since many people are adept at lying, they think they are good at sniffing out lies in others. This is highly questionable. We live in a country of lies, from the top down and the bottom up; propaganda and the everyday lies that grease the skids of social intercourse. Deceptions that deceive no one. Lying is the leading cause of spiritual death in the United States, even as devotion to truth is embraced as a national platitude. Even when such fealty to truthfulness isn't professed or implied and the lying is admitted, as with ex-CIA Director Mike Pompeo's 2019 remark about the CIA at Texas A&M university—"We lied, we cheated, we stole"—such an admission is uttered proudly and with a chuckle. It's what everybody knows and pretends they don't.

There are some intellectuals, like Noam Chomsky, who like to say that many who lie believe their own stories because of their institutional affiliations—e.g. journalists for the *BBC, The New York Times, CBS,* etc. (but not the Defense Department–funded MIT where he spent his career)—because such institutions require the employees they hire to have internalized the script in advance. But they don't call it lying, for it is built into the socialization process that leads to positions within such institutions. So presumably they are only doing their jobs and lack awareness of any duplicity. They are innocent of their own complicity in censorship and propaganda in stories they report. They have no knowledge of the fact that their mainstream employers have long been proven to be mouthpieces for the CIA, M-16, NSA, etc.

Focused exclusively on institutional analyses, Chomsky denies these people a place for individual freedom of thought and consciousness, as he does with his long-held absurd assertion that JFK's assassination is of little importance and his denial of the clearly documented facts that Kennedy took a radical turn toward peacemaking in the last year of his life, a metanoia that led directly to his death.

He is correct, however, that such MSM people don't need to self-censor, for their jobs require them to play the game according to the censorship rules under which they were hired, but he is very wrong to claim they therefore believe what they say. That assumes these people are very ignorant, which they are not; that they just obliviously do their jobs and collect their pay. He fails to distinguish between playing dumb and being dumb.

It would be more accurate to say that they live in what Jean Paul Sartre calls "bad faith" (*mauvaise foi*), for "the essence of a lie implies in fact that the liar actually is in complete possession of the truth which he is hiding. . . . The ideal description of a liar would be a cynical consciousness, affirming truth within himself, denying it in his words, and denying the negation as such."

You can't lie to yourself, for that would mean you were two people. But you can lie to others. And you can play dumb. It's called acting. And of course many journalists and academics hold dual positions, since they secretly work as assets for the intelligence services.

I begin with these thoughts about lying because a good number of the people who appear in *The Assassination and Mrs. Paine* have no ostensible institutional affiliation but may be working in some capacity for an invisible institutional paymaster who calls their tunes. No names required. They implicitly present themselves as disinterested pursuers of truth, yet viewers are forced to assess the veracity of their claims, including those of Ruth Paine who appears throughout, answering Max Good's interview questions.

Much has been written and filmed about the JFK assassination. Most take a broad perspective. This film is quite different because it approaches it through a personal focus on Ruth Paine who, for those who may not have heard of her, was the key witness against Lee Harvey Oswald at the Warren Commission (WC) hearings where she was asked more than five thousand questions (her husband Michel was asked 1,000 or so). She is the woman who invited Marina Oswald to live with her in her home in the Dallas suburb of Irving, Texas, where Lee Harvey Oswald also spent weekends from late September 1963 up until the morning of the Assassination on November 22, 1963. Her testimony led to the WC's conclusion that Oswald, and Oswald alone, shot the president.

The Assassination and Mrs. Paine is Max Good's second full-length documentary. He came to the subject after reading a section (pp. 168–72) on Ruth and Michael Paine in James W. Douglass's *JFK and the Unspeakable: Why He Died & Why It Matters,* a book considered by many to be the best on the JFK assassination. He felt the Paines' story shouted out for a documentary, and when he discovered that Ruth Paine was still alive, in her late eighties, lucid, and living near him in a Quaker retirement home in California, he contacted her and she agreed to be interviewed, something she has done for 59 years, always protesting her innocence, even though over the decades researchers have uncovered much evidence to the contrary.

Her ex-husband, Michael, also lived at the home but has since died. There's a brief interview of little consequence with him in the film since his memory was going, but I should note that he too is a crucial figure in the assassination story. Both he and Ruth have always denied involvement in the plot and coverup, yet much evidence connects them to it. Michael Paine's involvement is artfully suggested by the film's title—"Mrs. Paine" and not simply Ruth Paine, a woman acting alone. The Paines, who have claimed they are pacifists, might best be superficially described as unassuming, liberal Quaker/Unitarian do-gooders, whose wealth and astounding family and intelligence connections would make heads spin, if they were known. The film exposes many of those connections.

The fundamental undisputed facts are as follows. In February 1963, Ruth, who spoke and taught Russian, was invited to a party in Dallas, Texas by George de Mohrenschildt, a White Russian CIA asset who was "babysitting" Lee Harvey Oswald at the request of the CIA. There she met Oswald. Soon de Mohrenschildt would go to Haiti and Ruth would establish a relationship with Lee and Marina Oswald. In September, Ruth Hyde Paine visited family in eastern Massachusetts on Naushon Island, owned by the Forbes family. Michael Paine's mother, Ruth's mother-in-law, was Ruth Forbes Paine Young, from the blue-blood Forbes family of Boston. She was friends with the CIA's Allen Dulles since her best friend was Mary Bancroft, Dulles's mistress. They had stayed on the island.

From Massachusetts, Ruth drove to New Orleans to pick up the Russian speaking Marina Oswald and the Oswalds' belongings to bring her back to Dallas to live with her. It was a small, unassuming house, but there was room for Marina and her children because Michael Paine had conveniently moved out in the spring, allegedly because of marital problems, but would move back in the winter after the assassination and Marina's departure. Ruth says she did this to help a woman in need. On her long road trip south, she made numerous stops, including at her sister Sylvia Hyde Hoke's house in Falls Church, Virginia. Sylvia worked for the CIA, as documents have confirmed, and her husband worked for the agency's front, the U.S. Agency for International Development (AID), yet to this day—and in Good's interview in the film—she claims not to know where her sister worked. Ruth's father, William Avery Hyde, also worked for U.S. AID in Latin America and his reports went to the CIA. From her sister's house, Ruth proceeded to New Orleans where she picked up Marina and took her to her house in Irvington. In mid-October, again out of alleged kindness, she got Lee a job in the Texas School Book Depository, despite calls to her house from an employment agency offering him a much higher paying job. When asked about this by the Warren Commission, Ruth gave an evasive answer. Then when JFK was killed, an empty blanket roll that allegedly held Oswald's rifle was found in the Paines' garage. And Ruth claimed to have found a note—the "Walker Note" that was used to show his propensity for violence—and a letter also allegedly written by Oswald to the Russian Embassy that was used as evidence of his guilt. There is much more of a strange and suspicious nature involving Ruth and the Oswalds.

The Paines have always said that Oswald killed Kennedy to make a name for himself—the little man kills the big one syndrome. They repeat this in the documentary. Ruth says of Oswald, "He realized he had the opportunity to no longer be a little guy but someone extraordinary." But as Jim DiEugenio (one of the finest and most informed commentators in the film) says, if that were so, then why did Oswald always claim he was innocent, a patsy who didn't shoot anyone. Those who wish to kill to make a name for themselves obviously claim credit, but the Paines seem not to get this. Their claim makes no sense, yet they both repeat it in the film.

And although the film's focus is on Ruth, not Michael, there are other undisputed facts about him worth noting. As previously mentioned, his mother was Ruth Forbes Paine Young. After divorcing Michael's father, Lyman Paine, his mother married a man named Arthur Young. Among other strange facts about Young, he was the inventor of the Bell helicopter, which was the prototype for the infamous Huey helicopter used in Vietnam. Those helicopters were produced at the defense contractor Bell Helicopter in Fort Worth, Texas where Michael, the self-proclaimed pacifist, worked through his connection to Arthur Young. He had a security clearance; when the Warren Commission asked him what type of clearance, he said he didn't know. One of his cousins, Thomas Dudley Cabot (the Boston Cabots), was a former president of the United Fruit Company, and another, John Cabot, worked for the State Department where he exchanged information about the CIA-United Fruit coup d'état against Jacobo Arbenz. Later, he was president of the CIA front company Gibraltar Steamship Corporation that leased Swan Island in the Caribbean for the CIA, where the agency set up Radio Swan that was used during the Bay of Pigs invasion of Cuba, among other things (see pp.193–208 in James DiEugenio's *Destiny Betrayed*, second edition, for important information on the Paines).

All this factual background on the Paines doesn't definitively prove anything about them, but it is essential to assess their credibility, and *The Assassination and Mrs. Paine* is all about doing that.

The question about Ruth that the film asks is whether she is a truthful, naïve, Quaker do-gooder or a CIA asset, a pawn, or someone in deep denial.

She has her defenders and they appear in the film along with well-known supporters of her and the Warren Commission's conclusion that Oswald did the deed alone: Max Holland, Gerald Posner, Priscilla Johnson McMillan, Jack Valenti, Michael Beschloss, and Peter Jennings.

From the so-called prosecution side we hear from: Jim DiEugenio, Dr. Gary Aquilar, Dr. Martin Schotz, Vince Salandria, and Sue Wheaton.

Paine's defenders make sure to bash Oliver Stone and his film, *JFK*, and Ruth claims Stone never contacted her about her portrayal in the film. Stone denies this and says she would not talk to him. But she makes it clear that she is a big fan of various Network TV specials that support the WC, especially the London mock trial with Gerry Spence and Vincent Bugliosi, and a Peter Jennings ABC special.

Ruth Paine is given a lot of screen time between her defenders and accusers. As I said, Max Good is more than fair, perhaps too fair. Paine is a cool character who only rarely gets a bit flustered. She's been doing these interviews for a long time, and is either a good actor or an innocent bystander, as she says, "I'm kind of naïve. . . . But I think it's a blessing."

After giving both sides their say—and a few others, whom I won't mention, who make lawyerly-like slippery statements—Bill Simpich, a JFK assassination researcher, interjects that there is "something about the Ruth Paine story that simply doesn't jell," which is farcical in the extreme considering all the evidence against Paine. Good then proceeds to ask her a series of hard questions that viewers will find very interesting. But he never lets the audience know what he has concluded about her guilt or innocence. He is impartial to the end.

I am not. For before watching the film, I knew a great deal about the Paines and their roles in the assassination and its cover-up. I completely agree with the Philadelphia lawyer Vince Salandria, one of the earliest and most brilliant critics of the official story, when he says "You can't close the circle without the Paines. There is no way they can be innocent. No way."

And he added the film's penultimate statement about the assassination:

> There is no mystery here. It's all self-evident. It was a coup. It was designed to be a false mystery and the debate would be eternal and why it [killing JFK] was done—forgotten. In order to commit yourself to truth here, you're changing your real identity from a citizen

of a democracy to a subject of a military empire. A big step.

Ruth Paine, however, gets the final word. Regarding all the claims about her involvement with the CIA and the Oswalds: "Nonsense. Absolute nonsense. . . . I am interested in truth. . . . I'm a very independent person. Nobody tells me what to do."

I highly recommend that people watch this important film and reach a verdict based on the evidence it provides, which is plenty. Ruth Paine's cries of innocence are not believable. The film clearly shows that. If they need more, to read the works of Douglass and DiEugenio mentioned earlier, among others. As good as a film can be, it is only as good as the sources it relies upon and this movie has excellent sources.

Human duplicity is a marvel to contemplate. *The Assassination and Mrs. Paine* will force you to do that. Don't miss it. For you will learn much about a key piece in the CIA's conspiracy to assassinate President Kennedy—Ruth Paine.

The Roots of Radicalism and the Structure of Evil

My title is redundant for a reason, since the root of the word radical is the Latin word, *radix*, meaning root. For I mean to show how the use and misuse of language, its history or etymology, and ours as etymological animals as the Spanish philosopher José Ortega y Gassett called us, is crucial for understanding our world, a world once again teetering on the edge of a world war that will almost inexorably turn nuclear if events proceed as they are. If our language is corrupted, as it surely is, and political propaganda flourishes as a result, the correct use of our language and the meaning of words becomes an obligation of anyone who uses them—especially writers.

The United States government exists to wage war. In its present form, it would crumble without it; and in its present form, it will crumble with it. Only a radical structural change will prevent this. For warmaking is at the core of its budget, its raison d'être—895 billion dollars for the Fiscal 2025 National Defense Authorization Act alone—a deficit-financed sum that tells only part of the story since U.S. National security spending will approach 2 trillion dollars in 2025. This amount that finances the military-industrial complex and its blood money is ostensibly to defend a country that has never been invaded, is bordered by friendly neighbors, and is oceans away from the multitude of countries its leaders attack and call our enemies. The U.S. wages wars around the world because killing is the economy's lifeblood, its structural essence.

In writing of the misuse of language, George Orwell wrote, "It becomes ugly and inaccurate because our thoughts are foolish, but the slovenliness of our language makes it easier for us to have foolish thoughts." So with these words Orwell slyly places us within the enigma of the chicken and the egg, a conundrum or paradox that relates to my theme in a weird way, but which I will directly ignore.

By radical I do not mean the widespread political usage as in radical-right or radical-left or radical meaning one who plays the role through dress or demeanor. I am using the word in its primary meaning—a radical is one who is rooted in the earth, which means everyone. Everyone therefore is mortal, human, not a god, and comes from the earth and returns to it. Everyone is radical in this sense, although they may try to deny it. And the more one feels alive the more one senses one will die and doesn't like the thought, therefore many tamp down their aliveness in order to reduce their fear of death. The best way to do this is to disappear into the crowd, to become a conventional person. To act as if one didn't know that one's political leaders were in love with death and killing and were not obedient cogs in a vast systemic killing machine. Maybe the unconscious assumption is that these "leaders" can kill death for you by killing vast numbers of people and make you feel someone has control of this thing called death.

Rabbi Abraham Joshua Heschel, who stood strongly against the Vietnam War and marched with Dr. Martin Luther King, Jr., put the basic sense of radical well when he said:

> Our goal should be to live life in radical amazement. . . . get up in the morning and look at the world in a way that takes nothing for granted. Everything is phenomenal; everything is incredible; never treat life casually. To be spiritual is to be amazed.

To be radically amazed that we exist is to be equally amazed that we will die. And there's the rub.

Yesterday I got in our car and drove away to meet a journalist friend. It was evening and my wife had previously used the car. I had just spent time following all the dreadful news about the massive slaughter by Israel of more than 45,000 Palestinians in Gaza, including the death of more than 17,000 children whose numbers continue to climb (these are low estimates). Visions of those children and babies played havoc with my spirits, and I kept thinking of my own children and the love and tenderness that comes with being a parent. A musical CD that my wife had been listening to started playing. The case was on the console. It was *Sacred Arias* by Andrea Bocelli. He of the majestic voice was singing *Silent Night*. I was overwhelmed with tears by his passionate words:

> Silent night! Holy night!
> All is calm, all is bright
> round yon Virgin Mother and Child,
> Holy infant so tender and mild,
> sleep in Heavenly peace!
> sleep in Heavenly peace!

I saw nights in Gaza as Israeli bombs burst and shattered everyone and everything to bits, all the holy infants, the children and adults.

I felt beside myself with grief, a U.S. citizen driving down a safe country road contemplating the savagery of my nation and its support for the Israeli government's brutality and mass killings of Palestinians for all the world to see on screens everywhere.

I felt ashamed to live in a land where justice is a game reserved for rhetoric alone as it joins in the massacre of the innocent, as it always has, now together with the apartheid Israeli regime.

I thought of all the compromised politicians who pledge their allegiance to the killers, Biden, Trump, and all their presidential predecessors, now including the former candidate Robert F. Kennedy, Jr., a man with a conscience on many important issues whom I once supported in his quest for the presidency, but a man whose conscience has abandoned him when it comes to the Palestinians, as Scott Ritter and others have documented. For months I had privately urged Kennedy to reconsider his "unwavering, resolute, and practical" support for the Israeli government following the Gaza breakout of October 7, but to no avail.

I felt as betrayed again—perhaps you will call me naïve—as when I was young and last put my trust in voting for a U.S. presidential candidate in 1972. I thought then I had learned to radically grasp the systematically corrupt nature of the U.S. warfare state. Now that RFK, Jr. has remained silent for more than a year about the genocide and even teamed up with president-elect Trump, another fanatical Israel supporter, I realize how wrong I was. For the Palestinians, Kennedy has not a word of sympathy. Although he considers the Israeli-Palestinian situation complicated, there is nothing complicated about genocide; it doesn't necessitate long analyses and discussions with advisers. The facts of the Israeli slaughter of Palestinians in Gaza and the West Bank are evident for all to see, if they wish. Bobby Kennedy has turned away. And I have now sadly turned away from him.

I remembered the Gospel words I heard long ago about the fulfillment of the words of the prophet Jeremiah: "A voice was heard in Ramah, sobbing and loudly lamenting: it was Rachel weeping for her children, refusing to be comforted because they were no more." But this time it is not the Jewish Rachel, for Herod has assumed the name Netanyahu and his U.S. allies, and the weeping ones are Palestinian mothers and fathers. Nothing can justify such slaughter, not the killings of innocent Israelis on October 7; not the fear that the birth of messengers of peace might strike into Herod/Netanyahu's heart—nothing! Seventy-five years of ethnic cleansing of Palestinians continues apace. The Jewish child Jesus, the radical preacher of love and peace for all people, didn't die on a private cross, nor do the Palestinians. So it goes.

I thought of the indescribable sweet wonder of holding your baby in your arms while realizing how many Palestinian parents have been holding their dead children in theirs. Rage welled up in me at the obscenity of those who support this and those who shut their eyes to it and those who remain silent.

I realized that as a Christian I am baptized into the human family, not some special in-group, which is the opposite of Jesus's message. Every child is holy and innocent and to massacre them is evil. And to remain silent as it happens is to be complicit in evil.

I remembered how these many ongoing weeks of terror started and thought of a poem that is succinctly apposite: *Harlem* by Langston Hughes:

> What happens to a dream deferred?
> Does it dry up
> like a raison in the sun?
> Or fester like a sore-
> and then run?
> . . . .
> Maybe it just sags
> like a heavy load.
> *Or does it explode?*

And I thought that he could have omitted that final question mark because we have our answer then and now.

Then the music stopped and I arrived at my destination to meet my friend.

Yes, to be radical is to be rooted in the earth and to realize all people are part of the human family, each of us made of flesh and blood and therefore sisters and brothers deserving of justice, peace, and dignity. But this is just a first step in the grasping of the full dimension of the radical vision. It can end in fluff if a second step is not taken: to use our freedom to uproot ourselves from the conventional government and mass media propaganda and mind control that clouds our understanding of how the world works. This takes study and work and an understanding of the historical and systemic roots of all the alleged "unprovoked" violence that ravages our world.

Thus the existential and socio-historical merge in the radical vision that allows us to grasp the structures of evil and our personal responsibility.

Today that obligation is clear: To oppose the Israeli genocide of the Palestinians.

Otherwise we are guilty bystanders.

A Message to Donald Rumsfeld's Ghost about My Known Knowns

On February 12, 2002 at a Pentagon news conference, Secretary of Defense Donald Rumsfeld was asked by Jim Miklaszewski, the NBC Pentagon correspondent, if he had any *evidence* that Iraq had weapons of mass destruction and was supplying them to terrorists. Rumsfeld delivered his famous circumlocution, saying:

> Reports that say that something hasn't happened are always interesting to me, because as we know, there are known knowns; there are things we know we know. We also know there are known unknowns; that is to say we know there are some things we do not know. But there are also unknown unknowns—the ones we don't know we don't know.

When he was pressed by Jamie McIntyre, CNN's Pentagon correspondent, to answer the question about evidence, he talked gobbledygook, saying, "I could have said that the absence of evidence is not evidence of absence, or vice versa."

He never said he had evidence, because he didn't. He was lying.

Rumsfeld, who enjoyed his verbal games, was the quintessential bullshitter and liar for the warfare state. This encounter took place when Rumsfeld and his coconspirators were promoting lie after lie about the attacks of September 11, 2001 and conflating false stories about an alliance between Saddam Hussein and Osama bin Laden in order to build a case to wage another war against Iraq, in order to supplement the one in Afghanistan and the war on "terror" that they launched post September 11 and the subsequently linked anthrax attacks.

A year later on February 5, 2003, U. S. Secretary of State Colin Powell went before the U. N. Security Council and in a command performance assured the world that the U.S. had solid evidence that Iraq had "weapons of mass destruction," repeating that phrase seventeen times as he held up a stage prop vial of anthrax to make his point. He said, "My colleagues, every statement I make today is backed up by sources—solid sources. These are not assertions. What we're giving you are facts and conclusions based on solid intelligence." He was lying, but to this very day his defenders falsely claim he was the victim of an "intelligence failure," a typical deceitful excuse along with "it was a mistake." Of course, Iraq did not have "weapons of mass destruction" and the savage war waged on Iraq was not a mistake.

Scott Ritter, the former Marine U.N. weapons inspector, made it very clear back then that there was no evidence that Iraq had weapons of mass destruction, but his expertise was dismissed, just as his current analysis of the war in Ukraine is. See his recent tweet about Senator Diane Feinstein in this regard:

> I met Senator Diane Feinstein once, in the lead up to the 2003 invasion of Iraq. She had just recently been assigned to the Senate Select Committee on Intelligence (in 2001), and it was in that capacity that she had a senior staffer from the committee ask me to come to Washington, D.C. to brief her on Iraqi WMD and the allegations being made by the Bush administration that Iraq continued to possess them. We met in a secure conference room in the Capitol building—me, the Senator, and a half dozen staffers and aides. It was a polite, professional affair, with the Senator asking questions and taking notes. Eventually she confronted me—"Your position is causing us some difficulty. You

are making the U.S. look bad in the eyes of the world." I replied that my analysis and the underlying facts were rock solid, something she agreed with. I said that while I knew she couldn't reveal sensitive intelligence, if she could look me in the eye and say she has seen unequivocal proof that Iraq retained WMD, I'd shut up and go away. She looked at her retinue, and then me. "I have seen no such intelligence," she replied. She thanked me for the briefing, and said it provided her with "food for thought." On October 11, 2002, Senator Feinstein voted in favor of the resolution authorizing war with Iraq. Later, she said she had been misled by the Bush administration and bad intelligence. I will forever know Senator Feinstein as someone who had been empowered by the truth, and lacked the moral courage to act on it. The blood of thousands of Americans and hundreds of thousands of Iraqis stains her soul. I hope when she stands in judgment before her maker, she is punished accordingly.

Thirteen months after Rumsfeld's exchange at the news conference, the United States invaded Iraq on March 19, 2003, knowing it had no justification. It was an illegal war of aggression. Millions died as a result. And none of the killers have been prosecuted for their massive war crimes. The war was not launched on mistaken evidence; it was premeditated and based on lies easy to see. Very, very easy to see.

On January 28, 2003, eleven days before Powell performance, I, an independent writer with no insider connections, wrote a newspaper Op Ed, "The War Hoax," saying:

> The Bush administration has a problem: How to start a war without having a justifiable reason for one. No doubt they are working hard to solve this urgent problem. If they can't find a justification, they may have to create one. Or perhaps they will find what they have already created. . . . Yet once again, the American people

> are being played for fools, by the government and the media. The open secret, the insider's fact, is that the United States plans to attack Iraq in the near future. The administration knows this, the media knows it, but the Bush scenario, written many months ago, is to act as if it weren't so, to act as if a peaceful solution were being seriously considered. . . . Don't buy it.

Only one very small regional Massachusetts newspaper, the *North Adams Transcript*, was willing to publish the piece.

I mention this because I think it has been very obvious for a very long time that the evidence for United States' crimes of all sorts has been available to anyone who wished to face the truth. It does not take great expertise, just an eye for the obvious and the willingness to do a little homework. Despite this, I have noticed that journalists and writers on the left have continued to admit that they were beguiled by people such as Bill and Hillary Clinton, Barack Obama, and Joseph Biden, con men all. I do not mean writers for the mainstream press, but those considered oppositional. Many have, for reasons only they can answer, put hope in these obvious charlatans, and some prominent ones have refused to analyze such matters as the JFK assassination, September 11th, or COVID-19, to name a few issues. Was it because they considered these politicians and matters known unknowns, even when the writing was on the wall?

Those on the right have rolled with Reagan, the Bushes, and Trump in a similar manner, albeit for different reasons. It causes me to shake my head in amazement. When will people learn? How long does it take to realize that all these people are part of a vast criminal enterprise that has been continuously waging wars and lying while raking in vast spoils for the military-industrial complex. There is one party in the U.S.—the War Party.

If you have lived long enough, as have I, you reach a point when you have, through study and the accumulation of evidence, arrived at a long list of known knowns. So with a backhand slap to Donald Rumsfeld, that long serving servant of the U.S. war machine, I will list **a very partial number** of my known knowns in chronological order. Each could be greatly expanded. There is an abundance of easily available evidence for all of them—**nothing secret**—but one needs to have the will for truth and do one's homework. All of these known knowns are the result of U.S. deep state conspiracies and lies, aided and abetted by the lies of mass corporate media.

My Known Knowns:

- The U.S. national security state led by the CIA assassinated **President John F. Kennedy** on November 22, 1963. **This is The foundational event for everything that has followed.** It set the tone and sent the message that deep state forces will do anything to wage their wars at home and abroad. They killed JFK because he was ending the war against Vietnam, the Cold War, and the nuclear arms race.
- Those same forces assassinated **Malcolm X** fourteen months later on February 21, 1965 because he too had become a champion of peace, human rights, and racial and economic justice with his budding alliance with Rev. Martin Luther King, Jr. Such an alliance of these two black leaders posed too great a threat to the racist warfare state. This conspiracy was carried out by the Nation of Islam, the New York Police Department, and U.S. intelligence agencies.
- The **Indonesian** government's slaughter of more than one million mainly poor rice farmers in 1965–66 was the result of a scheme planned by ex-CIA Director Allen Dulles, whom JFK had fired. It was connected to Dulles's role in the assassination of JFK, the CIA-engineered coup against Indonesian President Sukarno, his replacement by the dictator Suharto, and his mass slaughter ten years later, starting in December 1975. The American-installed Indonesian dictator Suharto, after meeting with Henry Kissinger and President Ford and receiving their approval, would slaughter hundreds of thousands of **East-Timorese** with American-supplied weapons in

a repeat of the slaughter of more than a million Indonesians in 1965.

- In June of 1967, Israel, **a purported ally of the U.S.,** attacked and destroyed the Egyptian and Syrian armies, claiming falsely that Egypt was about to attack Israel. This was a lie that was later admitted by former Israeli Prime Minister Menachem Begin in a speech he gave in 1982 in Washington, D.C. Israel annexed the West Bank and Gaza and still occupies the Golan Heights as well. In June 1967, Israel also attacked and tried to sink the U.S. intelligence gathering ship the **U.S.S. *Liberty,*** killing 34 U.S. sailors and wounding 170 others. Washington covered up these intentional murders to protect Israel.

- On April 4, 1968, these same intelligence forces led by the FBI, assassinated **Martin Luther King, Jr.** in Memphis, Tennessee. He was not shot by James Earl Ray, the officially alleged assassin, but by a hit man who was part of another intricate government conspiracy. King was killed because of his work for racial and human rights and justice, his opposition to the Vietnam War, and his push for economic justice with the Poor People's Campaign.

- Two months later, **Senator Robert F. Kennedy,** on his way to the presidency, was also assassinated by deep state intelligence forces in another vastly intricate conspiracy. He was not killed by Sirhan Sirhan, who was a hypnotized patsy standing in front of RFK. He was assassinated by a CIA hit man who was standing behind him and shot him from close range. RFK, also, was assassinated because he was intent on ending the war against Vietnam, bringing racial and economic justice to the country, and pursuing the assassins of his brother John.

- The escalation of the war against **Vietnam** by Pres. **Lyndon Johnson** was based on the Tonkin Gulf lies. It's savage waging by **Richard Nixon** for eight years was based on endless lies. These men were war criminals of the highest order. Nixon's 1968 election was facilitated by the "October Surprise" when South Vietnam withdrew from peace negotiations to end the war. This was secretly arraigned by Nixon and his intermediaries.

- The well-known **Watergate** scandal story, as told by Woodward and Bernstein of *The Washington Post*, that led to Richard Nixon's resignation in August 1974, is an entertaining fiction concealing intelligence operations.

- Another October Surprise was arranged for the 1980 presidential election. It was linked to the subsequent Iran-Contra scandal during the **Reagan** administration, led by future CIA Director under Reagan, **William Casey,** and former CIA Director and Vice-President under Reagan, **George H. W. Bush.** As in 1968, a secret deal was made to secure the Republican's election by making a deal with Iran to withhold releasing the American hostages they held until after the election. They were released minutes after Reagan was sworn in on January 20, 1981.

- American presidential elections have been fraught with scandals, as in 2000 when George W. Bush and team stole the election from Democrat Al Gore, and Russia-gate was conjured up by the Democrats in 2016 to try to prevent Trump's election.

- **The Reagan administration,** together with the CIA, armed the so-called **"Contras"** to wage war against the Sandinista government of Nicaragua that had overthrown the vicious U.S. supported dictator Anastasio Somoza. The Contras were Somoza supporters and part of a long line of terrorists that the U.S. had used throughout Latin America where supported dictators and death squads to squelch democratic movements. Such state terrorism was of a piece with the September 11, 1973 U.S. engineered coup against the democratic government of **President Salvadore Allende** in Chile and his replacement with the dictator Augusto Pinochet.

- **The Persian Gulf War** waged by **George H.W. Bush** in 1991—the first made for TV war—was based on lie upon lie promoted by the administration and their public relations firm. It was a war of aggression celebrated by CNN and other media as a joyous July 4th fireworks display.

- Then the neoliberal phony **William Clinton** spent eight years bombing Iraq, dismantling the social safety net, deregulating the banks, attacking and dismantling Yugoslavia, savagely bombing Serbia, etc. In a span of four months in 1999 he bombed four countries: Afghanistan, Sudan, Iraq, and Yugoslavia. He maintained the U.S. sanctions placed on Iraq following the Gulf War that resulted in the death of 500,000 Iraqi children. When his Secretary of State Madeleine Albright was asked by Lesley Stahl of *60 Minutes* if the price was worth it, Albright said, "We think the price is worth it."

- The attacks of **September 11, 2001,** referred to as 9/11 in an act of linguistic mind control in order to create an ongoing sense of national emergency, and the anthrax attacks that followed, were a joint inside operation—a false flag—carried out by elements within the U.S. deep state. Together with the CIA assassination of JFK, these acts of state terrorism mark **a second fundamental turning point** in efforts to extinguish any sense of democratic control in the United States. Hence, The Patriot Act, government spying, censorship, and ongoing attacks on individual rights.

- The **George W. Bush**–led U.S. invasion of Afghanistan, Iraq, etc. and its "war on terror" were efforts to terrorize and control the Middle East, Southwest Asia, as well as the people of the U.S. The aforementioned Mr. Rumsfeld, along with his partner in crime, Dick Cheney, carried out Bush's known known war crimes justified by the crimes of Sept 11 as they simultaneously created a vast Homeland Security spying network while eliminating Americans basic freedoms.

- **Barack Obama** was one of the most effective imperialist presidents in U.S. history. Although this is factually true, he was able to provide a smiling veneer to his work at institutionalizing the permanent warfare state. When first entering office, he finished George W. Bush's unfinished task of bailing out the finance capitalist class of Wall St. Having hoodwinked liberals of his bona fides, he then spent eight years presiding over extrajudicial murders, drone attacks, the destruction of Libya, a terrorist aided "secret" war against Syria, a coup in Ukraine bringing neo-Nazis to power, etc. In 2016 alone he bombed seven countries: Pakistan, Libya, Yemen, Afghanistan, Syria, Somalia, and Iraq. He expanded U.S. military bases throughout the world and sent special forces throughout Africa and Latin America. He supported the new Cold War with sanctions on Russia. He was a fitting successor to Bush junior.

- **Donald Trump,** a New York City reality TV star and real estate tycoon, the surprise winner of the 2016 U.S. presidential election despite the Democratic Party's false Russia-gate propaganda, attacked Syria from sea and air in the first two years of his presidency, claiming falsely that these strikes were for Syria's use of chemical weapons at Douma and for producing chemical weapons. In doing so, he warned Russia not to be associated with Syrian President Assad, a "mass murderer of men, women, and children." He did not criticize Israel that to the present day regularly and continuously bombs Syria while committing genocide against the Palestinians, but he recognized Jerusalem as the capital of Israel. He ordered the assassination by drone of Iranian General Qasem Soleimani near Baghdad International Airport who was on a peacemaking visit to meet with Iraq's prime minister. As an insider contrary to all portrayals, Trump presided over Operation Warp Speed COVID vaccination development and deployment, which was a military-pharmaceutical-CIA program, whose key player was Robert Kadlec (former colleague of Donal Rumsfeld with deep ties to spy agencies), Trump's Assistant Secretary of Health and Human Services for Preparedness and Response and an ally of Dr. Anthony Fauci and Bill Gates. On December 8, 2020 Trump joyously declared: "Before Operation Warp Speed, the typical time-frame for development and approval [for vaccines], as you know, could be infinity. And we were very, very happy that we were able to get things done at a level that nobody has ever seen before. The gold standard vaccine has been done in less than nine months." And he announced they he would quickly distribute such a "verifiably safe and effective vaccine" as soon as the FDA approved it because "We are the most exceptional nation in the history of the world. Today, we're on the verge of another American medical miracle." The Pfizer/BioNTech vaccine was approved three days later. Moderna's COVID-19 vaccine received FDA emergency use authorization a week later. Now that he has been reelected, Trump has "ironically" nominated RFK, Jr. to be secretary of HHS and "remedy" the situation.

- This **COVID-19** medical miracle was a con-job from the start. The official COVID operation launched in March 11, 2020 with worldwide lockdowns that destroyed economies while enriching the super-rich and devastating regular people, was a propaganda achievement carried out by intelligence and military apparatuses in conjunction with Big Pharma, the WHO, the World Economic Forum, etc. and promulgated by a vast around-the-clock corporate media disinformation campaign. It was **the third fundamental turning point—following the JFK assassination and the attacks of September 11, 2001 and anthrax**—in destabilizing the economic, social and political life of all nations while undermining their sovereignty. It was based on false science in the interests of further establishing a biosecurity state. The intelligence agency planners who had conducted many germ wargame simulations leading up to COVID-19 referred to a future arising out of such "attacks," as the "New Normal." A close study of these precedents, game-planning, and players makes this evident. The aim was to militarize medicine and produce a centralized authoritarian state. Its use of the PCR "test" to detect the virus was a lie from the start. The Nobel Award winning scientist who developed the test, Kary Mullis, made it clear that *"the*

PCR is a process. It does not tell you that you are sick." It is a process "to make a whole lot of something out of something," but it cannot detect a specific virus. That it was used to detect all these COVID "cases" is all one needs to know about the fraud.

- **Joseph Biden,** who was **Obama's point man for Ukraine** while vice-president and the U.S. engineered the 2014 coup d'état in Ukraine, came into office intent on promoting the New Cold War with Russia and refused all Russian efforts to peacefully settle the Ukrainian crisis. He pushed NATO to further provoke Russia by moving farther to the east, surrounding Russia's borders. He supported the neo-Nazi Ukrainian elements and its government's continuous attacks on the Russian speaking Donbass region in eastern Ukraine. In doing so, he clearly provoked Russian into sending troops into Ukraine on 24 February 2022. He has fueled this war relentlessly and has pushed the world to the brink of nuclear annihilation. He supported the invasion of Afghanistan and Iraq and Israel genocide of the Palestinians. He currently presides over an aggressive provocation of China. And like his predecessor Trump, he promotes the COVID disinformation campaign and the use of "vaccines," urging people to get their jabs.

Throughout all these decades and the matters touched upon here—some of my known knowns—there is another dominant theme that recurs again and again. It is the **support for Israel and its evil apartheid regime's repeated slaughters and persecution of the Palestinian people** after having dispossessed them of most of their ancestral land. This has been a constant fact throughout all U.S. administrations since the JFK assassination and Israel's subsequent acquisition of nuclear weapons that Kennedy opposed. It has been aided and abetted by the rise of the neocon elements within the U.S. government and the 1997 formation of the **Project for the New American Century,** founded by William Kristol and Donald Kagan, whose signees included Donald

Rumsfeld, Dick Cheney, Paul Wolfowitz, et al., and claimed the need "for a new Pearl Harbor." Many of these people, who held dual U.S. and Israeli citizenship, became members of the Bush, Jr. administration. Once a summer of moviegoers watching the new film *Pearl Harbor* had passed, and the attacks of September 11th occurred, George W. Bush and the corporate media immediately and repeatedly proclaimed the attacks a new Pearl Harbor. Once again, the Palestinians and Hamas's Oct. 7, 2023 attack on Israel that is widely and falsely reported as **unprovoked, as is Russia's invasion of Ukraine,** has been referred to as "a Pearl Harbor Moment." President Biden has already given full U.S. support to Israel as it savagely attacks Gaza and has said that additional assistance for the Israeli Defense Forces is now on its way to Israel with more to follow. The U.S./Israel has killed tens of thousands of innocent Palestinians, mostly children and women in a campaign of genocide. Rather than acting as an instrument for peace, the U.S. government continues its support for Israel's crimes as if they were the same country. The Israel Lobby and the government of Israel has for decades exerted a powerful control over U.S. Middle East policies and much more as well. The Mossad has often worked closely under the aegis of the CIA together with Britain's M16 to assassinate opponents and provoke war after war.

Donald Rumsfeld, as a key long-time insider to U.S. deep state operations, was surely aware of my list of known knowns. He was just one of many such slick talkers involved in demonic U.S. operations that have always been justified, denied, or kept secret by him and his ilk.

One does not have to be a criminologist to realize these things. It is easy to imagine that Rumsfeld's forlorn ghost is wandering since he went to his grave with his false secrets tucked away.

When he said, "I could have said that the absence of evidence is not evidence of absence, or vice-versa," he then did say it, of course. Despite double-talkers like him, evidence of decades of U.S. propaganda is easy to see through if one is compelled by the will-to-truth.

Sea Monsters Threaten the World With Their Tridents

Sometimes you wake up from a dream to realize it is telling you to pay close attention to the depth of its message, especially when it is linked to what you have been thinking about for days. I have just come up from a dream in which I went down to the cellar of the house I grew up in because the basement light was on and the back cellar door had been opened by a mysterious man who stood outside.

I will spare you additional details or an interpretation, except to say that my daytime thoughts concerned the media spectacle surrounding the Titan submersible that imploded two miles down in the ocean's cellar while trying to give its passengers a view of the wreck of the Titanic, the "unsinkable" ship nicknamed "the Millionaire's Special." The ship that no one could sink except an ice cube in the drink that swallowed it.

Cellar dreams are well-known as the place where we as individuals and societies can face the flickering shadows that we refuse to face in conscious life. Carl Jung called it "the shadow." Such shadows, when unacknowledged and repressed, have a tendency to autonomously surface and erupt, not only leading to personal self-destruction but that of whole societies. History is replete with examples. My dream's mysterious stranger had lit my way through some dark thoughts and opened the door to a possible escape. He got me thinking about what all of us tend to want to deny or avoid because its implications are so monstrous.

The obsession with the alleged marvels of technology together with naming them after ancient Greek and Roman gods are fixations of elite technologues who have lost what Oswald Spengler called "living inner religiousness" but wish to show they know the classical names even though they miss the meaning of these myths. Such myths tell the stories of things that never happened but always are. Appropriating the ancient names without irony—such as naming a boat Titanic or a submersible Titan—unveils the hubristic ignorance of people who have never descended to the underworld to learn its lessons. Relinquishing their sense of god-like power doesn't occur to them, nor does the shadow side of their Faustian dreams.

They will never name some machine Nemesis, for that would expose the fact that they have exceeded the eternal limits with their maniacal technological extremism, and, to paraphrase Camus, dark Furies will swoop down to destroy them.

Nietzsche termed the result nihilism. Once people have killed God, machines are a handy replacement in societies that worship the illusion of technique and are scared to death of death and the machines that they invented to administer it.

The latter is not a matter fit to print since it must remain in the dark basement of the public's consciousness. If it were publicized, the game of nihilistic death-dealing would be exposed. Because power, money, and technology are the ruling deities today, the mass media revolve around publicizing their marvels in spectacular fashion, and when "accidents" occur, they never point out the myth of the machines, or what Lewis Mumford called "The Pentagon of Power." Tragedies occur, they tell us, but they are minor by-products of the marvels of technology.

But if these media would take us down to see the truth beneath the oceans' surfaces, we would see not false monsters such as the Titanic or Moby Dick or cartoon fictions such as Disney's Monstro the whale, but the handiwork of thousands of mad Captain Ahabs who have attached the technologues' "greatest" invention—nuclear weapons—to nuclear-powered ballistic submarines.

Trident submarines. First strike submarines, such as the USS *Ohio*.

These Trident subs live and breathe in the cellars of our minds where few dare descend. They are controlled by jackals in Washington and the Pentagon with polished faces in well-appointed offices with coffee machines and tasty snacks. Madmen. They hum through the deep waters ready to strike and destroy the world. Few hear them, almost none see them, most prefer not to know of them.

But wait, what's the buzz, tell me what's happening: the Titan and the Titanic, wealthy voyeurs intent on getting a glance into the sepulchres of those long dead, while six hundred or so desperate migrants drown in the Mediterranean sea from which the ancient gods were born. These are the priorities of a society that worships the wealthy; a society of the spectacle that entertains and distracts while the end of the world cruises below consciousness.

The United States alone has fourteen such submarines armed with Trident missiles constantly prowling the ocean depths, while the British have four. Named for the three-pronged weapon of the Greek and Roman sea gods, Poseidon and Neptune respectively, these submarines launch ballistic missiles, manufactured by Lockheed Martin ("We deliver innovative solutions to the world's toughest challenges"), that can destroy the world in a flash. Destroy it many times over, as if that were possible. A final solution.

While the United States has abrogated all treaties that offered some protection from their use and has declared their right of first use, it has consistently pushed toward a nuclear confrontation with Russia and China. Today we stand on the precipice of nuclear annihilation as never before.

A single Trident submarine has 20 Trident missiles, each carrying 12 independently targeted warheads for a total of 240 warheads, with each warhead approximately 40 times more destructive than the Hiroshima bomb. Fourteen submarines times 240 equals 3,360 nuclear warheads times 40 equals 134,400 Hiroshimas. Such are the lessons of mathematics in absurd times.

Author James W. Douglass, a longtime activist against the Tridents at Ground Zero Center for Non-Violent Action outside the Bangor Submarine Base in Washington state, put it this way in 2015 when asked about Robert Aldridge, the heroic Lockheed

Trident missile designer who resigned his position in an act of conscience and became an inspirational force for the campaign against the Tridents and nuclear weapons:

Question: "What did the Nuremberg attorneys say about war crimes that had such a deep impact on Robert Aldridge?"

Douglass: "They said that first-strike weapons and weapons that directly target a civilian population were war crimes in violation of the Nuremberg principles. Those Nuremberg principles, which are the foundations of international law, are violated by both electronic warfare—which is why we poured blood on the files for electronic warfare [at the base]—and also by the Trident missile system, which is what Robert Aldridge was building."

Robert Aldridge saw his shadow side. He went to the cellar of his darkest dreams. He refused to turn away. He became an inspiration for James and Shelley Douglass and so many others. He was a man in and of the system, who saw the truth of his complicity in radical evil and underwent a metanoia. It is possible.

If those missiles are ever launched from the monsters that carry them through the hidden recesses of the world's oceans, there will never be another Nuremberg Trial to judge the guilty, for the innocent and the guilty will all be dead.

We will have failed to shed light on our darkest shadows.

We turn away at our peril.

Listening To the Silence with Don DeLillo

In 1997, Don DeLillo, the author of seventeen novels, published what many consider his masterpiece, *Underworld*. It was a prophetic book in many ways, especially with its focus on the World Trade Towers and the way the book's cover, front and back, pictured the towers shrouded in smoke or clouds with what seemed like a large bird approaching it at its upper floors. That the front cover had a positive image and the rear a negative one with the light and dark inverted gave it a ghostly look that was haunting. I remember when I first saw the book, I wondered if the photograph was showing a plane or a bird approaching the north tower near what looked like twenty or so floors from the top. I concluded it was probably a bird, but four years later reality entered the picture with a plane exploding into the side of the building twenty or so floors from the top.

The photo is ambiguous but eerily suggestive, especially in retrospect. Below the towers we see a cross atop the local church seemingly holding the towers together, as if to announce the future of the new Crusade against Islam, or perhaps the connection between God and Mammon, or maybe a reminder that "you cannot serve both God and mammon." Who knows?

No one seeing it now could avoid thinking of the attacks of September 11, 2001, but remember, this was published in 1997. And reading the words of the novel's character Brian, who is in the waste management business, one realizes why the cover photos were an appropriate choice and how they captured DeLillo's story and the terrible future. Fresh kills and burials. Waste. The underworld. Brian thinks as he stands atop the mountains of waste at the Fresh Kills landfill on Staten Island where the remains of the Twin Towers will be buried and looks at the Twin Towers across the harbor: "The towers of the World Trade Center were visible in the distance and he sensed a poetic balance between that idea [trade and commerce] and this one [waste and a burial grounds]." Does Brian know that soon nearly three thousand people will be wasted there? And that his twinning of the towers with waste in four years would take on the creepiest of meanings. "The wind carried the stink [of death and decay]across the kill," he thinks, comparing it all to "an omnivorous movie terror."

Ezra Pound once said that artists are the antennae of the race. He seemed to be speaking of DeLillo, among others. Can artists intuit the future? Did DeLillo apprehend the fate of the Twin Towers? How?

When I read *Underworld*, I was struck by its uncanny brilliance. This was in 1998. I recommended it to everyone I knew. No one would read it. It was too long—827 pages—and maybe something closer to the bone dissuaded them, as if its title was announcing dread and death and they preferred smiley faces. Then, after the attacks of September 11, 2001, I again recommended it. No one took my suggestion to read it. Perhaps then it wasn't the length but its eerie insights. Its prescience. Its weirdness. Its references to the Twin Towers, terrorists, the view of the Towers from the Fresh Kills landfill where the debris from the attack was in fact later taken and laid to waste as fast as possible to avoid inspection, buried, with a reference to germs and the fear of them, the need to wash your hands over and over, the traumatic looping of images on television, so much repetition, such frantic sex, loss of faith, nuclear dread, etc. The book was capacious and captivating and unnerving.

"What's your argument?" one character asks another.

"You asked, so I'll tell you. That the biggest secrets are staring us straight in the face and we don't see a thing."

Or don't want to.

What are those open secrets now?

DeLillo's latest book is *The Silence*, which is called a novel but is really a long short story or a novella. But the categories don't matter. It's a meditation in words on silence, death, technology, and loss, always the heart of the matter and DeLillo's core themes. It is very short—117 pages of big print. All the characters talk gibberish, inanities that cut to the bone. It's hard to know whether to laugh or cry when hearing them talk. Yet much of their talk is frightening because it is the way people do talk to each other. The sounds of silence. What did you say? What? What did you say? I don't remember, I was texting.

And like *Underworld*, whose first 150 pages are devoted to the first nationally televised baseball game played on October 3, 1951 at New York's Polo Grounds that ended with a ninth inning home run by the Giants' Bobby Thompson that came to be called "the shot heard round the world," *The Silence* centers around a group of five people gathering in 2022 to watch the Superbowl on a super screen TV in a Manhattan apartment.

"Filling time. Being boring. Living life," says Tessa to Jim who are on a plane returning from France. Jim is fixated on the screen in front of him that is flashing the plane's altitude, the temperature, time to destination. Tessa is writing in a small notebook her memories of what they saw on their trip so that in the years to come she may realize what she had missed, "something I don't see right now." Both killing time. Jim jabbers on about nothing, but he "wasn't listening to what he was saying because he knew it was stale air."

Back in the NYC apartment a threesome is awaiting their arrival for the big viewing of the Superbowl. Drinks and snacks are ready. There sit Diane, Max, and Diane's former student, Martin, who is in his early thirties. Routine, boredom, and ennui await the kickoff and the arrival of the other couple and expected excitement. The national diversion on a small scale. A question hovers in the air: "What are we doing here, that is the question," says Vladimir in Samuel Becket's *Waiting for Godot*. "And we are blessed in this, that we happen to know the answer."

Do we?

Back on the plane, something happens, "a massive knocking somewhere below them. The screen went blank." Knock, Knock. Who's there? Death. "Are we afraid?" she said. The plane crash-lands because all the electronics have failed.

Back in the high-rise aerie, the threesome talk in clipped voices like the robotic Alexa. While her husband Max sits and drinks bourbon and stares at the big screen, Diane, in search of something to excite her, prods the gangling Martin with absurd questions to which he quickly responds with gibberish that gives her a sexual frisson. Boredom is a powerful force.

The kickoff is minutes away. "Something happened then." The images on the screen shake, get distorted, and then the screen goes blank. Their phones go dead. At first they think it is a local outage, but it soon becomes apparent that what happened on the plane was happening everywhere and that the entire electronic grid was down, all electricity, the internet out. Max keeps staring at the blank screen, cursing. He starts announcing out loud the invisible game:

Play resumes, quarter two, hands, feet, knees, head, chest, crotch, hitting and getting hit. Super Bowl Fifty-Six. Our National Death Wish.

Martin tells Diane he is taking a medication, and a side effect can be that others can hear your thoughts or control your behavior. "Yes, we all do this," he says. "A little white pill."

It seems madness has walked in. Blank screens. Disoriented minds.

Soon Tess and Jim, after visiting the darkened hospital with others from the plane crash to have Jim's head wound attended to, walk to the apartment through darkening empty streets for the absent game. Martin says, "Are we living in a makeshift reality? Have I already said this? A future that isn't supposed to take form just yet?"

The five sit and eat by candlelight as cold joins the darkness of the encroaching night. "Was each a mystery to the others, however close their involvement, each individual so naturally encased that he or she escapes a final determination, a fixed appraisal by the others in the room?"

No one knows what has happened, who or what is behind the digital takedown. Or who they really are. Martin says, "Nobody want to call it World War III but this is what it is." His madness pours from his mouth, a ranting filled with the kinds of questions and thoughts many would think if the digital takedown really happened, the kinds of questions more and more people are now asking. Will DeLillo be prescient again: Is a digital "attack" coming soon?

Martin's words:

> Certain countries. Once rabid proponents of nuclear arms, now speaking the language of living weaponry. Germs, genes, spores, powders.

DeLillo:

> Cyberattacks, digital intrusions, biological aggressions. Anthrax, smallpox, pathogens. The dead and the disabled. Starvation, plague, and what else. Power grids collapsing. Our personal perception sinking into quantum dominance.... And isn't it strange that certain individuals have seemed to have accepted the shutdown, the burnout?"

The five of them sit and talk on and on in the silence. Each delivers a closing monologue, as if it's closing time and the last drinks have been served. Say what you want. What has happened? Speak. Was this foreseeable? Have we been zombified? Lost our ability to think, to communicate, to grasp what's happening around and within us? Have our digital addictions destroyed our humanity? Have we reached our expiration dates? Who is doing this to us?

Your phone is wasted; don't seek its advice.

Just as he seemed to perceive the attacks of September 11, 2001 four years before they occurred, does DeLillo know something that most would prefer to avoid? Are we like Tessa, who wishes to just go home and return to normality but who feels she is "in a tumbling void"?

When her husband Jim hears her say something about home, "he realizes it is simply fake, a dead language."

"Home," he says finally. "Where is that?"

DeLillo has been asking that for decades.

Are we and he like Max, who ends the book understanding nothing and staring into a blank screen?

Or can we see the biggest secret staring us straight in the face?

I can't help thinking that DeLillo tipped his hand at the end of *Underworld* when he has the book's protagonist, Nick Shay, born and bred like his creator in the Italian Arthur Ave. section of the Bronx, say what he longs for:

> I long for the days of disorder. I want them back, the days when I was alive on the earth, rippling in the quick of my skin, heedless and real. I was dumb-muscled and angry and real. This is what I long for, the breach of peace, the days of disarray when I walked real streets and did things slap-bang and felt angry and ready all the time, a danger to others and a distant mystery to myself.

Can we get back into our skins or are we doomed to tumble into a void? The signs are not too encouraging.

My wife and I were recently hiking on a narrow mountain trail along which we encountered not a soul. We came to an isolated spot overlooking a valley to the east. We stopped, looked, and listened. Not a sound. Not even birds. Just beautiful silence. There was so much to hear there. When we continued on, we saw a couple with a dog up ahead. The man and woman each wore a mask. When they saw us, mask-less criminals, they quickly stepped off the trail. The woman pulled the dog close to her and the man took out and checked his phone. As we passed, they said not a word, but their eyes spoke fear. I was wondering if the man was texting the police.

Numbed by Numbers on the Way to the Digital Palace

"But yet mathematical certainty is after all, something insufferable. Twice two makes four seems to me simply a piece of insolence. Twice two makes four is a pert coxcomb who stands with arms akimbo barring your path and spitting. I admit that twice two makes four is an excellent thing, but if we are to give everything its due, twice two makes five is sometimes a very charming thing too."

—FYODOR DOSTOEVSKY, *Notes from the Underground*

Everybody knows that 2 + 2 = 4 since 4 = 2 + 2. They know that excellent thing with certainty but generally fail to appreciate the charming nature of 2 + 2 = 5. Tautologies are usually preferred to choices that seem to contradict the "laws of nature." Mind-forged manacles are popular because freedom from the laws of nature, while desired, is feared because it suggests that liberty is a fundamental existential truth.

Don't get me wrong, I can count. I am drinking my second cup of coffee. Number one has disappeared down my throat, but the second coffee tastes fine. It is real and still exists. The first is just an abstraction now—number 1—a simple vertical line on the page.

We are pissing our lives away on abstractions, forgetting that notation is a system of symbols that direct us to what they intend. The key is to grasp what is intended. The cognitive construction of the number system is a useful tool, but when it is pushed as the essential tool to grasp the meaning of life it has become a tool of control. That is the case today.

The Internet, cell phones, and digital media are the greatest propaganda tools ever invented. They have come to us on the wings of numbers. They are insidious in the extreme, for, as the etymology of "insidious" tells us—Latin, *insidere*, to sit on, occupy—for over the last few decades they have acted as an invading army occupying our minds with numbers in a cunning attempt to mathematize our lives for techno-scientific, financialized neoliberal capitalist purposes. To prepare us for the Great Reset when people and machines will be indistinguishable, Artificial Intelligence (AI), 5-G ultra microwaves, and Agenda 2030 will be fully established, and when human life has become part of The Internet of Things.

That, at least, is what the builders of the new Crystal Palace [the Great Exhibition, London, 1851] intend. At the moment, their Digital Palace seems like a stone wall that is here to stay, but as Fyodor has said, people are strange creatures and will sometimes refuse to be reconciled to the impossibility of "stone walls if it disgusts you to be reconciled to it." I am disgusted.

The construction of the Digital Palace is the long goal that has been underway for decades. To erase lived time and space, flesh and blood humans, and by transfixing people with numbers, to create an abstract and ephemeral reality through a constantly evoked sense of emergency. Living the machine/Internet life would never be acceptable if people had not been subjected to an onslaught of numbers/statistics/data that has accustomed them to think like computers. The great Jacques Ellul made it clear in his classic work, *Propaganda*, that propaganda is much more than the waving of a magic wand and lying, although it is that. It is a long process, slow constant impregnation.

The mathematization of our thinking has been the essential first step in addicting people to the internet complex where mind-control is so effective. I say first step, yet it has been concomitantly accompanied by daily litanies of lies about world events through what Ray McGovern aptly terms the

Military-Industrial-Congressional-Media-Academia-Think-Tank complex (MICIMATT). In his usually masterful way, the great late journalist John Pilger pointed out so many of those grotesque lies about U.S. wars of aggression around the world. Their numbers are legion, but not the kind of numbers you will find in the mainstream media. We are drowning in lies and numbers produced by a nihilistic elite in love with power, money, mayhem, and murder.

Twenty or so years ago a massive push was organized to give prime emphasis throughout the educational system to what is termed STEM subjects—science, technology, engineering, and mathematics. This has been implemented at the expense of subjects that have traditionally been associated with the liberal arts—philosophy, history, literature, art, music, etc., subjects that introduce students to thinking in the widest and deepest ways. It is no accident that instrumental logic has replaced deep thought for so many people and the poets have been replaced by intellectual pimps. The emphasis on STEM subjects has paralleled the rise of the Internet with its drumbeat of numbers, statistics, and data. Let me offer just a few examples, which may seem innocuous unless seen in their larger context.

- The switch from analog to digital clocks and watches and their omnipresence.
- Referring to the week as 24/7 and the writing of dates as numbers such as 08/30/2023.
- The use-by-date numbers on all products, soon to be applied to commoditized people.
- The use of the term 9/11 to refer to the events of September 11, 2001.
- The listing by numbers of the best colleges, mascara, underwear, corkscrews, etc.
- The hilarious dating of the earth's age to the current 4.4 billion as if that meant anything to anyone.

- The computer generated weather forecasts with their 10 and 30 day forecasts with precise numerical percentages for rain, snow, etc.

- The analytics that dominate the world of sports, the posting of numbers for everything from the speed a ball leaves a baseball bat, a tennis ball a racket, and in golf the speed, height, curve, apex, carry, and launch angle when a ball is driven—all these numbers changing as a computer measures the ball in flight.

- The "helpful" messages on restaurant receipts where the tips are recorded in descending order and exactitude from 18% to 20% to 25%.

- Manipulated statistics for everything under the sun, such as COVID cases and deaths, Ukrainian military casualties, unemployment numbers, etc.

- The way people's health is assessed by the use of numbers on blood tests rather than how they feel.

It is easy for one to add to this small list of the use of numbers. They are everywhere and are intended to be—in people's heads, as the saying goes. They are intended to induce mass production of thought and behavior that is numb and that tranquilizes real thought and oppositional action. The more this is so, the more the schooling institutions will loudly announce how well they are teaching "critical thinking" skills. All our institutions have become complicit in 24/7 capitalism and the mind-control of deep-state forces.

In his brilliant new book, *Scorched Earth: Beyond the Digital Age to a Post-Capitalist World,* Jonathan Crary, sums it up nicely: "One of the foremost achievements of the so-called knowledge economy is the mass production of ignorance, stupidity, and hatefulness. . . . programmed unintelligibility and duplicity."

The reality of everyday life used to revolve around our bodies in place and time. Now that time and place have been jumbled, it revolves for so many around the cell phones in which people live a weird disembodied existence. Sensory life is being annihilated.

This is the era of virtual people, shadows of shadows, abstractions upon screens. Our connections to nature, to the seasons, to the sacred ways of our ancestors are being discarded for the machine life in the Digital Palace.

Dostoevsky's underground man wasn't playing a silly game when he suggested that 2 + 2 = 5. He was saying that free will is more important than reason which just satisfies the rational side of our nature. Without it we are sub-human, machines in a vast prison of our own making. His words are more important today than when he wrote them in 1864, the time of The Crystal Palace with its promotion of the Industrial Revolution's technological marvels. Today's Digital Palace marks a far greater threat to our humanity, and so his words are worth attending to:

. . . man everywhere and at all times, whoever he may be, has preferred to act as he chose and not in the least as his reason and advantage dictated. And one may choose what is contrary to one's interests, and sometimes one *positively ought* (that is my idea). One's own free unfettered choice, one's own caprice, however wild it may be, one's own fancy worked up at times to frenzy—that is that "most advantageous advantage" which we have overlooked, which comes under no classification and against which all systems and theories are continually being shattered to atoms. And how do these wiseacres know that man wants a normal, virtuous choice? What man wants is simply *independent* choice, whatever that independence may cost and wherever it may lead. And choice, of course, the devil only knows what choice.

And if you are apt to raise a finger in warning about such wild advice about existential freedom, let Dostoevsky ask you this rhetorical question about the reasonable and logical ones: "Have you noticed that it is the most civilized gentlemen who have been the subtlest slaughterers, to whom the Attilas and Stenka Razins could not hold a candle, and if they are not so conspicuous as the Attilas and Stenka Razins it is because they are so often met with, are so ordinary and have become so familiar to us."

As mundane as numbers.

— EPILOGUE —

Mr. Blue and Maria: A Musical Dream

Sixty years ago in the late fall and early winter, a seventeen-year-old blue-eyed Bronx boy went by himself to see an afternoon showing of *West Side Story* on Fordham Road in the north Bronx. He took the bus to the theater but walked the few miles home in a romantic daze, in love with Maria and yearning for a girl like her for himself. The movie had mesmerized him, and though he knew about gang fights and the enmity between different ethnic groups, especially white prejudice against Puerto Ricans and blacks, he had never been involved in such violence. It was real and not-real for him, and he was smart enough to realize that a movie was not real life and that great music had the anodyne power to enchant, and together with colorful moving pictures it could put one into a dream state that could be very powerful. There was a reason why Hollywood was called the "Dream Factory." But he liked to dream and went to the movies to lose himself in fantasy like so many others. But *West Side Story* had hit him especially hard, and as he walked home through the winding streets, he felt unreal, as though the spell the movie cast on him was everlasting. He wanted to be Tony, not dead but alive, and Tony taking Maria away from the violent streets to a somewhere place where love and happiness were possible. His fascination, however, was tinged with foreboding, a sense that despite what felt like a window of optimism and hope in 1961 with the new young president John Kennedy in the White House, something bad was coming round the corner or cannonballing down through the sky since shortly before the U.S. and the Soviet Union had faced off with tanks at the recently erected Berlin Wall, and weird things were happening around the world such as the Bay of Pigs invasion earlier in the year and the recent death of the Secretary General of the UN Dag Hammarskjöld, one of the boy's heroes. In those years before cynicism swept the country, people had heroes, as did the boy: his father, JFK, Hammarskjöld, Paul Newman, and the basketball star Bob Cousy, obviously different in kind and stature. For the boy was a romantic at heart but his head thought dark thoughts. He didn't know why, but he felt an odd mixture of hope and dread, and he kept thinking of Tony and Maria and how they fell in love at first sight. He wondered if this was just a movie thing. Was it fate that Tony got shot? He kept thinking back to seven years earlier when his seven-year-old cousin accidentally shot and killed his nine-year-old brother and the weirdness of accidents and horrible evil and love and sex and death and how his blue-eyed red-haired sister had married her Puerto Rican boyfriend despite the sick norms of the time—his mind was a merry-go-round of inchoate thoughts and impressions going in circles till the music stopped when he got home without a partner to share his deepest thoughts with, and no hand to hold—and so he went twice more by himself to see the movie, hoping to discover some secret embedded in its tale, thinking that perhaps the beautiful music hid a revelation and so he would have to listen again and again. He kept all this to himself, not daring to share his heart's desires and fears with anyone, since he was an athlete and the only boy with seven sisters and his role was to be strong and brave and stoic and swallow his loneliness. The previous month he had come out of high school basketball practice on East 85th St. in Manhattan in the early evening only to ask a stranger for the time. The stranger in the tan cap and coat was his hero Paul Newman, the star of the recently released movie *The Hustler* in which he played Fast Eddie Felson, the pool hustler. The boy, who loved movies and went dreaming in them, had identified with Newman and his character's desire to win, and when Newman, who introduced himself as Paul, very nicely took a few minutes to ask his name and talk to the boy about his school and basketball, the boy was thrilled, and the thrill was compounded when Newman called after him as the boy was leaving, "See you later, Fast Eddie." They shared blue eyes and for some reason blue now seemed to color so much of what the boy saw and felt, the blue of the open sky's freedom and the blueness of Tony's eyes and his death and the Virgin Mary blueness of the aptly named Maria of the dark eyes, just like the talismanic miraculous medal of Blessed Mary that hung around the boy's neck, kept there to protect and guide him to something that felt just out of reach and that perhaps he needed a miracle to reach. Who knows? He didn't, but he felt that something was coming if he could only wait in hope, something very hard to do with his impetuous and passionate nature. He had just gotten into a stupid fight at a basketball practice with Louis Alcindor, who later became Kareem Abdul-Jabbar the great NBA basketball player, which left him feeling weird and wondering about young men and fighting and now he had just seen Tony get killed in a tragic twist of fate in a game run by forces bigger than the Sharks and the Jets could imagine. What did it mean to win? And even though Tony wasn't real, only an actor playing a part, his death resounded in the boy's mind, just as did Maria's anguish as she held her dying lover. Somewhere someday, he thought, love might conquer all this madness and we'll find a new way of living and I'll find my Maria and it will be love at first sight. The next year the boy went with a friend to The Gaslight Café in Greenwich Village. It was around the time of the Cuban Missile Crisis when the world teetered on the edge of nuclear war. The unknown Bob Dylan was performing there that fall and it was when he first sang "A Hard Rain's A-Gonna Fall." The boy kept hearing his words: "And what'll you do now, my blue-eyed son? And what'll you do now, my darling young one?" And a hard rain did fall, although nuclear war was avoided, Kennedy was soon shot dead for seeking peace between two gangs far more deadly than the Sharks and the Jets. And the boy had to decide what he would do, for the music played on but nobody was listening and there were guns and sharp swords in the hands of young children and napalm and rifles in the hands of young men in distant jungles. He wondered if there really was a place for us somewhere, a place to find a new way of living, for it didn't seem like this was the time for it with blood everywhere, bad blood, good blood, puddles of blood, streams of blood, blood in the songs and songs in the blood, Dallas, New York, Memphis, the city of Angels, Saigon, San Juan, Hanoi down through the years as he wandered in tears and wondered where it was all going, all this blood. Blue entered his soul, a blueness of the deepest deep that was not a technicolor blue but a Billie Holiday blue, the Bronx buried Billie near the boy's dead young cousin Jimmy, dead with a bullet to the heart because of an adult's carelessness, the adults who made the wars in the ghettos and the jungles and caused the deaths of so many all across the world, those unfeeling ones who killed Billie and Bobby and Jimmy and Tony and Johnny and Bernardo, and did their best to try to extinguish blue skies in the hearts of young people everywhere, to drug them and wipe their minds clean of hope and idealism and the feeling that miracles could happen and the world is full of light with suns and moons all over the place, wild and bright going mad, shooting sparks into space because love is found and love abides. For the boy, as he walked through the years and became a man, the blueness in his soul always also harbored a certain blue that counteracted the blues, a blue like singing the blues defeats the darkness. For him it was this inner image of Maria, Mary, Marie, the lady in blue, the Blessed one, the mother of all sorrows and hope that kept him company all along his journeys and sang to him as she held his hand. Who can explain it, who can tell you why? He wasn't foolish enough to try. One day, the boy who became the man, now a reluctant young professor, walked into a room to teach a course on death and meaning, and there was his beautiful Maria looking at him, she of the long dark hair and dark eyes, resurrected, and he saw her and the world went away, death departed, they stared at each other spell-bound, and he knew this wasn't a movie but was real love at first sight. Time flew away and yet a hard rain kept falling and it's falling still. The sky still weeps and the blood keeps a-flowing. The boy learned to tell it and "speak it and think it and breathe it and reflect from the mountain so all souls can see it," and is still doing his best. He and Maria, no longer young, just went to the movies together to see the remake of *West Side Story.* The theater was nearly empty. He was expecting to find much to criticize. Instead, he found Tony and Maria again and the same old story, the fight for love and glory for a new time and place but with new faces in the same race to defeat the old hate that never seems to die. It was only a movie. But as he took Maria's hand he knew that love abides, and he whispered to himself: "Always you, every thought I'll ever know/Everywhere I go you'll be, you and me." It was a miracle, not a dream.